CIPS Study Matters

Level 4

Foundation Diploma in Purchasing and Supply

Measuring Purchasing Pe

Bryan Jones and John Oliver
Supply Chain Projects Ltd

THE
CHARTERED INSTITUTE OF
PURCHASING & SUPPLY

Published by

The Chartered Institute of Purchasing and Supply
Easton House, Easton on the Hill, Stamford, Lincolnshire PE9 3NZ
Tel: +44 (0) 1780 756 777
Fax: +44 (0) 1780 751 610
Email: info@cips.org
Website: http://www.cips.org

First published June 2006

While every effort has been made to ensure that references to websites are correct at time of going to press, the world wide web is a constantly changing environment and CIPS cannot accept any responsibility for any changes to addresses.

CIPS acknowledges product, service and company names referred to in this publication, many of which are trade names, service marks, trademarks or registered trademarks.

CIPS, The Chartered Institute of Purchasing & Supply and its logo are all trademarks of the Chartered Institute of Purchasing & Supply.

The right of Bryan Jones and John Oliver to be identified as authors of this work has been asserted by them in accordance with the Copyright, Designs and Patents Act, 1988 in force or as amended from time to time.

Technical reviewer: Anne Ball, University of Derby

Instructional design and publishing project management by Wordhouse Ltd, Reading, UK

Content management system, instructional editing and pre-press by Echelon Learning Ltd, London, UK

Index prepared by Indexing Specialists (UK) Ltd, Hove, UK

ISBN 1-86124-154-2
ISBN 978-186124-154-2

Contents

Introduction **vii**

Unit content coverage **xi**

Study session 1: Introduction to performance management in purchasing
and supply **1**
The importance of performance management in business **2**
Introduction to performance management in general and purchasing
and supply in particular **5**
Introduction to cost management in organisations and the link with
purchasing performance **6**
Continuous improvement in business, and the link with purchasing
performance management **8**
Continuity of supply, and the link to measuring purchasing
performance **10**
The importance of measuring purchasing and supply chain performance
in public and private sector organisations **12**

Study session 2: Adding value to the business **19**
Added value performance management in corporate business
operations: general principles **20**
Added value opportunities **22**
Measuring value added performance achieved by purchasing and
supply **23**
Adding value by reducing inventory costs and administration and using
consignment stocks **25**
Added value opportunities of negotiating: improved procurement and
contract terms with suppliers **26**
Adding value by improving operational efficiency **28**

Study session 3: Categories of performance measurement **37**
How do purchasing and supply managers contribute to the KPI targets
set by corporate management? **38**
How do purchasing and supply managers select and set KPIs for their
core: business operation? **41**
Purchasing's contribution to improved service and the bottom-line
profit **43**
Selecting KPIs to measure management of departmental purchasing
process and supply chain costs **45**
Selecting KPIs that link to the purchasing infrastructure within an
organisation **47**
Purchasing competence and the link to business objectives **49**

Study session 4: Cost and price measures **57**
The bigger picture: costs and forces that determine a price within a
market **59**
Basic cost analysis: how costs are allocated and accounted for in a
commercial organisation? **60**
Introduction to cost price analysis: how are variable costs managed? **62**
Using cost analysis and measuring your purchasing performance **64**

How are fixed costs managed? **66**

Study session 5: Inventory management measures **73**
Stock: its place and value in business operations **75**
The cost of holding stock **77**
Building up the stockholding cost base and identifying links to performance management **78**
Stores and inventory key performance indicators **79**
Managing inventory KPIs within the wider supply chain **82**

Study session 6: IT and data management **89**
Information systems in business, and the links with supply chain systems used to measure performance **90**
The key elements of a purchasing IT system **93**
The added value issues and linked performance indicators for managing the purchasing function **95**
The added value issues and processes in managing the performance of suppliers **96**
The added value issues and processes in managing the performance of buyers **98**
Best practice: which KPIs will help supply chain managers reduce cost and improve service? **99**

Study session 7: Why measure suppliers? **107**
Supplier performance and business success. **108**
Supplier performance measures within the procurement function **110**
Performance measurement and 'quality management' **112**
Supplier measurement and the building of relationships **114**
Measurement in supplier selection and supplier evaluation **117**
Performance measurement for mutual advantage **118**

Study session 8: Steps in the supplier measurement process **125**
The key stages in the buying process **126**
Steps in a pre-award assessment **129**
Steps in a post-award evaluation **131**
Internal and external supplier feedback and corrective action **134**
Continuous review and the supplier measurement process **136**

Study session 9: About measurement tools **141**
Using the right performance measurement 'tools' **142**
Qualitative and quantitative measures of performance **145**
Planning measurement systems and ensuring data availability **148**
Involving others in the measurement process **149**
A desk-based or visit-based approach? **151**

Study session 10: Performance measurement **157**
Generic methodologies for post-award performance measurement **158**
Simple vendor rating **160**
Perception-based rating **162**
The benefits of using weighted measurements **164**
Third party involvement and testing procedures **166**
Audit and the planning of an audit trail **168**

Study session 11: Communication **175**
  Communication and business relationships at strategic, tactical and operational levels **176**
  Communication, performance measurement and relationship-building **178**
  The importance of good communication mechanisms within performance measurement systems **181**
  Good communications and the resolution of disputes and management of conflict **183**
  Types of communication mechanism **186**

Study session 12: Financial appraisal **193**
  The role and input for the finance department **194**
  The benefits of undertaking corporate financial appraisal **197**
  Specialist third-party versus internally led financial appraisal **198**
  Financial appraisal measurement tools **201**

Study session 13: Other performance measures **211**
  Internal and external commercial relationships **212**
  Other areas of measurement activity **215**
  Joint performance measurement initiatives **217**
  Benchmarking and supplier surveys **220**

Study session 14: Supplier development and supplier account management **227**
  Developing and controlling suppliers in a more positive way **228**
  The need to identify key suppliers **230**
  About supplier development **232**
  About supplier account management **235**

Study session 15: Why measure buyers' performance? **243**
  Performance management and the buyer **244**
  Performance management and the organisation **246**
  Periodic, ongoing and annual measurement **247**
  The links with reward and advancement **249**
  Problems with poorly managed measurement schemes **250**
  The wider view, and Investors in People **252**

Study session 16: Cascading targets and objectives **259**
  Managing by objectives **260**
  Targets and objectives, and the business-planning process **261**
  Designing positive and SMART objectives **263**
  Timescales for objectives **266**
  Problems with objective-setting **267**
  Feedback, audit and review of the objective-setting process **268**

Study session 17: Appraisal and evaluation techniques **275**
  Formal and informal appraisal and evaluation techniques **276**
  Quantitative and qualitative measurement approaches **277**
  Interview-based appraisal **279**
  Self-assessment **281**
  Involving others in the appraisal process **282**

Problems with the appraisal process **284**

Study session 18: Training and staff development **289**
Developing a training needs analysis **290**
Job profiles, job descriptions and their influence on a TNA **292**
Focused versus non-focused training and development **294**
The different types of training available **296**
Continuous professional development **298**
Evaluating the success of training **299**

Study session 19: Information and individual performance
management **305**
The importance of data in the measurement process **306**
Accessing corporate and departmental planning **308**
Types of data used **311**
Sources of usable data **313**

Study session 20: Buyer and supplier performance links **319**
The weaknesses of existing approaches to performance
measurement **320**
The wider involvement of stakeholders **322**
Performance measurement links to suppliers **325**
Performance links with other stakeholders **327**

Revision questions **333**

Feedback on revision questions **341**

References and bibliography **355**

Index **357**

Introduction

This course book has been designed to assist you in studying for the CIPS Measuring Purchasing Performance unit in the Level 4 Foundation Diploma in Purchasing and Supply. The book covers all topics in the official CIPS unit content document, as illustrated in the table beginning on page xi.

Increasingly both public and private sector organisations are taking advantage of the gains good purchasing can bring in terms of improved service and product quality and contribution to the bottom line. Within such organisations there is generally a recognition that good purchasing does not 'just happen' and that there are many factors which need to come together for the best results to be obtained. Such organisations also recognise that, as with most aspects of business, purchasing performance needs to be measured if it is to be fully recognised and understood.

Whilst there can be many facets in the measurement of purchasing performance, this course book views some of the key basic issues from three perspectives.

Firstly we consider the measurement of procurement as a business function – how effective is it on behalf of the business or organisation in which it operates. This is particularly important because it affects the overall profile of procurement and the way the function is perceived by its stakeholders. This is an area is of increasing interest to authors and researchers with a growing body of literature available to students.

Secondly we move away from the business contribution to consider the performance of suppliers. It is often said that purchasing is 'only as good as its suppliers', and there is much truth in this as supplier performance plays a major part in forming the opinions of users of procurement services. For this reason, and because there are many practical activities which can be involved, there is plenty of information available in this area for students to access.

Lastly we consider the performance of the buyers. In our opinion this area is overlooked in many books and publications, and indeed there is some 'blurring' between the procurement and human resources approaches. However it is critical for the success of procurement that staff performance is measured *and* that the information is used to train and develop buyers to meet organisational expectations.

Performance measurement is a complex and involving subject – we hope you will enjoy this course book.

How to use this book

The course book will take you step by step through the unit content in a series of carefully planned 'study sessions' and provides you with learning activities, self-assessment questions and revision questions to help you master the subject matter. The guide should help you organise and carry out your studies in a methodical, logical and effective way, but if you have your own study preferences you will find it a flexible resource too.

Before you begin using course this book, make sure you are familiar with any advice provided by CIPS on such things as study skills, revision techniques or support and how to handle formal assessments.

If you are on a taught course, it will be up to your tutor to explain how to use the book – when to read the study sessions, when to tackle the activities and questions, and so on.

If you are on a self-study course, or studying independently, you can use the course book in the following way:

Scan the whole book to get a feel for the nature and content of the subject matter.

Plan your overall study schedule so that you allow enough time to complete all 20 study sessions well before your examinations – in other words, leaving plenty of time for revision.

For each session, set aside enough time for reading the text, tackling all the learning activities and self-assessment questions, and the revision question at the end of the session, and for the suggested further reading. Guidance on roughly how long you should set aside for studying each session is given at the beginning of the session.

Now let's take a look at the structure and content of the individual study sessions.

Overview of the study sessions

The course book breaks the content down into 20 sessions, which vary from three to six or seven hours' duration each. However, we are not advising you to study for this sort of time without a break! The sessions are simply a convenient way of breaking the syllabus into manageable chunks. Most people would try to study one or two sessions a week, taking one or two breaks within each session. You will quickly find out what suits you best.

Each session begins with a brief **introduction** which sets out the areas of the syllabus being covered and explains, if necessary, how the session fits in with the topics that come before and after.

After the introduction there is a statement of the **session learning objectives**. The objectives are designed to help you understand exactly what you should be able to do after you've studied the session. You might find it helpful to tick them off as you progress through the session. You will also find them useful during revision. There is one session learning objective for each numbered subsection of the session.

After this, there is a brief section reproducing the learning objectives and indicative content from the official **unit content document**. This will help you to understand exactly which part of the syllabus you are studying in the current session.

Following this, there are **prior knowledge** and **resources** sections if necessary. These will let you know if there are any topics you need to be familiar with before tackling each particular session, or any special resources you might need, such as a calculator or graph paper.

Then the main part of the study session begins, with the first of the numbered main subsections. At regular intervals in each study session, we have provided you with **learning activities**, which are designed to get you actively involved in the learning process. You should always try to complete the activities – usually on a separate sheet of your own paper – before reading on. You will learn much more effectively if you are actively involved in doing something as you study, rather than just passively reading the text in front of you. The feedback or answers to the activities are provided at the end of the session. Do not be tempted to skip the activity.

We also provide a number of **self-assessment questions** in each study session. These are to help you to decide for yourself whether or not you have achieved the learning objectives set out at the beginning of the session. As with the activities, you should always tackle them – usually on a separate sheet of paper. Don't be tempted to skip them. The feedback or answers are again at the end of the session. If you still do not understand a topic having attempted the self-assessment question, always try to re-read the relevant passages in the textbook readings or session, or follow the advice on further reading at the end of the session. If this still doesn't work, you should contact the CIPS Membership and Qualification Advice team.

For most of the learning activities and self assessment questions you will need to use separate sheets of paper for your answers or responses. Some of the activities or questions require you to complete a table or form, in which case you could write your response in the study guide itself, or photocopy the page.

At the end of the session are three final sections.

The first is the **summary**. Use it to remind yourself or check off what you have just studied, or later on during revision.

Then follows the **suggested further reading** section. This section, if it appears, contains recommendations for further reading which you can follow up if you would like to read alternative treatments of the topics. If for any reason you are having difficulty understanding the course book on a particular topic, try one of the alternative treatments recommended. If you are keen to read around and beyond the syllabus, to help you pick up extra points in the examination for example, you may like to try some of the additional readings recommended. If this section does not appear at the end of a session, it usually means that further reading for the session topics is not necessary.

At the end of the session we direct you to a **revision question**, which you will find in a separate section at the end of the course book. Feedback on the questions is also given.

Reading lists

CIPS produces an official reading list, which recommends essential and desirable texts for augmenting your studies. This reading list is available on the CIPS website or from the CIPS Bookshop. This course book is one of the essential texts for this unit. In this section we describe the main characteristics of the other essential text for this unit, which you are strongly urged to buy and use throughout your course.

The other essential text is:

The Performance Prism by Andy Neely, Chris Adams, Mike Kennerley (0-273-65334-2, 1ˢᵗ edition, 2002, Pearson).

This is a comprehensive and interesting book on performance management in general, and its approach is very much based on the need to understand the performance required by different stakeholders before deciding on the measures and systems to be put in place.

It's approach can therefore be said to be 'top down', making it particularly relevant to the first part of this course book, though there are useful sections on suppliers and alliances and employee relationships which relate to the rest of the course book.

This is *not* a purchasing book as such and students will need to consider how best to apply it to the specifics of procurement, whilst bearing in mind that the book argues in favour of taking a holistic rather than a fragmented approach.

Unit content coverage

In this section we reproduce the whole of the official CIPS unit content document for this unit. The overall unit characteristics and learning outcomes for the unit are given first. Then, in the table that follows, the learning objectives and indicative content are given in the left hand column. In the right hand column are the study sessions, or subsections, in which you will find coverage of the various topics.

Unit Characteristics

This unit is designed to help students to measure the effectiveness of the supply chain and its contribution towards aiding the competitiveness and effectiveness of the organisation.

Students taking this unit should be able to apply a range of measurement techniques used to monitor the performance of a variety of individual suppliers, how they perform financially versus target, compliance to contract/specification, and potential risks that they may present.

Measurement will take place on three levels, organisational, functional and individual.

Students should be able apply a range of techniques and provide results that evaluate supplier performance, and make suggestions for future improvements

Learning Outcomes

On completion of this unit students should be able to:

- Determine how measuring performance in supply chain activities fits into the overall management process of an organisation
- Discuss the benefits of implementing a well structured approach to measuring organisational, functional and individual performance
- Categorise types of performance measures that are available to supply chain managers
- Argue the reasons for measuring a suppliers performance
- Appraise measures that can be used to improve supplier performance
- Use a range of accounting techniques to measure organisational efficiency
- Interpret and apply statistical data used to measure performance

Learning objectives and indicative content

1.0 Measuring and evaluating the performance of the purchasing and supply function (Weighting 40%)

1.1 Describe the role and importance of measuring performance, how it fits into the overall management decision-making process, and how it contributes to continuous improvement and continuity of supply.
- Importance of performance measurement for control purposes
- Link to organisations mission and strategic goals/objectives
- Its role in the purchasing management process
- Advantages and disadvantages of performance measurement for the purchasing function.

Study session 1

1.2 Explain the concept and forms of added value and evaluate the benefits of value-added solutions including:
- Savings resulting from improved performance
- Reducing inventory costs and administration
- Extending payment and warranty terms
- Using consignment stock
- Improving operational efficiency

Study session 2

1.3 Classify the information required to perform purchasing activities and to measure and evaluate purchasing performance.
- Departmental versus strategic goals of the organisation
- Resource requirements
- Costing, pricing, inventory management
- Supplier/vendor information
- Product/Service specifications

Study session 4

1.4 Outline and appraise the types and categories of key performance measures available to organisations including:
- Contributions to profitability - savings, service and inventory
- Basic workload control
- Infrastructure and competency

Study session 3

1.5 Demonstrate an understanding of how an organisation's purchase and supply function can manage and reduce inventory costs, and outline the methods available to do so.
- Economy: achieving best value for money. Managing the cost of the supply operation
- Efficiency: use of appropriate inventory management systems/techniques.
- Effectiveness: level of service provided by the inventory function to its end users.

Study session 5

1.6 Suggest how the use of information technology may help in the acquisition of purchase and supply performance data.   Study session 6
- Use of appropriate management information systems to capture and record information relating to all related costs re: stock/inventory levels and use; and overall costs relating to the purchasing function
- Databases for recording/storing supplier/vendor information
- Stock movement/monitoring systems, including point-of-sale data capture and delivery details
- Statistical database for quality monitoring purposes

2.0 Measuring and evaluating the performance of the supplier (Weighting 30%)

2.1 Demonstrate an understanding of the key areas associated with supplier selection and evaluation.   Study session 8
- The key stages in the buying process
- The variables considered when making the purchasing decision

2.2 Explain the importance of measuring a supplier's performance and distinguish from supplier appraisal.   Study session 7
- Supplier appraisal: assessment of supplier capability to control quality, quantity and price
- Supplier performance: comparison against a standard, performance on previous orders and against other supplier's performances

2.3 Discuss the impact of supplier performance on an organisation's quality and productivity.
- Good suppliers allow an organisation to perform efficiently and effectively. Issue of right-first-time-every-time. Lower costs of operation
- Poor suppliers adversely affect performance. Knock-on effect of sub-standard goods and services, plus untimely deliveries all add cost to an organisation.

2.4 Apply and evaluate appropriate measures to develop sustained improvement of supplier performance including: Study session 9 / Study session 10
- Carters Model of performance measures (9Cs)
- Simple vendor rating calculations
- Use of financial ratios

2.5 Discuss the importance of close and frequent buyer-supplier communication and of its importance within supply contracts.   Study session 11 / Study session 14
- Demand-supply chain relationships
- Inter-organisational partnering and long-term commitment
- Benefits relating to working together: cost reduction, joint product and service development, joint performance measurement and appraisal

2.6 Outline how a shared measurement approach will inform a process of continuous improvement, and employ appropriate financial and accounting tools to assess organisational efficiency including:
- Cash flow analysis
- Use of appropriate ratios – activity ratio, liquidity ratio, working capital – to assess organisational efficiency
- Identification of supplier fraud

Study session 12

2.7 Discuss the use of performance measurement as a tool for supplier relationship development.
- Measurement as a motivating factor for both parties
- Mutual opportunities to create understanding to improve performance
- Positive approach to relationship building and continuous improvement
- Identification of weaknesses and problems

Study session 14

2.8 Discuss possible measures relating to a supplier's research and development, cultural adaptation and similar qualitative performance.
- Compare conformance to international and recognised industry standards or benchmarks

Study session 13

2.9 Determine ways of measuring supplier achievement of service levels. Use of evaluation reports relating to:
- Cost of initial purchasing measure
- On-going levels of performance in carrying out the service: quality, after-sales service, price, consistency of performance

Study session 10

3.0 Measuring and evaluating the performance of the buyer (Weighting 30%)

3.1 Discuss the benefits of a well-managed and structured approach to measuring an individual's performance including:
- Investors in people guidelines and structure
- Performance against target assessments
- Planning for improvements

Study session 15

3.2 Outline the appraisal and evaluation techniques that can be employed within such an approach.
- Periodic reviews
- Informal and formal appraisals

Study session 17

3.3 Review how individual components of a purchasing job link to the overall objectives of the organisation.
- Contribution of individuals to an organisation's profitability
- Management of basic workload
- Development of purchasing infrastructure

Study session 16

3.4 Discuss and demonstrate how an individual's knowledge, expertise and skills can be developed to the benefit of both that individual and the organisation.
- Individual benefits: level of responsibility, job satisfaction, career progression, skills development
- Organisational benefits: better-trained workforce
- Improved productivity and profitability
- Competitive advantages

Study session 15

3.5 Identify and appraise the training needs of individuals, using   Study session 18
appropriate analytical approaches, including:
- Job profiles
- Key objectives
- Performance measures
- Appraisals

3.6 Suggest and evaluate relevant statistical data and/or information   Study session 19
as a basis for measuring an individual's performance including:
- Measuring performance against pre-set targets relating to
cost reduction, profitability and productivity

3.7 Compare the relative performance measures of the buyer with   Study session 20
those of his/her respective suppliers.
- Key measures of supplier performance: competency,
commitment, capacity, control
- Key measures of buyer performance: skill and knowledge,
plus contribution to an organisation's goals and targets

Study session 1

Introduction to performance management in purchasing and supply

'If you can't measure it, you can't manage it.'

This business axiom implies that performance measurement is critical to core business activities. This principle is valid for all organisations.

Introduction

This course book – *Measuring Purchasing Performance* – is divided into three parts:

- measuring and evaluating the performance of the purchasing and supply function (sessions 1–6)
- measuring and evaluating the performance of the supplier (sessions 7–14)
- measuring and evaluating the performance of the buyer (sessions 15–20).

The whole course book will review all aspects of performance management for procurement professionals working in any business sector or organisation.

Performance management is not just the prerogative of large corporations; it is equally important for enterprises of all size and structure.

There are 20 study sessions in this course book. This first session lays the foundation stone for the subject.

Session learning objectives

After completing this session you should be able to:

1.1 State the principles of performance management in corporate business operations.
1.2 Explain how performance management is undertaken within purchasing and supply operations.
1.3 Explain how costs are identified and built up in business processes, from the acquisition of goods and services to added value, and to final delivery to customers.
1.4 Give examples of how performance measures are used as part of the wider principle of continuous improvement in business.
1.5 Assess how performance management is linked to the need for continuity of supply in a business operation.
1.6 Demonstrate the importance of effective supply chain performance management within the management of a successful operation.

Unit content coverage

This study session covers the following topics from the official CIPS unit content document:

1

Learning outcomes

- Determine how measuring performance in supply chain activities fits into the overall management process of an organisation.
- Discuss the benefits of implementing a well-structured approach to measuring organisational, functional and individual performance.

Learning objective

1.1 Describe the role and importance of measuring performance, how it fits into the overall management decision-making process, and how it contributes to continuous improvement and continuity of supply.
  - Importance of performance measurement for control purposes
  - Link to organisations mission and strategic goals/objectives
  - Its role in the purchasing management process
  - Advantages and disadvantages of performance measurement for the purchasing function.

Prior knowledge

You should have some general knowledge of the supply chain process, and the basics of costs involved in managing a business operation and the goods and services used. You also need to have some financial/value analytical skills.

Resources

No specific resources are required, but it will be useful to be or to have been involved in some aspects of performance monitoring. This might be either in a general business operating environment or more specifically in measuring or monitoring purchasing-related issues. If not, you may find it useful to discuss this issue with other students or colleagues, or with a manager.

Timing

You should set aside about 6 hours to read and complete this session, including learning activities, self-assessment questions, the suggested further reading (if any) and the revision question.

1.1 The importance of performance management in business

Organisations in all sectors take many forms and functions, but they all have a common need to manage their business needs efficiently and effectively in line with their stated business objectives.

Most businesses set out a business plan, which begins with both a mission statement and a vision statement, and then set out a plan of how the business will be managed over time. Business management matters are led by strategic plans, which are delivered by tactical and operational methods. Management is then effected by implementing the longer-term strategy, executing medium-term tactical management, and directing the day-to-day operational processes.

Most organisations have a planned management structure that includes some, if not all, of the following interrelated management functions:

- finance
- human resources
- design
- production/service operations
- marketing
- purchasing
- administration.

Whatever the size of the business, success is judged by the result of the whole organisation's performance, and each element depends on all the others for corporate success. This first study session takes an overview of how the organisation is judged as a whole; in subsequent sessions we shall then move on to focus on how purchasing management plays its part in this corporate result.

In the opening sentence of this session we used the terms 'effectively' and 'efficiently' in describing how the achievement of business objectives is assessed. In considering performance management we need to understand the meaning of both effectiveness and efficiency before we move on to consider performance measurement in subsequent study sessions:

- **Effectiveness** is measured by the extent to which stakeholders' or customers' requirements are met over time.
- **Efficiency** is measured in terms of how economically the organisation's resources are utilised in providing a given level of stakeholder/customer satisfaction.

These two terms identify the dimensions of performance measurement for corporate managers in general, and for purchasing managers in particular.

The selected performance indicators are called **key performance indicators** (KPIs).

You can view performance management in terms of a process diagram, as illustrated in figure 1.1.

1

Figure 1.1: Purchasing performance management within the organisation

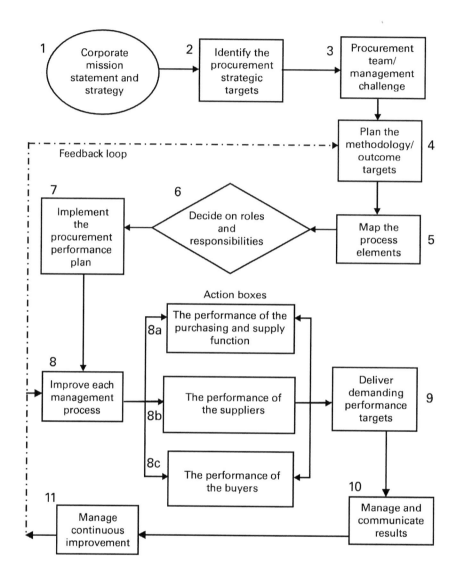

The numbered boxes in this diagram set out the key steps in purchasing performance management within corporate strategy:

1   The business management team or board establish the organisation's mission statement.
2   They then establish the purchasing function's strategic targets.
3   The procurement management team accept the challenge.
4   The purchasing manager or managers decide on their methodology and targets.
5   The manager or management team map out their plan.
6   Decision point: who does what?
7   Start the implementation plan.
8   Start the action plan: subdivide it into purchasing function performance, suppliers' performance, and buyers' performance.
9   Deliver the KPIs.

10   Communicate the KPIs.

11   Manage continuous improvement of the KPIs.

See also the dotted feedback loop: repeat the process as necessary.

Learning activity 1.1

Based on your organisation or experience, review the process diagram above and create a KPI checklist of purchasing points that you recommend should be measured in the action boxes 8a, 8b and 8c.

Feedback on page 14

Now tackle the following self-assessment question.

Self-assessment question 1.1

Based on the list you created in learning activity 1.1 above, categorise the performance indicators (KPIs) that you identified for your organisation to achieve operational and/or business success under the following three headings:

1   Strategic performance measures (longer-term senior management targets and issues)

2   Tactical performance measures (medium-term executive/supervisory management performance issues)

3   Operational performance measures (shorter-term process/transactional data and issues).

Feedback on page 15

1.2   Introduction to performance management in general and purchasing and supply in particular

Purchasing is an important function in any management team. Depending on the nature of the business, a significant percentage of turnover is spent through purchasing.

In this course book you will be focusing on purchasing, but the wider term **supply chain management** is implied in many cases. Supply chain management covers the whole process of managing goods and services into, through and out from the business. Supply chain management can and does have a direct effect on the profitability and performance of the business. The supply chain management functions interface both with the external environment and with internal management and processes. They fall into three supply chain or logistics categories:

- inbound supply issues
- intra-site management
- outbound delivery of goods and services to stakeholders or customers.

The broad process flow can be illustrated as in figure 1.2.

1

Figure 1.2: Supply chain performance measurement processes

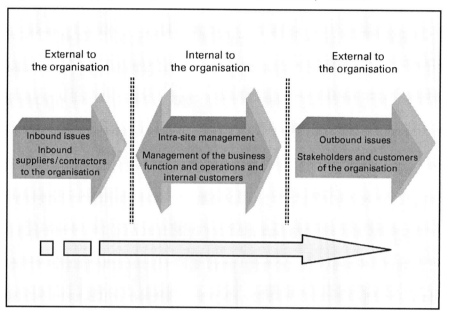

Now tackle the following self-assessment question.

1.3 Introduction to cost management in organisations and the link with purchasing performance

Financial management, budgeting, cost management and accounting procedures are fundamental to organisations, irrespective of their size or the market sector they are in. Private sector organisations measure percentage profitability and return on capital employed (ROCE) as key financial indicators. Public sector organisations have strict budgets, but usually measure service levels delivered as performance indicators. All organisations – private and public – need to manage their costs in order to achieve their strategic targets.

Products and services are costed and sold to consumers. The main elements of building a commercial cost model are labour, materials, overheads and profit. Public bodies and not-for-profit organisations (NPOs) may not make a profit as such, but they usually have to recover their service costs within their budget limits. However, whether you are a buyer for a private or a public organisation, you need to know how costs are accumulated, how they are accounted for, and how prices are determined.

There is not always a direct relationship between the cost of an item or service and the price you pay. There are many other market factors, some of which can be quantified and valued objectively, such as money, time, and level of quality. Other issues are more subjective: service quality, artistic or aesthetic value, business relationships and similar qualitative issues.

There is an old adage: 'There are some people who know the cost of everything but the value of nothing.' In commercial purchasing we *do* need to know the costs and, where appropriate, how they are made up, but in some cases market or category knowledge is equally important.

The measurement of purchasing performance, then, is a skill that requires us to consider both objective information and subjective opinion.

Mini case study: Cost analysis

You are managing a contract to supply office desks. The current price is £269 per desk. You request a cost analysis from your regular supplier, who replies with the information shown in figure 1.3.

Figure 1.3: Mini case study

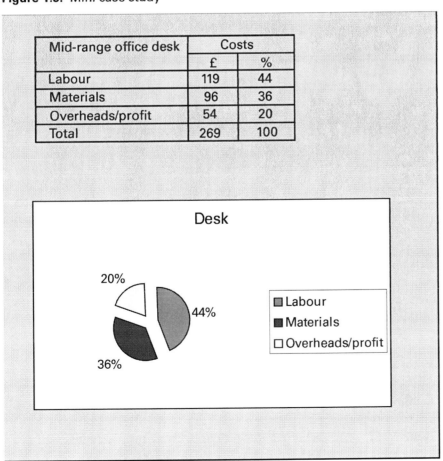

Mid-range office desk	Costs	
	£	%
Labour	119	44
Materials	96	36
Overheads/profit	54	20
Total	269	100

1

You now have some better cost information about the product you are purchasing. You can see where the costs occur, and can use this information for a variety of purchasing purposes: comparison, price monitoring over time, and so on.

Obviously the costs for different goods and services will vary greatly. Some are labour-intensive, some are dominated by the price of materials, and some carry different overhead or profit levels. The main point here is that, by having a more detailed cost analysis, a buyer has better information to link to performance management tasks.

You will have the opportunity to develop the principles of cost and price analysis further in study session 4.

Learning activity 1.3

Explain how costs are identified and built up for a product or service with which you are familiar.

Feedback on page 16

Now tackle the following self-assessment question.

Self-assessment question 1.3

You wish to find out more about the cost of items you buy. Draft a table or form for your suppliers to complete when they next quote a price for goods or services.

Feedback on page 16

1.4 Continuous improvement in business, and the link with purchasing performance management

The principle of **continuous improvement**is common to many successful business operations where there is an ongoing culture of developing and improving processes and products over time. Continuous improvement organisations foster improvements in product quality, which often produce simultaneous reductions in costs.

Various quality 'gurus' have developed the principles of continuous improvement, and some milestones include the following:

- Demming (1982): his 14 points, moving from the product 'price tag' to a total cost philosophy
- Ishikawa (1985): quality circles and continuous improvement principles
- Taguchi (1986): improvement by statistical process control (SPC).

The Japanese philosophy of continuous improvement has developed as part of both just-in-time (JIT) and the more recent lean supply culture in industry.

In both research and development and, later, the production environment the learning curve principle will apply. When a new product is developed, the prototype and early product runs will take longer to make than subsequent runs. Manufacturing tasks are performed more quickly with each subsequent repetition (up to a certain limit). Therefore the process labour costs will reduce as we 'learn'. This is one practical example of continuous improvement in production management operations.

The Japanese word *kaizen* means 'improvement'. Kaizen strategy calls for everyone linked to the organisation to make never-ending efforts to improve – managers, workers, suppliers, stakeholders and customers alike.

Based on this philosophy we shall now focus on the contribution that purchasing performance measurement can make to the wider process of continuous improvement.

Purchasing can ensure improvements at all stages in the supply chain. Here are some examples:

- managing the quality and service delivery of inbound supplies
- ensuring continuity of supplies to the organisation by means of best purchasing practice tactics
- ensuring selection of the best suppliers for the business
- reviewing the transactional processes in purchasing (i.e. the many transactions that take place in the supply chain)
- ensuring adequate stockholding where appropriate
- managing the purchasing process to best effect
- managing cost reductions as suppliers make 'learning curve' savings
- feeding back vendor performance rating to existing suppliers
- ensuring that outbound processes and services satisfy customer needs.

No doubt you could add to this list based on your own experience or business needs. The main point here is that you need to recognise how we in purchasing can be proactive in the process of managing continuous improvement, whatever our role and responsibility.

Look back at the process diagram in figure 1.1. Point 11 in the diagram marks the continuous improvement point of review. This is where you can identify opportunities and follow the feedback loop to undertake continuous improvement in purchasing performance.

Learning activity 1.4

Identify three ways in which you can achieve continuous improvement gains over time with a supply partner.

Feedback on page 16

Now tackle the following self-assessment question.

Self-assessment question 1.4

Explain the process of continuous improvement with respect to the concept of the learning curve.

Feedback on page 17

1.5 Continuity of supply, and the link to measuring purchasing performance

One of the buyer's most important roles for his or her organisation is to ensure **continuity of supply** – the availability of materials or services to the organisation when they are needed.

Figure 1.4 illustrates several 'core tasks' that are the role and responsibility of purchasing in the business. They involve short-, medium- and longer-term actions incorporated in the purchasing strategic plan.

Figure 1.4: Purchasing: the key tasks within a business or organisation

You may need to refer to this diagram several times as you progress through this course book. Depending on the nature of the organisation you may need to consider other tasks, but this model summarises the core tasks for a purchasing manager.

Ensuring continuity of supply to the organisation is shown as one of the core tasks, along with the need to produce verified performance indicators.

Most organisations need some form of goods or services to run their business – raw materials, components, consumables, equipment, repairs

1

and maintenance, wholesale/retail stock etc, depending on the business needs. Without these basics businesses could not continue, but that does not mean that purchasing should obtain them at any price. Purchasing's role is to manage the supply inputs regularly and consistently over time to meet the business's needs. The measurement of this core task must provide a meaningful indicator of purchasing performance.

Continuity of supply can be achieved in many ways; some of them are listed below (you should remember, however, that buyers must consider the cost–benefit consequences of each action relevant to their particular organisational and financial needs):

- multi-source supplies
- single-source agreements
- developing a strategic partnership
- managing stock and stockholding
- market research and knowledge
- collaboration/cooperative strategies.

These opportunities offer different benefits in the short, medium and longer term. They can be used independently, or together; they are not mutually exclusive.

Having made operational choices, managers can then measure the outcomes and the performance indicators, which are thus a measure of the success or failure of the strategy or tactic adopted.

The measurement of supply continuity outputs would address such issues as:

- customer service/product delivery performance
- number of production line hold-ups due to non-supply
- the cost of holding stock as 'insurance'
- the cost of being without supplies
- the acquisition costs of obtaining supplies.

Learning activity 1.5

Supply continuity is an important core activity. However, we have emphasised the need to be aware of cost–benefit issues. Purchasing costs money; holding stock costs money. Organisations can choose to have more or less of each.

Using these two terms create a list of costs that you would include under these two headings:

1 What is the cost of acquiring goods and services?
2 How much does it cost to hold inventory/stock?

Feedback on page 17

Now tackle the following self-assessment question.

Self-assessment question 1.5

What are the costs of non-supply of goods and services to your business operation?

Feedback on page 17

1.6 The importance of measuring purchasing and supply chain performance in public and private sector organisations

So far in this first study session we have introduced the wider context of performance management in general and the measurement of purchasing performance in particular.

The holistic concept of measuring purchasing performance was illustrated in the steps of the process flow diagram in figure 1.1. This diagram included three action boxes:

- 8a The performance of the purchasing and supply function
- 8b The performance of suppliers
- 8c The performance of buyers.

You will see that these purchasing actions are preceded by planning and policy actions. When the performance in boxes 8a, 8b and 8c is measured, the flow diagram shows that the next step is to communicate the results and then link them to the process of continuous improvement within the business.

In an organisation that has chosen to manage performance across all three functions – supply, suppliers and buyers – each departmental area of operation would be managing its own set of action boxes in order to make its input to the corporate performance objectives. Thus the individual departments or functions work as a team in achieving the corporate performance goals.

Purchasing plays a key role in this corporate process, and in task 6 of figure 1.1 the purchasing team players agree their roles and responsibilities linked to the purchasing targets.

We have now introduced the main elements of purchasing performance management. As you worked through each of these you had an opportunity to identify some specific purchasing performance measures.

You now need to start on your own path to continuous improvement by looking back over your work and improving the outputs, aiming at effective and efficient measurements of purchasing performance.

In the spirit of continuous improvement you will develop your skill and understanding further as you work through the course book.

We now focus on the way in which purchasing has a direct effect on all organisations, even though they may measure their performance in different ways:

- private sector businesses: company profits, ROCE, value for money (VFM), cost reduction, reduced stockholding, customer service
- public sector/NPOs: service to users, utilisation of funds, profitability, response and service times, stock availability.

We can classify measurable improvements linked to purchasing under various headings:

- cost reduction
- service improvement
- continuous improvement progress
- improved/reduced stockholding
- improved quality outputs
- improved delivery/schedules
- improves process control/systems
- reduced transaction costs
- improved supplier base management
- improved communications
- measures specific to the organisation.

We can view the above issues as long-, medium- or short-term indicators: the strategic or longer-term issues measured over 1–4 years, tactical or medium-term issues measured over 1–2 years, and the shorter-term transaction/operational issues measured over 6–12 months. Each may also be part of a wider continuous improvement development programme within the organisation. Each is important to the organisation plan in general and to purchasing management in particular.

Having discussed the theory you now need to put purchasing performance management into practice by using your own skill and judgement in selecting practical measures that will contribute to your organisation's success.

Learning activity 1.6

Develop a checklist of purchasing performance indicators at the strategic, tactical and operational levels that could be applied to a chosen working environment.

Feedback on page 18

Now tackle the following self-assessment question.

Self-assessment question 1.6

For a given operational environment select the four best practice purchasing performance indicators.

Feedback on page 18

Revision question

Now try the revision question for this session on page 333.

Summary

This session opened with the wider corporate view of performance measurement within the whole organisation, and showed where the purchasing role fits into that process.

The session then developed the issue of performance management elements, cost and price management, links to continuous improvement, and the importance of continuity of supply to all organisations. Each of these is equally relevant in any business sector, whether public or private.

The final section developed the many and various opportunities to measure performance, and encouraged students to relate the theory they are studying to practical situations in their own experience.

Suggested further reading

Students will find Neely et al (2002) particularly useful supplementary reading, providing a higher level overview relevant to study sessions 1 to 6. Lysons and Farrington (2006) provides excellent and detailed information on strategy and strategic procurement theories, and chapter 9 of Poister (2003) provides a perspective on how to apply measures at a strategic level, all of which is also relevant to these six sessions.

For this session in particular students will find more information about the works and theories of the quality 'gurus' (Deming, Ishkawa and Taguchi) in Lysons and Farrington (2006), chapter 9, pages 271–2.

Feedback on learning activities and self-assessment questions

Feedback on learning activity 1.1

The purpose of this activity was to set the scene for the course book by first understanding that purchasing is an important part of any management team, in terms of its contribution to success as measured by the achievement of agreed targets set in the business plan.

You should have identified a minimum of three KPIs for each action box.

8a KPIs related to the management and organisation of the purchasing function.

For example, the KPI process time for processing a customer requisition to order:

KPI versus actual over the last quarter.

8b KPIs related to performance of suppliers selected by the purchasing managers

For example, the published performance levels for a category of suppliers:

- KPI: delivery performance of top five suppliers last quarter.

8c KPIs related to personal performance of buyers in the organisation

For example, the savings target versus actual.

- KPI: target for a buyer group over the last quarter.

Any of these examples can be expanded. For example, a KPI developed under 8b could be fleshed out in detail for a specific supplier:

- Delivery performance for a specific product from key supplier ABC Ltd.
- Target: 95% of 'on-time' deliveries as per dates agreed.
- Measured: monthly, giving percentage result and variance from target.
- Feedback and actions: on results and variance.

Feedback on self-assessment question 1.1

There is no right or wrong answer here. This is your list, and the object of the question was for you to understand the differences in timescale and actions related to business strategy management, tactical management targets and process/transactional issues that exist in any organisation.

Feedback on learning activity 1.2

We can generate a useful general management checklist for this type of question by asking the questions How? What? Where? Why? and When?

At this stage you are being asked to decide 'where' and 'what' to measure on the basis of information given to you up to this point.

As you progress you will be more selective in your answers, but you should have identified some performance indicator suggestions for each of the three stages in the flow diagram.

Generic examples might include the following:

- inbound: supplier delivery/quality KPIs
- intra-site: stock and warehouse management KPIs
- outbound: transport and distribution KPIs.

1

Feedback on self-assessment question 1.2

As we have seen, there are many issues and actions that can be measured, and which you might have listed. The point of this question is to develop your skill and judgement in assessing which measures are the most useful and relevant to meet your success criteria.

The purpose of ranking them in order of importance is to show that you must be selective in deciding on the indicators and on how you will measure them for best effect.

Feedback on learning activity 1.3

The purpose of this activity was for you to understand the elements of cost for goods and services supplied, and how they are broadly classified in a cost accounting price build-up format.

You should have chosen a product or service that you offer or consume, and have should have researched the basis of the main cost headers that we introduced above.

You may have accurate cost analysis data, or you may have made a reasonably informed judgement on the item or service that you have chosen.

You should have subdivided the costs into labour, materials, overhead and profit, and have calculated the percentage make-up of the total you pay.

Feedback on self-assessment question 1.3

You need to undertake this activity selectively for key items only, and not for everything you buy. Table 1.1 shows the basic data we would expect you to include on such a form.

Table 1.1 Cost information

Product	Cost	Percentage %
....		
Labour costs		
Material costs		
Overheads		
Profit		
Selling price/total		

Feedback on learning activity 1.4

This activity takes you to the beginning of the supply chain – inbound – where buyers agree the purchase of goods, stock, services etc The use of the term 'supply partner' implies the existence of a longer-term relationship with a vendor. If both parties – buyer and supplier – wish to maintain that relationship, it is in both their interests to work together and follow a continuous improvement strategy by:

- the buyer giving clear and timely notice of needs
- the seller being open with cost information
- the buyer reducing transactional costs to a minimum and paying suppliers on time
- the seller passing on process/manufacturing improvement costs as the learning curve effect progresses
- the seller looking for cost reductions or service improvements that have mutual value for the relationship.

These are just some of the ways you can achieve continuous improvement gains in purchasing management. How did your list of three ways compare?

Feedback on self-assessment question 1.4

As you have read in this session, a basic form of continuous improvement is linked to the management theory of the learning curve.

Most people improve their skill or competence when undertaking the same task after several repetitions. In a manufacturing context we can negotiate cost reductions as the workforce make improvements in manufacturing time or associated costs, including:

- improved speed and efficiency in producing the product
- less scrap generated
- improved process controls/methods
- investment in capital equipment to speed up the process for longer runs.

Feedback on learning activity 1.5

It is important to ensuring continuity of supply, but there are cost–benefit limits in achieving this objective.

By listing the costs under each heading you will now be in a position to review the balance between costs and benefits. We shall develop these issues further as we progress through this course book.

Feedback on self-assessment question 1.5

The cost of not having goods and or services when they are needed can far outweigh the cost of acquiring or of holding stock. For example:

- In a retail situation customers will migrate away from stores that do not have the range or depth of stock they are looking for.
- In a manufacturing operation a production line can be halted for the lack of a key component. Just-in-time can become 'just-too-late'.

You will no doubt be able to add other examples based on your own experience.

Feedback on learning activity 1.6

This activity develops from the concluding paragraph of this study session. There is no right or wrong answer, but rather your own informed view of how to put theory into practice in your own organisation so that you can relate the study material to practical situations.

Feedback on self-assessment question 1.6

This question adds value to learning activity 1.6, in which you developed a list of performance indicators.

In any business you have to prioritise time and effort. This question requires you to do this by ranking the issues in order of importance and then listing the top four: that is, those that you would act on first for best effect.

As an example, consider an answer for a private sector wholesale business that supplies and distributes engineering tools. What KPIs would senior managers be most interested in?

- stock availability: linked to stock/stores management
- market price: linked to buyers' performance
- delivery service: linked to stock distribution management
- gross/net profit: linked to overall business costs and profitability
- customer service: customers' views/loyalty.

Adding value to the business

Introduction

When we buy goods or services there is a usually an actual monetary cost, but 'value' is more subjective. Quality, on-time delivery or service, or indeed a better discount or a reduced cost – these and other factors all add value to a transaction. In a manufacturing operation the business can add further value in the production process.

A purchasing manager's task is twofold:

1 to establish a competitive cost
2 to gain added value or business benefits for the process through good purchasing/commercial management.

'Some people know the cost of everything and the value of nothing.'

In daily life and in business operations we all want value for money – but what *is* value? By understanding what value is we can then develop the principle of added value, and how we can achieve it.

Session learning objectives

After completing this session you should be able to:

2.1 State the principle of added value with respect to the role of purchasing and supply in a business operation, and describe how it can be measured.
2.2 Give examples of added value opportunities that purchasing and supply managers can offer to a business.
2.3 Assess the added value opportunities afforded by improved performance in purchasing and supply, and describe how these can be measured.
2.4 Assess the added value opportunities afforded by reducing inventory costs and administration and the use of consignment stocks in purchasing and supply, and describe how these can be measured.
2.5 Assess the added value opportunities afforded by purchasing and supply managers negotiating improved procurement and contract terms with suppliers, and describe how these can be measured.
2.6 Assess the added value opportunities afforded by improving operational efficiency in purchasing and supply, and describe how these can be measured.

Unit content coverage

This study session covers the following topics from the official CIPS unit content document:

Learning outcomes

- Discuss the benefits of implementing a well-structured approach to measuring organisational, functional and individual performance.

- Categorise types of performance measures that are available to supply chain managers
- Argue the reasons for measuring a supplier's performance.
- Appraise measures that can be used to improve supplier performance.

Learning objective

1.2 Explain the concept and forms of added value and evaluate the benefits of value-added solutions including:
- Savings resulting from improved performance
- Reducing inventory costs and administration
- Extending payment and warranty terms
- Using consignment stock
- Improving operational efficiency

Prior knowledge

You should have a basic understanding of the business concept of adding value in a business operation. From this basis of knowledge, the study session develops the concept with respect to purchasing and supply at the strategic, tactical and operational levels of management.

Resources

No specific resources are required for this session.

In order to apply the concepts described, it would be useful to have access to some cost information on goods or services you are or have been involved with. However, we do give examples if no direct information is available.

Timing

You should set aside about 5 hours to read and complete this session, including learning activities, self-assessment questions, the suggested further reading (if any) and the revision question.

2.1 Added value performance management in corporate business operations: general principles

One definition of **added value** could be the achievement of equivalent financial savings or benefits that are not based on a movement in unit price only.

The monetary benefits of added value are sometimes estimated subjectively, because by their nature they will often be less tangible than a specific price benefit, which is more easily quantified.

The wider corporate principle of the **value chain** was illustrated by Michael Porter in his classic model (figure 2.1). It shows how margin is created as functions add value, which is created by process flow both through primary activities and through associated 'support' activities. The resulting 'margin' is a direct function of how well these primary and secondary activities are managed.

Figure 2.1: The value chain: creating and sustaining superior performance

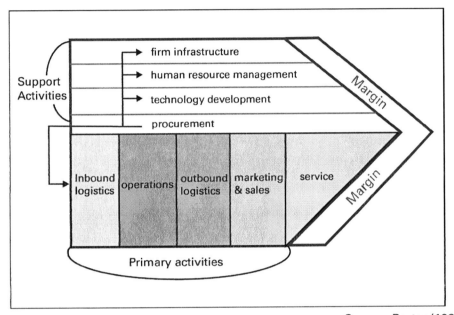

Source: Porter (1985)

Each function or activity is part of the corporate management, and either contributes to or diminishes the operating margin. Thus the members of the corporate management team all have a role and responsibility in generating the business margin.

In this model we see that Porter listed procurement as a support activity, which then feeds into the primary added value processes that feed forward to the business/profit margin.

You can see that procurement can and does have a direct effect on the value added business margin with each of the functions within the primary value-adding activities illustrated in figure 2.1.

Learning activity 2.1

Based on your experience, and on the definition of added value given above, create a list of opportunities where purchasing and supply managers can achieve added value for the business operation.

Feedback on page 30

Now tackle the following self-assessment question.

2

2.2 Added value opportunities

We now move from the general corporate added value added to the specific contribution that can be made via the purchasing function. The Porter model is based on a manufacturing or process type of operation, but of course there are similar value-adding opportunities within public service and NPO organisations.

Examples of purchasing-related savings that can contribute to the corporate value added chain include:

- eliminating or changing the initial requirement specified by the end user or customer
- changing the product/service specification or standard
- substituting lower-cost items – links to value analysis techniques
- extended payment terms
- extended warranty terms
- reducing stock or using a consignment stock facility
- improved operational efficiency – links to learning curve theory
- lower administration costs
- lower transactional costs.

There may be other opportunities within different organisations – some general, some specific to the organisation.

As some of these procurement issues are subjective rather than quantifiable, added value savings or benefits can be more difficult to substantiate and audit, but they are no less important to the organisation.

To summarise, the performance targets can be said to fall under the following headings:

- the same goods or services for lower cost, or
- the same costs but improved goods or services, or

- both lower costs and improved goods or services – the ultimate target!

Self-assessment question 2.2

Based on figure 2.2, give one example of an added value measure that a purchasing and supply manager can achieve at each main stage of the supply chain: that is, inbound, intra-site, and outbound.

Feedback on page 31

2.3 Measuring value added performance achieved by purchasing and supply

Having established some added value opportunities offered by improved purchasing and supply performance, we now need to consider how they can best be measured.

Setting, achieving, reporting on, and constantly revising purchasing and supply performance measures help the department improve its strategic position in the organisation.

Organisations may be at different points in their business evolution. If an organisation is just beginning, the 'best' performance measurements will depend on where the purchasing and supply department is in the development of the organisation and its supply base.

For a young or newly formed purchasing and supply department, the focus may be on cost reduction, supply base reduction, and service-level measurements.

As purchasing and supply departments mature, so do performance measures, to match and service more advanced relationships between the purchasing organisation and its key suppliers.

In section 2.1 above we looked at the broad principles of what purchasing and supply managers can offer to the business. We shall now focus on specific tasks that are the role and responsibility of the buyer, and on how these can be measured.

The term 'buyer' is a broad one: it covers the sourcing of goods and establishing prices and subsequent placing of orders to meet business needs. This role embodies a front-end supply chain process, and is the point of contact and interface between the organisation and the external supply market.

There are various titles for the jobs that involve work within the purchasing and supply function at this part of the chain, including order clerk, buyer, purchasing manager, procurement officer, agreements manager, and

2

contract manager. All work within an organisation and are responsible for soliciting information and prices from potential suppliers in a market sector and entering into contracts for supply.

Thus if the job is to buy goods and services to meet the needs of the next step of the supply chain (figure 2.2), we can measure efficiency and effectiveness in various ways. To take the buyer as an example:

- Efficiency:
    - actual costs of the buying process
    - buyers' cost per order, or per pound or euro spent
    - the cost of acquisition
    - savings achieved
    - added value gained
    - cycle times (network flow)
    - use of information technology
    - organisational structure
    - supplier management
    - work force assessment.
- Effectiveness:
    - customer service levels
    - goods/services within budget
    - quality levels
    - goods and services reach customers on time
    - service delivery to customers
    - improved relationships
    - impact on capital efficiency, asset management and profits.

Having read the efficiency and effectiveness issues in this list you should now be in a position to review your organisation's needs and add points relative to your own operation. When this is done you are ready to begin or revamp your purchasing and supply department's purchasing performance measures.

What is the first step in achieving this? If there is one consistent piece of advice, it is to make sure your purchasing performance measures reflect your own organisation's goals. Most purchasing and supply professionals start with the 'macro' goals and work down. Little value is found in a measure developed by a purchasing department if the measurement does not follow the stated organisation's wider goals.

Learning activity 2.3

Write a report on the merits of a bonus payment system based on measurable savings achieved by purchasing managers.

Feedback on page 32

Now tackle the following self-assessment question.

Self-assessment question 2.3

List three added value opportunities that you would recommend for a middle manager to take in order to improve his or her performance and contribution to the organisation. Write a short note on each.

Feedback on page 32

2.4 Adding value by reducing inventory costs and administration and using consignment stocks

Not all organisations hold stock; indeed, with the development of materials requirements planning (MRP) and the just-in-time philosophy (JIT), the holding of stock has been dramatically reduced in process and manufacturing industries. But there are still many other businesses and organisations that trade or rely on stockholding to achieve their business needs. The important point here is that stock has value, but also carries costs. Organisations need to identify where those costs lie in order to make a value judgement on the need to have or hold stock.

In the broadest terms stock is an asset; accountants include it as part of working capital on the balance sheet. Cash is the most liquid asset a business can have; although stock is an asset, it is not 'liquid' until it is sold. Excess stock ties up cash and reduces liquidity. Insufficient stock may reduce levels of service to customers (whether internal or external). So how much stock do we need to hold?

Study session 5 will analyse these cost–benefit issues in detail; at this point you need to understand the basic issues relating to added value within the broader supply chain.

Look again at figure 2.2. The centre link in the chain refers to stock management, stock control and work in progress (WIP). At these points in the chain goods have arrived in, perhaps as raw materials, or stock items, or components or sub-assemblies.

In a business operation some of the costs of stock are operational: those costs that accrue as part of the stockholding and handling process.

A second category of costs are financial: the costs of financing the acquisition of stock from working capital. These costs are linked to bank interest rates.

Still other costs are described as **opportunity costs**. This is an economics term. It means, with respect to stock, that we have an opportunity to invest our working capital in business stock or elsewhere. That decision can be based on a financial cost–benefit analysis: which is the best opportunity to utilise the money/working capital for a business.

2

In a manufacturing organisation business stock aggregates up as work in progress towards finished goods stock. There are process costs along the chain: buying the goods, handling the stock, assembling and moving the stock, and finally issuing and despatching the finished stock produced.

In wholesale, retail and service operations the goods are not processed as such. Bulk stock arrives and is stored, and then sales unit items are issued to users or customers.

In several industries, including retailing and manufacturing, buyers use consignment stock to reduce inventory costs. Where demand is independent but usage is regular, stock is delivered 'on consignment' to the point of use. As the need or sale arises, stock is issued and paid for when used. This has the benefit of stock availability and reduced cashflow for the buyer. There are still administrative and physical storage costs associated with the consignment stock, but the principle has worked well in many retail and maintenance operations.

Having identified where costs can accrue in managing inventory, you can see there are many opportunities for purchasing managers to reduce those costs.

Learning activity 2.4

Draw a process diagram showing how cost accrues to stock items as they pass through a stores/stock control system.

Feedback on page 33

Now tackle the following self-assessment question.

Self-assessment question 2.4

What do you understand by the term 'opportunity cost' with respect to stock held by a business organisation?

Feedback on page 33

2.5 Added value opportunities of negotiating: improved procurement and contract terms with suppliers

The quality of the agreements that buyers enter into with their suppliers can make a contribution to added value. The terms and conditions (T&Cs) of the agreement or contract can and will have an effect on the price.

The general concept here is the **total cost of acquisition** (TCA) and the wider concept of **total cost of ownership** (TCO): that is, not just how much the item or service costs but rather what its corporate life costs are, as set out in the cost equation (figure 2.4).

Figure 2.4: The cost equation

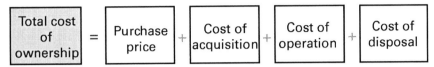

In this section we focus on the buying TCA/TCO in general, and in particular on how a buyer can add value by improving the T&Cs of the agreement.

Most agreements are covered by general terms of trade linked, where applicable, to express product or service conditions.

A buyer may have the opportunity to apply leverage to a proposed or negotiated deal based on various circumstances and needs.

Some negotiations result in objective, quantitative reductions: price, time, trade discount percentage, settlement discount. Some negotiations result in more subjective improvements or values: better quality, improved service, or extra warranty.

Other savings can accrue from reduced transaction costs of buying: fewer orders, call-off orders, procurement card usage, reduced transaction time, streamlined processing/systems resulting in reduced administration costs.

In summary, buyers can add value based on their skill and competence in both the TCA and TCO issues concerning the acquisition of goods and services by obtaining cost reductions or service improvements linked to negotiation of the commercial T&Cs of the agreement or contract.

Learning activity 2.5

Prepare a brief set of discussion points to be discussed at a planned negotiation meeting with a supplier.

Feedback on page 34

Now tackle the following self-assessment question.

Self-assessment question 2.5

How would you assess the effectiveness of a business negotiation meeting with a supplier?

Feedback on page 34

2.6 Adding value by improving operational efficiency

A key element in the cost of acquisition of goods and services is the actual cost of buying itself. The buying costs include:

the wages and salaries of buyers and purchasing staff

the cost of office premises and support costs

the cost of systems – both paper-based and IT/IS.

Operational efficiency is based on:

- HR factors: buyers' personal and or professional competence – skill, knowledge, experience, qualifications and attitude
- system and process factors: purchasing procedures, strategy, tactics, transactions, relationships, business IT systems and communications.

The operation of a buying person or team costs money and time, and as in all investment there is in effect a cost–benefit decision to be made. But if we assume that we have an existing team of buyers, then we need to measure their operational efficiency based on quantifiable volumes and values.

The principles set out here are developed in more detail in subsequent sessions, but at this point you need to consider issues based on:

- the volume of purchasing work
- the value of purchasing work.

The first step is to understand the current 'where are we now?' issues in order to establish a baseline for both the volume and value of work undertaken.

We can then go on to assess how buyers can improve their working operation, in both effectiveness and efficiency terms.

- The volume of work. This will include:
  - the numbers of orders placed over time
  - the number of items/services undertaken
  - the number of queries dealt with – how well the buying process works.
- The value of work. This will include:
  - the monetary value of those orders
  - the transactional costs involved – enquiries, evaluation, meetings etc
  - the savings made against budget.

The key question is: how are the volume and value of work managed by buyers? The answer to this question will vary from business to business, depending on the type of operation, its size and its complexity. For example, in a small business, is buying done by one person or several? Is buying general, or based on commodity knowledge or skill?

In a larger operation, with several geographic locations, is buying centralised at one site, or undertaken at every site?

There are many operational business buying combinations for managing the purchasing process, and they all have their respective advantages and disadvantages in terms of cost and efficiency. Your job is to be aware of the opportunities and then to assess how to evaluate both the purchasing efficiency and the effectiveness of the chosen application of the resources available to provide service and add value to the business.

Learning activity 2.6

List the advantages and disadvantages of a central purchasing operation for a UK manufacturer that has three separate production sites in the north, centre and south of the country.

Feedback on page 34

Now tackle the final self-assessment question in this study session.

Self-assessment question 2.6

Describe, in terms of added value, the operational efficiency advantages of having a fully integrated IT/IS system for an organisation.

(Fully integrated IT/IS systems are known as **enterprise resource planning** (ERP) systems; examples include SAP and Oracle.)

Feedback on page 35

Revision question

Now try the revision question for this session on page 333.

Summary

Added value is an important business and management concept. In this session you were introduced to Porter's value chain, which illustrates the contribution to margin made by the various business activities. In this session we have focused, in particular, on how the purchasing function can add value and create margin.

Value can be added both to manufactured goods and to services provided in any business sector. We considered each part of the supply chain, and reviewed the various ways in which value is added along it.

We then moved on to the wider consideration of how the concept of added value can be measured to ensure efficiency and effectiveness in parallel with continuous improvement targets.

2

Suggested further reading

Students can find more detail of the works of Michael Porter, particularly the concept of 'the value chain', in Lysons and Farrington (2006), chapter 3, pages 101–2.

Feedback on learning activities and self-assessment questions

Feedback on learning activity 2.1

The purpose of this activity is for you to recognise where value can be added. Using the Porter's value chain concept illustrated in figure 2.1 you can focus on the opportunities where purchasing and supply's value added inputs correlate to the wider supply chain or logistics concepts or terms noted in the diagram.

You could classify your list of purchasing and supply opportunities against each of the primary activities in the model, and decide on appropriate KPIs as follows:

- Inbound logistics: costs of acquisition, costs of bringing goods in, handling inbound goods.
- Operations: availability and costs of goods to the operations, manufacturing or process functions.
- Outbound logistics: costs of packing, picking and moving finished goods outbound to the customer.
- Marketing and sales: working with this function on product development and on products as they progress through their marketing life cycle.
- Service: costs of services that relate directly to the added value production process.

Feedback on self-assessment question 2.1

You identified some specific procurement measurement opportunities in learning activity 2.1. This question asks you to build on this by giving some examples of how to manage the process of reporting and achieving the chosen performance measures.

This relates to the opening statement in the previous study session: 'If you can't measure it, you can't manage it.' Having chosen some performance measures, how do you manage purchasing performance?

To help answer this, look back to figure 1.1. It shows that, once the agreed measurements are chosen, you should set demanding performance targets (process point 9) and then manage and communicate the results (process point 10).

Feedback on learning activity 2.2

Figure 2.2 is one representation of a supply chain flow model. The chain link elements overlap as the process flows from beginning to end.

Figure 2.2: A supply chain flow model from suppliers to customers

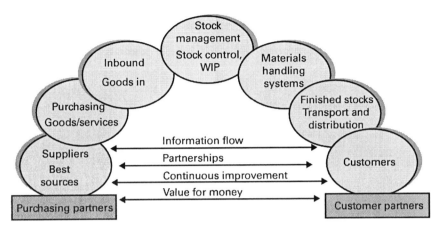

Source: Supply Chain Projects Ltd

The first link of the chain represents the upstream or inbound flow of goods or services into an organisation as they are sourced and bought by purchasing managers.

As these goods enter the process they are managed as stock and/or converted into products. Purchasing and materials managers have further opportunities to create added value within each link of the chain.

As goods are taken from stock and sold, or complete their process of manufacture, they move downstream into the outbound distribution chain, where purchasing managers can add further value.

Finally, as goods arrive at the end user or customer, purchasing managers can make further outbound added value contributions.

So we can see that a supply chain is only as strong as its weakest link. The purchasing manager's role is to ensure strength in every link of the chain.

In order to maximise the added value opportunities the four supply chain cross-links in the figure must also be robust:

- information flow
- partnerships
- continuous improvement
- value for money (VFM) criteria.

Feedback on self-assessment question 2.2

- Inbound. A key measurable here is supplier performance.
- Intra-site. In manufacturing or process operations this is where the materials are converted into assemblies and products. At this stage there are many performance measures. One key measurable here is inventory management.
- Outbound. At this end of the chain purchasing managers interface with distribution management. There are several outbound measures that fall under the general heading of distribution resource planning (DRP) performance management.

Feedback on learning activity 2.3

Most frontline sales staff have the opportunity to earn bonus based on sales success, in terms of value and/or volume. Is there an equal case for offering an incentive to buyers?

There is no single right or wrong answer, but – as for most questions of this nature – you could list points for and against in order to develop your understanding.

Consider the following points, which you might include in your report.

There is a basic difference here between public sector and private sector organisations. In the private sector the key driver is return on capital invested (ROCI), as measured in terms of profitability and shareholder value. In the public sector the key driver is service delivery. There is no profit as such; any savings or added value gains allow more of the budget to be spent on service delivery opportunity.

Thus the payment of a bonus – in cash terms at least – becomes a problem in the public sector for reasons of public accountability, because payment to one group may reflect and include the effort of others.

There are of course many ways in which value added savings are rewarded, rather than payment of a bonus as such: they include professional and job motivation linked to the organisation's vision and values, which ensure that buyers do contribute to the process. In effect the organisation receives the bonus of value contributed by the whole management team, including purchasing managers.

Feedback on self-assessment question 2.3

In most management organisations there are three broad levels of management:

- senior managers: the board, making strategic long-term decisions
- middle managers: aware of the business strategy, and tactically exercising management control of medium-term management operations
- supervision and operational workforce employees: undertaking the volume of transactional and operational work on a shorter-term timescale.

This self-assessment question focuses on the middle managers in the business. A purchasing manager within this group would have many opportunities to obtain and retain added value and set appropriate KPIs based on:

- understanding the purchasing issues set out in the strategic business plan
- setting up a purchasing business plan to manage his or her own area of responsibility
- identifying those medium-term tactical tasks that purchasing can undertake.

A list of tactical management issues might include:

- market analysis, knowledge and information sources
- understanding the demand for goods and services in the business operation
- source management of new and existing suppliers
- ensuring that robust procedures and processes exist to manage purchasing
- utilising the best available IT systems to support purchasing.

Your answer could have included three points from the above summary, with notes on how you would measure them.

Feedback on learning activity 2.4

Figure 2.3 shows a cut-away view of a typical industrial stores. The key costs associated with holding stock are annotated alongside.

Figure 2.3

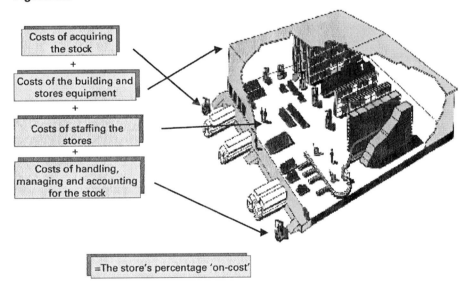

Costs of acquiring the stock
+
Costs of the building and stores equipment
+
Costs of staffing the stores
+
Costs of handling, managing and accounting for the stock

=The store's percentage 'on-cost'

Feedback on self-assessment question 2.4

In this section you were introduced to the term 'opportunity cost' with respect to stockholding. You were told that stock is valued as part of a company's working capital, and thus the more stock you hold the more cash is tied up.

Your answer should consider the cost–benefit opportunity decisions to be considered for holding stock, based on such questions as:

- How much cash should be tied up in stock?
- What is the cost of not having stock – lost sales or delayed production time?
- How else could working capital be used in the business – equipment, staff, systems?
- Could you obtain a better return on business cash from any other investment?

The opportunity cost of stock is based on these and similar business opportunity assessments.

Feedback on learning activity 2.5

Preparation for any negotiation is always based on good planning and market knowledge. In this section we are concerned with issues of added value accruing from better T&Cs obtained by the buyer from a supplier.

This learning activity is a broadly based task, which will vary from case to case. However, a general list of discussion points would include those set out in table 2.1.

Table 2.1

T&C discussion point	Opportunity
Purchase price	Can it be reduced?
Current discount structure	Can this be improved, based on this deal or on longer-term commitment?
Settlement terms	Can these be extended in the buyer's favour without increasing the price?
Warranty terms	Can we obtain a longer warranty on parts and labour at no extra cost?
Quality/service	Can we have better quality/service for the same price?
Transaction and administration costs	Can the number of paper/electronic transactions be reduced?

Feedback on self-assessment question 2.5

You would be able to do this by measuring the 'before' and 'after' values of the price or deal agreed.

- Some of these values are objective, eg actual price reductions.
- Some are subjective, eg better quality for the same price.

You would need to quantify and add up the objective values, and agree a notional value to the business for the subjective vales.

Feedback on learning activity 2.6

This learning activity is designed for you to assess the organisational aspect of purchasing operational efficiency in a larger business. The discussion about centralising or decentralising operations often arises in business. A basic list could include some of the following points:

Advantages of centralisation:

- Buyers can aggregate demand for maximum leverage with suppliers.
- Buyers may specialise in commodity sectors.
- Buyers can cover each other more effectively over time.
- Fewer orders are placed, resulting in improved control over costs and budgets.
- Administration costs are reduced.

Disadvantages of centralisation:

- It may take longer to process orders centrally.
- Buying staff may not understand local management or production needs.
- Buyers are not part of the respective regional management team.
- Buyers don't know the local market or suppliers as well.
- There is some duplication of costs of buying and administration.

Feedback on self-assessment question 2.6

This question looks at the value of IT/IS processes used to support buying and thus improve that particular aspect of operational efficiency.

Most organisations need an IT system to support their purchasing managers. There are many good stand-alone systems that can achieve this. The purpose of this question was not to identify this need, but to describe how this can be improved by the use of ERP systems.

Enterprise resource planning (ERP) systems integrate all data management and information systems for the whole organisation: finance, HR, marketing, production and administration. The key point is the word 'integrate': all the systems draw on a central database and cross-communicate one with another.

For example, in a manufacturing environment the buyer can interface with production needs, and check supplier payments, goods received, stock positions and supplier history, all on the one system, thus improving purchasing efficiency and the effectiveness of data/information transfer.

Categories of performance measurement

'Performance indicators – why do we bother? Just what are these performance indicators?'

Introduction

Having established the importance of performance measurement within business in general and in purchasing operations in particular, we now need some quantitative and qualitative markers. These are the **key performance indicators** (KPIs).

In purchasing, both efficiency measures and effectiveness measures are critical to long-term success. Purchasers should be careful to not confuse the two concepts, and to balance the energies devoted to each.

These approaches are useful in assessing not only purchasing, but also the entire supply chain. As chains become more sophisticated and complex, new and more bespoke means of measuring performance need to be devised and implemented.

The management guru Peter Drucker stated: 'In comparing efficiency and effectiveness it is more important to do the right things (improve effectiveness) than to do things right (improve efficiency).

'Thus, if an organization is doing the right things wrong (that is, is effective but not efficient), it can outperform organizations that are doing the wrong things right (that is, are efficient but not effective).'

There is no one best set of solutions for performance measurement in purchasing, but there is no better endeavour on which to expend purchasing efforts and resources than working to strengthen the skills, techniques and perspectives used to enhance overall professional performance. We therefore need a wide cross-section of key performance indicators (KPIs) to measure progress.

This study session sets out the main groups of purchasing KPIs that will achieve this objective. We also consider the 'how, why, which, when and where' questions for selecting appropriate measures for short-, medium- and long-term objectives.

Session learning objectives

After completing this session you should be able to:

3.1 Describe how purchasing and supply expertise can contribute to KPIs for a corporate business team.
3.2 List the main categories of KPI within a purchasing and supply management operational department.
3.3 Define the most appropriate KPIs that will contribute to profitability with respect to cost savings, services and inventory management.

3

3.4 Define the most appropriate KPIs that will contribute to profitability with respect to basic workload control within a purchasing operation.

3.5 Define the most appropriate KPIs that will contribute to profitability with respect to purchasing infrastructure and organisation.

3.6 Define which purchasing and supply competences are required to contribute effectively to profitability.

Unit content coverage

This study session covers the following topics from the official CIPS unit content document:

Learning outcomes

- Categorise types of performance measures that are available to supply chain managers.
- Interpret and apply statistical data used to measure performance.
- Appraise measures that can be used to improve supplier performance.

Learning objective

1.4 Outline and appraise the types and categories of key performance measures available to organisations including:
   - Contributions to profitability - savings, service and inventory
   - Basic workload control
   - Infrastructure and competency

Prior knowledge

You need to have completed study sessions 1 and 2.

Resources

No specific resources are required for this session.

Timing

You should set aside about 5.25 hours to read and complete this session, including learning activities, self-assessment questions, the suggested further reading (if any) and the revision question.

3.1 How do purchasing and supply managers contribute to the KPI targets set by corporate management?

Corporate management structures and business plans vary with the nature of the business, but in a general manufacturing organisation the functional and business planning structure may well be set out as in figure 3.1.

Figure 3.1: Purchasing within a corporate business planning and management structure

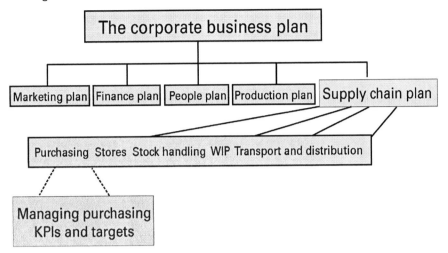

Each department and functional unit has its own business plan, which feeds upwards to the corporate business plan as set out by the strategic management team.

The strategic management team set the vision and values, and incorporate these and other management issues in the corporate business plan. The operational and functional department managers then generate their own business plans as part of the team, and set their respective KPIs and targets as their contribution to the corporate plan.

Before progressing further, tackle this learning activity.

Learning activity 3.1

Create a list of KPIs for a business operation at the strategic level.

Feedback on page 51

In figure 3.1 you can see that the purchasing managers are contributing to the supply chain plan. Purchasing is one of the five departments that are managing their respective departmental business plans.

Before we discuss the detail of how purchasing can contribute to the corporate planning structure, we need to reflect on some of the basic issues and terminology that are used in performance measurement and the links to the continuous improvement process.

Careful selection of performance measures is vital if we are to achieve meaningful outcomes. Figure 3.1 reminds us how important it is to link all departments to the corporate objectives and planned outcomes.

When selecting categories for performance measurement it is important to consider the following questions, in terms of both the efficiency and the effectiveness of the outcome.

- Why are we measuring this?
- What are we trying to achieve?

3

- What is our core business product or service?
- Who are our key customers – both internal and external?
- Who are our key suppliers?
- How and when do we obtain and disclose the performance KPI results?
- Do we have robust processes to support our core business?
- Do we have excellent information and communication channels?

Once we have answered these basic questions we can use the following six-point guide, which will assist in the process of selecting categories for performance measurement.

Performance measures should:

1   *Be reliable.* Basic data is gathered from robust, reliable and consistent information sources. The best sources come from established quality data, which is updated regularly as part of the day-to-day business transaction process.

2   *Be meaningful.* The KPI is relevant; it is the 'right' measure, which has meaning for and value to you and others. It must be clear to recipients, and not be chosen just because it is easy to obtain, or to 'make weight' in a list of KPIs.

3   *Be focused.* The measures should be focused on the core business or operational issues, not just on interesting facts. A focused measure measures only what we planned to measure.

4   *Be fair and balanced.* The KPIs should reflect your operation in all respects, not just the parts that make the organisation 'look good'. Aim to select a good balance of objective and subjective issues in the selected KPIs.

5   *Be capable of change and improvement.* Continuous improvement leads to change. Can your selected KPI adapt to change too?

6   *Manage the target.* The objective is not just to hit a target but rather to improve the output within agreed timescales. Individual 'quantum' measurements could just be manipulated – eg how many orders are placed per month. For example, a buyer might simply place more one-line orders so that a numerical target was achieved.

The process of selecting categories for performance measurement indicators requires a considerable investment of time at all management levels.

How can we judge whether the chosen measures are going to meet the targets set?

Targets are quantified objectives, set by management, to be attained at a future date. The setting of targets is an important part of a measurement process. The target is the objective and the measurement tells us how fast or well we are approaching that objective.

Targets may take various forms. For example:

- A simple yes/no target: Did we do that?
- An achievement target: Did we increase sales by x%?
- A reduction target: Did we reduce the number of queries/complaints by y%?
- An outcome target: Did the project complete to time/budget?

- A quality target: Did we improve quality/service over time?

One of the management tools that can be used to judge the quality of targets is to apply the **SMART** criteria. SMART is an acronym that crops up in many areas of general management. We can apply this general management tool to the selection of categories for performance measurement:

- S = specific (specific, clear unambiguous easily understood)
- M = measurable (being capable of reasonable measurement)
- A = achievable (a target that can reasonably be achieved)
- R = relevant (to the core business or service)
- T = timed (should have an agreed timescale).

Self-assessment question 3.1

The management board of Alltrading UK plc set a corporate target of a 5% growth in sales over the last financial year as part of its annual business plan.

You have the task of assessing this particular corporate target by using the SMART criteria. Complete table 3.1 with your comments on each SMART element of this target.

Table 3.1

SMART criteria review Alltrading UK plc	The corporate target of a 5% growth in sales over the last financial year
S Specific	
M Measurable	
A Achievable	
R Relevant	
T Timed	

Feedback on page 51

3.2 How do purchasing and supply managers select and set KPIs for their core: business operation?

We can now move from general, corporate management issues to the specific selection of categories of performance measurement for purchasing managers.

The main criteria for effectiveness and efficiency still apply at this level, and we can use the six-point selection guide and SMART assessment tools here too.

Referring back to figure 3.1, we are now focusing on the supply chain plan. The supply chain manager will be concerned with all elements of the supply chain: inbound, intra-site and outbound.

3

In this section we shall focus on the front – upstream – element of the supply chain, and specifically on purchasing management's input.

At this point the purchasing role is to interface with external suppliers and internal customers or user departments. (See also figure 2.2.) In basic terms, purchasing managers receive instructions on supply needs from users, source supply, and raise orders for goods and services.

Having revisited these basic core tasks for purchasing managers, we can now consider the selection of appropriate purchasing KPIs.

For the purposes of this selection process we shall be considering various purchasing roles:

- order placing
- spot purchasing
- creating agreements
- setting up contracts
- managing longer-term agreements.

These tasks and terms are not mutually exclusive, and often overlap, depending on role and job title. The work may be undertaken with the purchasing department at the strategic, tactical or transactional level.

In order to select KPIs in purchasing we need to develop this range of work tasks. See table 3.3.

Table 3.3 Categories of performance measurement

Purchasing business planning headers	Typical purchasing business plan tasks	General purchasing KPI headers
Strategic	Working with key stakeholders/users	Managing the supplier base
	Managing key suppliers	Managing long-term relationships
	Developing internal and external relationships	Managing cost reduction plan
		Undertaking purchasing research
	Establishing long-term agreements/partnerships	
Tactical	Obtaining/evaluating quotes, proposals bids	Planning medium-term supply/service delivery
	Managing general suppliers	Managing current supplier relationships
	Working with operational departments	Interfacing customer needs with supply market
Transactional	Obtaining and checking prices	Number of orders to place per week/month
	Placing stock and non-stock orders	Number of queries raised per week
	Managing data input process	

Learning activity 3.2

From your knowledge or experience create a list of three specific KPIs for a manager operating at the middle management/tactical level in a purchasing team.

Feedback on page 52

Now go on to tackle self-assessment question 3.2 below. Completing these two tasks will enable you to apply this knowledge in various practical situations.

Self-assessment question 3.2

Draft up a simple process diagram to show the key steps in selecting a purchasing and supply KPI.

Feedback on page 52

3.3 Purchasing's contribution to improved service and the bottom-line profit

Purchasing managers are responsible for various costs within a business, and the management of these costs has a direct effect on the business in terms of profitability and/or customer service delivery.

Goods and services fall into various categories of purchasing management. Some of the main groupings are:

- raw materials
- components and sub-assemblies
- repair and maintenance items
- capital equipment
- stock and non-stock
- service contracts
- facilities management contracts.

In a private sector business the cost-of-sales items have a direct impact on trading accounts and the bottom-line profit and loss account. The amount of stock held is part of the company balance sheet, and excess stock can affect liquidity ratios.

In public sector organisations and NPOs there is no profit as such, but the general supplies – goods and services purchased with the budget – have a direct effect on service provision opportunity.

3

Thus in all sectors of an economy and for all organisations, whether large or small, purchasing has a direct effect on outputs and on financial and service performance. Buyers are not alone in this role, but they are key team players in this area of cost management and subsequent performance.

In this section we shall review the selection of KPIs for one of the most important buyer contributions to profit: materials cost saving. By understanding the principles here, buyers can identify cost analysis data and develop similar models for other areas of the supply chain, such as service contract management, stores and inventory management, or distribution.

Each of these supply chain headings will be developed later in this course text. Our objective here is to explain the importance of the principles by using the example of materials cost savings, and thus show how purchasing managers can have an effect on other supply-chain-related business outcomes.

Materials cost savings

In basic terms the measure is: how much can we save on cost from some agreed base? That base may be the last price paid, the budgeted price, or an estimated target cost. All these cost bases are linked to price movement over time.

For example, we can claim a cost saving if we pay the same price now that we paid, say, 12 months ago. If inflation increased prices in the market by 2.5% in the last year, then if we pay the same price there is an effective saving of at least the 2.5% expected inflation increase. The guide here is to track prices and aim to be equal to or lower than the tracked increase.

There are many cost-saving opportunities and techniques open to buyers, and we can apply them as appropriate within a supply market. In terms of measuring performance it is important to establish a base price, track market movements, buy items, and then measure the differential.

The savings described above are based on single event or spot purchases. There are many other opportunities for buyers to contribute to profit or service improvement. The principles of total cost of acquisition (TCA) and total cost of ownership (TCO) were introduced in study session 2. By applying purchasing skills and tactics the buyer will also contribute to these evaluations; however, the calculations are more detailed, and the profit impact may take time to be assessed.

The effect on profitability can be illustrated by some basic calculations. Consider the basic profit and loss account shown in table 3.4.

Table 3.4

		£000s	%		£'000	%
				Sales	325.0	100.0
Less cost of sales	Labour	149	51.0			
	Materials	109	37.3			
	Overheads	34	11.6			
	Total	292	100.0	Costs	292.0	89.8
				Profit	33.0	10.2

Here the profit on sales turnover is £33,000 (10.2%) where the cost of sales is £292,000. The materials element of the cost of sales is £109,000 (37.3%)

Now consider the following example (table 3.5)

Table 3.5

		£'000	%	Sales	£'000	%
					325.0	100.0
Less cost of sales	Labour	149	52.0			
	Materials	**103.55**	**36.1**			
	Overheads	34	11.9			
	Totals	286.55	100.0	Costs	286.6	88.2
				Profit	38.5	**11.8**

Here the purchasing manager has been able to reduce the material costs to £103,550: a reduction of 5%. This saving has a direct effect on the profit, which is now £38,500: in percentage terms +1.6% extra profit for this business.

Learning activity 3.3

Prepare a plan of action to achieve direct cost savings/service improvements in a business operation and set achievable targets that can be measured over time.

Feedback on page 53

Now tackle the following self-assessment question.

Self-assessment question 3.3

Take an example from your own organisation/experience. What is the effect on the bottom-line profit achieved by a direct material cost saving?

Feedback on page 53

3.4 Selecting KPIs to measure management of departmental purchasing process and supply chain costs

Within a typical management structure (figure 3.1) each departmental business plan will be underpinned by a robust process of system and control. These processes will link to the basic business transactions and will be managed at that level. Middle and senior managers will manage the medium-term and longer-term tactics and strategy associated with the transactions and data that are created.

There are several processes within the supply chain:

- purchasing
- stores and inventory management

- links to added value manufacturing (production management, MRP, JIT options)
- storage and delivery of finished goods
- customer relationships.

In this study session we shall now focus on the purchasing process, but the principles of process review linked to improvement management would follow a similar pattern if we were reviewing any of the other direct or indirect supply chain processes mentioned above.

Figure 3.3 is a flow diagram showing the detailed links associated with the purchasing process within most organisations, both public and private. Each link is reviewed and assessed in order to develop the strength of the whole chain.

Figure 3.3: The purchasing process links

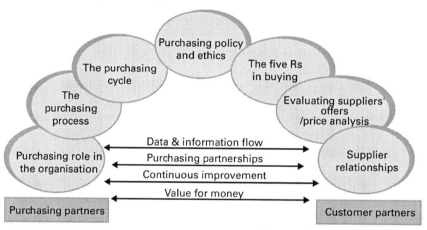

Source: Supply Chain Projects Ltd

This simple diagram covers the key process points involved in managing purchasing. The total cost of acquisition (TCA) and total cost of ownership (TCO) include the costs involved in purchasing the goods and services that are needed by an organisation.

Once again we see that the terms 'efficiency' and 'effectiveness' describe measures of how well the process is managed and delivered to users.

In order to review how efficient and effective this process is, we need first to understand the elements of the process and be capable of undertaking a benchmark comparison with industrial or professional 'best practice'. On the basis that any process is capable of some improvement, this task becomes an ongoing need if the principle of continuous improvement is to be effected.

The basic best practice tests of this process flow diagram include the following:

- Is the role of purchasing clearly set out and understood?
- Is there a purchasing manual or process flow chart of how a buyer is expected to work?
- Does the manual follow clear sequential steps that should be followed?
- Are purchasing policy and ethics standards set out in the corporate business plan?

- Are all purchasing basics understood (the 5Rs: right place, right price, right quality, right quantity and right time)?
- Do staff know and understand the bid evaluation and contract award criteria?
- Do we 'manage' customers, both internal and external?
- Do we have robust IT systems?

The efficiency and effectiveness of the purchasing process are thus functions of all these elements. Once purchasing managers have studied their own system, the continuous improvement process requires them to periodically address and re-address these questions, and then set targets and select measures to review and improve the purchasing process.

Learning activity 3.4

Prepare a plan of action to achieve measurable savings and/or process improvements by re-engineering the operational management and processes in purchasing and supply.

Feedback on page 53

Now tackle self-assessment question 3.4 below to develop your skill in this area.

Self-assessment question 3.4

List three methods for improving departmental acquisition costs by reviewing purchasing and supply transactions and process time.

Feedback on page 54

3.5 Selecting KPIs that link to the purchasing infrastructure within an organisation

Where does purchasing sit in the business infrastructure? In figure 3.1 we showed a typical structure for the supply chain and purchasing in a single-site organisation. In larger organisations the structure can be much more complicated, with, for example:

- several sites in one country
- several sites in several countries
- head office in one country with operational or retail divisions in other countries
- manufacturing subsidiaries or supply partners in various places
- companies with stock and distribution
- companies without stock.

This is just a representative selection of business infrastructures; you may recognise others. The question is: where does purchasing fit best in the infrastructure in terms of efficiency and effectiveness?

3

As in many similar business situations, there is no single answer, but managers aim to review the costs and benefits and come to a view. This section therefore sets out some of the possible options, and describes how purchasing can fit into the infrastructure.

First, how is purchasing organised itself? Here are some options:

- central purchasing departments
- decentralised purchasing – full delegation to operational divisions or subsidiaries
- centre-led action networks (CLAN) – a combination of centrally led management with agreed delegation of category or common needs being undertaken within divisions.
- category purchasing – specialist buyers for specific categories of goods and services
- consortium purchasing – mainly public service for operations with similar non-competing services, eg university or local government consortiums
- cooperative purchasing between groups with similar needs.

Each of these options has advantages and disadvantages, and carries costs and benefits in its application.

The purchasing infrastructure can also be influenced by the location of the supply market, but this factor is of less importance in the modern world of high-speed communications, logistics supply and distribution operations.

The decision on purchasing infrastructure is a strategic one. Setting up and commissioning a purchasing infrastructure is a medium- to long-term decision, and will have a direct effect on costs, and on operational effectiveness and efficiency. In any organisation the decision needs to be carefully considered at senior management/board level, and the costs and benefits of 'commercial risk' need to be fully reviewed. There is never one single best solution, but rather what works best for a particular organisation and its needs. Having taken the decision within a strategic life cycle the effects can have long-term consequences for a business or service organisation.

Learning activity 3.5

Look at the structure of an existing purchasing and supply operation, and list three issues that you would recommend for review in order to reduce transactional purchasing costs.

Directly following this learning activity try self-assessment question 3.5 below to link these issues. By doing this you develop your skill of applying theory to practice.

Feedback on page 54

Now tackle the following self-assessment question.

Self-assessment question 3.5

How would you improve the purchasing and supply infrastructure in an organisation that was expanding from one operational division to three sites?

Feedback on page 55

3.6 Purchasing competence and the link to business objectives

Competence in any field is important, but competence does not mean you have to 'know all' before acting. For example, a newly qualified lawyer may not be competent to handle a complex litigation because of his or her lack of courtroom experience or skills. Competence is acquired and developed over time, and through real situations.

Competence is measured by several elements, including skill, experience, knowledge and attitude, and when combined with a qualification will have best effect.

Many leading businesspeople have achieved much without all of the perceived competence elements; however, a balanced selection of each marks out progressive degrees of competence linked to business or organisational needs.

Some learning may major on academic knowledge alone, whereas other learning requires a wider basis of practical skill and experience: for example, NVQs are based on this latter format.

Competence to work in an environment is important, but in many situations individuals need only agreed levels of competence, whether implied or evidenced. In the context of this study session the issue is: what categories and measures are relevant to the competence of purchasing staff who need to achieve business deliverables?

In many organisations purchasing is delegated with budgetary control to staff and managers who may be full-time or only part-time purchasing people. Managers may have purchasing responsibilities as part of other roles, or they may move into purchasing from other disciplines.

The key to managing this situation is to look at the competences required and then assess the 'gaps'. Based on this assessment, the organisation should decide its purchasing competence needs and assess and train staff up to that level, by facilitating training or skill development to develop the required competences.

The measures can be objective or subjective.

- Objective:
  - Based on an agreed set of competences, how many 'gaps' are there to be filled?

3

- What is the timescale to achieve the competence level, by individual, team or category?
    - Are there measurable improvements?
- Subjective:
    - How well is the person doing?
    - How is the mentoring and/or training programme progressing?
    - Are teamwork and/or business relationships improving?

Learning activity 3.6

Review a purchasing and supply job description and identify four key competences that the post-holder would need.

Feedback on page 55

Now tackle the following self-assessment question:

Self-assessment question 3.6

Create a list of the purchasing competences that will have the most effect on business profitability.

Rank your list in order of priority for your organisation.

Feedback on page 55

Revision question

Now try the revision question for this session on page 334.

Summary

This study session was concerned with categories of performance measures and their selection in a purchasing environment.

It reviewed how purchasing fits into an organisation management planning structure and thus how it can first support the business planning corporate aims and then manage its own agreed plan.

In order to do this various categories of purchasing KPIs were discussed, and how these achievements contribute to business mission, vision values and financial targets.

In undertaking this form of review you were reminded that such an assessment was judged at three levels or over timescales. The categories of measures and results selected can be grouped in various formats or models, but the common theme would be to analyse them as:

- short-term transactional measures
- medium-term tactical measures
- longer-term strategic measures.

At every level there should be selection tests based on the six-point guide to selecting performance measures.

Suggested further reading

In this session we have referred extensively to the theories of Peter Drucker, one of America's leading authors on management and business. Students wishing for an overview of his work could do worse than read Drucker (2003) which contains much of his best work. Any good on-line bookshops will have details of his work. Drucker is also quoted in Neely et al (2002) on pages 24 and 190.

Feedback on learning activities and self-assessment questions

Feedback on learning activity 3.1

You should be thinking at the corporate level, and, with reference to figure 3.1, have selected KPIs linked to the main business plan. Strategic KPIs are part of an organisation's long-term planning, and when deciding on this set of performance measures managers should be sure that they can access the relevant data as and when they need it.

Suitable strategic KPIs would include:

- profitability
- return on investment
- cashflow
- customer service levels
- sales growth
- production/productivity levels
- performance against budget
- cost management
- HR targets
- R&D developments.

This list of KPIs reflects corporate targets and key departmental targets within set time periods.

Feedback on self-assessment question 3.1

See table 3.2.

Table 3.2

SMART Criteria review Alltrading UK plc	A corporate target of a 5% growth in sales over the last financial year
S Specific	Yes, the target was specific in specifying all sales/turnover generated by the company in one financial year.
M Measurable	Yes, it is measurable from prime documents. Sales money value is an objective measurement.

(continued on next page)

Table 3.2 *(continued)*

SMART Criteria review Alltrading UK plc	A corporate target of a 5% growth in sales over the last financial year
A Achievable	This depends on the market in which the business is operating. In general terms a 5% target is a realistic positive target.
R Relevant	The measure is relevant to the core business of a trading company.
T Timed	Yes there was a clear timed element – one full financial year.

Feedback on learning activity 3.2

The list will vary according to your experience, or the business area you choose. However, you should have referred to table 3.3 and developed your specific KPI list from this guideline.

Feedback on self-assessment question 3.2

Based on the study session so far, your flowchart should have included the elements shown in figure 3.2.

Figure 3.2

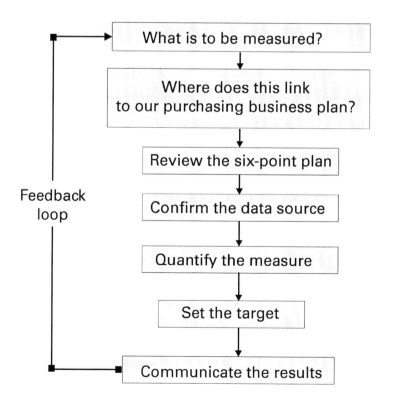

Feedback on learning activity 3.3

A basic action plan should identify the action, the target date, the person responsible for delivering the action, and the timescale. See table 3.4.

Table 3.6

Buyer action plan		
Subject: Materials cost reduction		
Issue	**Description and details**	**Action list and results**
		Dates and times
Product or service		
Present cost		
Target saving		
By when		
By whom		

Feedback on self-assessment question 3.3

On the basis that you have some information on the price of the item or service selected, you can create a simple cost analysis before and after the purchasing action and calculate what the materials cost was as a percentage before and after cost reduction, and thus estimate the percentage contribution to profit.

Feedback on learning activity 3.4

We introduced a basic action plan in learning activity 3.3. This activity requires you to produce a more detailed version of an action plan that should be capable of application to any aspect of the process. For the purposes of illustration we have chosen an operational aspect of basic purchasing: obtaining an outside supplier's quotations or bid price for an internal customer.

The performance measure may be to calculate internal response time to obtain priced quotations for internal customers, and to measure how those customers perceived the quality of that service.

In basic terms the efficiency and effectiveness can be measured as follows.

- Efficiency: How long did it take?
- Effectiveness: Did it meet all the customer needs?

See table 3.7.

Table 3.7

Action plan: Review of a purchasing process	Process element: Obtaining an outside suppliers quotations/bids price for an internal customer	Action	
Efficiency: How long did it take this time?	A time measure in days	By whom	By when
		Can the process be improved to do the job in less time?	Target date for improvement
Effectiveness: Did it meet all the customer's needs?	Did the customer consider that purchasing obtained VFM?		Target date for improvement
		How could we obtain better VFM?	
Linked issues	Number of quotes obtained		
	Delivery times offered		
	Quality measures/standard		

Feedback on self-assessment question 3.4

'Time is money', so process time improvement can be achieved by streamlining the task process time to be more efficient.

You could have selected any of the process steps from figure 3.3 and illustrated or suggested improvements in transactional time, procurement methods and general time management issues, which will in effect manage TCA purchasing costs.

Specific techniques could be:

- measuring the number of transactions
- measuring the volume and value of purchase order transactions in a set time period
- measuring the average time taken to process transactions, say on a weekly basis.

By managing TCA, purchasing managers contribute further to business benefits of cost reduction, efficiency and effectiveness.

Feedback on learning activity 3.5

This activity is part of a strategic review, but you were asked to focus on one area of cost management – transactional costs.

The first task is to quantify the transactions and their costs. These fall into three broad categories:

- inbound transactional costs: number of quotes/orders/supplier queries etc

3

- intra-site transactional costs: number of goods in, stores movements, inventory transactions
- outbound transactional costs: picking, issue, distribution, customer transactions.

The second part of the activity would be a discussion and review of the number, size and value of transactions, and a debate as to whether some aspect of purchasing organisation and/or methodology would lead to fewer transactions or reduced operational costs. You should use the text and content of this session to lead your thoughts and suggestions in answering this question relative to a chosen organisation.

Feedback on self-assessment question 3.5

Based on the text you may want to consider the following options:

- Retain full central purchasing control.
- Delegate all budgets to each site and allow them to operate as independent self-managing units and cost/profit centres
- Agree categories of supply management and location within the new three-division structure

There may be other relevant options based on supply sources, logistics infrastructure or divisional needs that could form part of your answer.

Feedback on learning activity 3.6

Taking a basic purchasing job description involving process and practice, you could have selected the following.

- What skills are required to do this job?
- What knowledge or experience is needed to do the job?
- What targets must be achieved (volume, value)?
- What – if any – are the recognised qualifications to do this job?

Your task would then be to review the 'gap' between the ideal and the actual competence and close the 'gap'.

Feedback on self-assessment question 3.6

The question focuses on competences that have an effect on business profitability.

The yardstick is: which purchasing actions will improve bottom-line profit? As we have seen in this study session, these can include:

- Objective measures (quantitative):
    - cost reduction
    - improved quality at no additional cost
    - better delivery
    - reduced stockholding

3

- improved efficiency
- fewer complaints.
- Subjective measures (qualitative):
  - better business relationships
  - better customer service
  - more long-term agreements
  - better process management and teamwork
  - improved assertiveness/confidence
  - better use of IT.

The second part of the question is designed to put theory into practice. The basic list is, in effect, a professional best practice list, but the issues will have different values for each organisation. Your task is to prioritise such a best practice list into a practical solution for your particular needs.

Study session 4
Cost and price measures

Introduction

- Just what is a price?
- When do we need to know about cost elements?
- How are costs and prices determined?
- In business, just what do we need to know about cost and price in order to improve our purchasing performance?

The cost is not always a function of the price; price is not always based on cost.

4

'I am always very fearful of markets and very respectful of them, and I intend to watch them closely.'

Dr Alan Greenspan, Chairman of the United States Federal Reserve Board, on his appointment to that office.

One of the basics of economics is the **law of supply and demand**, which states that, in a perfect marketplace, price will be a direct function of supply. So how are costs and prices related in other markets?

Many international commodities are traded, with price being a function of supply. Following this economic rule, if we have a bumper wheat harvest the price of grain in a free market will fall, whereas in a poor-yield year the price will rise. In both cases it probably costs the same to grow and harvest the grain, but the price is different because of economic laws of supply and demand.

There are other examples. For instance, in the world of fashion, a sought-after garment or brand may cost thousands of pounds. The actual materials and labour are only a small percentage of the cost, so why do some people pay so much? Here we see the subjective value of brand, design, limited availability and current fashion, where price has almost no relationship to product production costs.

In manufacturing and service provision costs are more closely related to price. There are, of course, many other factors, but if we know the process costs we can start to correlate the price in a more commercial way.

Purchasing managers therefore need to understand costs and prices, and how they are related in business.

In this session we shall focus on issues of commercial pricing strategy, and on how an understanding of this can contribute to both profit and service delivery. Commercial pricing strategy is linked to the supply of goods and services. A key element of the measurement of purchasing performance is thus a function of the management of both cost and price.

57

4

Session learning objectives

After completing this session you should be able to:

4.1 Describe the market forces that determine a price within a market.
4.2 Define, in cost accountancy terms, the main elements in building up the costs of a product or service.
4.3 Analyse the cost information provided for a given product into the main percentages, and illustrate this in a graphical format.
4.4 Undertake a detailed cost breakdown example as part of a negotiation with a supplier claiming a price increase due to an annual increase in labour costs.
4.5 Give examples of cost elements that are not subject to increase over time for a given product.

Unit content coverage

This study session covers the following topics from the official CIPS unit content document:

Learning outcomes

- Categorise types of performance measures that are available to supply chain managers.
- Use a range of accounting techniques to measure organisational efficiency.
- Interpret and apply statistical data used to measure performance.

Learning objective

1.3 Classify the information required to perform purchasing activities and to measure and evaluate purchasing performance.
  - Departmental versus strategic goals of the organisation
  - Resource requirements
  - Costing, pricing, inventory management
  - Supplier/vendor information
  - Product/Service specifications

Prior knowledge

You need to have completed study sessions 1, 2 and 3.

Resources

No specific resources are required for this session.

4

Timing

You should set aside about 5 hours to read and complete this session, including learning activities, self-assessment questions, the suggested further reading (if any) and the revision question.

4.1 The bigger picture: costs and forces that determine a price within a market

Before we look at the issues of commercial pricing strategy we need to think about the terms 'cost' and 'price'.

As we stated in the introduction, these two terms have different meanings. In order to measure purchasing performance we need to look further at each term, if cost or price is to be used as a measurement criterion:

- **Cost** is the total of the various individual costs involved in making a product or providing a service.
- **Price** is the sum for which the product or service can be sold in its market. It is almost certainly *not* the cost.

First, consider the many factors that a supplier may review when setting a commercial price. In manufacturing or service delivery a cost accountant would work with internal information from marketing, process/production, purchasing and others, while also being aware of relevant economic and market issues. Business traders will need to know their markets and customers in order to make their decisions. There is no single formula or method, but some of the main issues in this information-gathering/decision process are listed in table 4.1.

Table 4.1 Commercial pricing strategy checklist

Economic and marketing pressures (local, national or international)	Management and cost accounting information-gathering and decisions options
Market competition Supply and demand Value to customer Profit opportunity	Basic costs Direct labour costs to make the product Direct material costs for the product Fixed overheads for the business Profit margin
Price elasticity Market segmentation Market forces Alternatives available Possible new entrants to this market	Cost comparison/benchmarking Profit target/return/mark-up Contracting price format: fixed price, target price, cost plus, etc
Volume – size of run – order Time period of production/order/contract Buyer power Seller power	Price calculations Cost/capital/tooling apportionment policy Traditional overhead apportionment Activity-based costing (ABC) cost apportionment of overheads Cost/volume profit calculations Breakeven price/marginal costing Accounting procedures Finance legislation/tax rules

4

In many cases a buyer just needs to establish a selling price and compare this with other prices for similar specifications (**price analysis**). In manufacturing and more complex goods and service contracts, which may run over longer time periods, it is important to understand the cost base of the item (**cost analysis**).

From this understanding, purchasing performance can be measured relative to cost/price movements in a market.

Learning activity 4.1

Read the financial sections of the business press or professional periodicals and identify the major commodity prices or labour rates that will directly affect your business or operation.

Feedback on page 68

Now go on to tackle the following self-assessment question.

Self-assessment question 4.1

Based on your selection of commodities from learning activity 4.1 above, create a graph illustrating the price movements of these commodities over the last 24 months.

Feedback on page 68

4.2 Basic cost analysis: how costs are allocated and accounted for in a commercial organisation?

In many businesses, prices are built up by aggregating various categories of cost and then setting a selling price. You need to understand the basic principles of this part of cost accountancy, and how purchasing contributes to the process.

In the commercial pricing strategy checklist in table 4.1 there are two column headings:

- economic and marketing pressures
- management and cost accounting information-gathering and decision options.

As a purchasing manager you may be involved at two levels:

providing cost information to your own cost accountants as part of setting a selling price for your goods and services

4

requesting cost information from a supplier so that you have a cost analysis of the goods or services you wish to purchase.

In either case you need to understand the basis of costs. Using the principle of **cost price analysis** (CPA) a cost breakdown can be divided into cost centre categories. The usual main headers are: labour, materials, overheads and profit. These headers are grouped as variable and fixed costs, as listed below and illustrated in figure 4.1.

Variable production costs for the product or service:

- direct cost of raw materials/components
- direct cost of production (production managers/supervisors/labour)
- direct manufacturing consumption costs, eg power/energy
- fixed business/indirect overhead costs and profit for the business operation.

Indirect business overheads:

- indirect general management/staff/labour
- profit and margin amount/percentage.

The exact allocation of costs into cost centres is based on accounting best practice and principles, but for the purposes of this study session these are the main groups.

Figure 4.1: fixed and variable costs

Variable costs
Costs that vary directly with activity levels, eg raw materials, components, labour, energy
Each sale must cover this cost before a margin is generated

+

Fixed costs
Those costs (not overheads) not directly related to the activity (eg security, premises, management, plant, sales force)
They must be paid for however much or little the firm produces - they are paid for by the margin generated from a sale after the variable cost has been covered

=

Total costs of production
The sum of the fixed and variable costs, which together give the total cost of production

Marginal costs
The cost incurred by the supplier in producing one additional unit of output, which is the same as the increment of variable cost

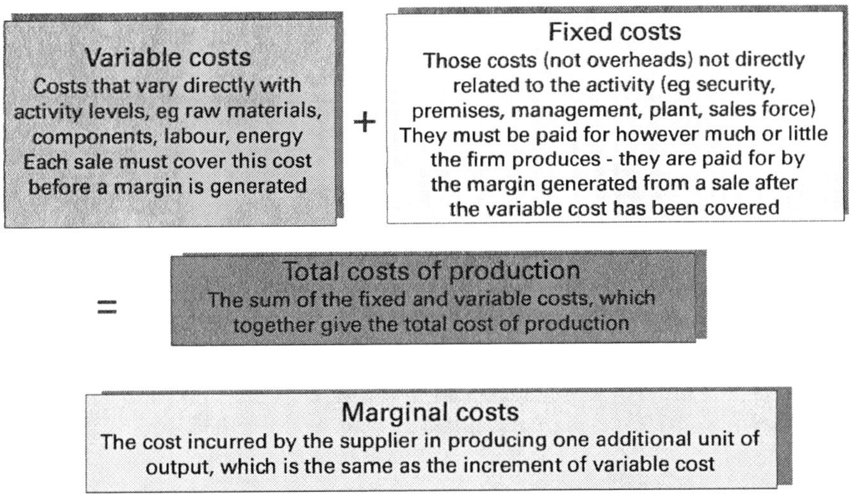

Learning activity 4.2

Choose a product or service with which you are familiar and analyse all the elements of cost that make up the total.

When you have done this, move straight on to self-assessment question 4.2 below.

Feedback on page 69

Now go on to tackle the following self-assessment question.

Self-assessment question 4.2

What is the difference between the direct costs and indirect overhead costs of a product or service?

Feedback on page 69

4.3 Introduction to cost price analysis: how are variable costs managed?

Undertaking this class of analysis will give you a clearer perspective on what is, otherwise, purely numerical information on the final selling price.

The direct or variable costs are the cost centre data on the actual cost of sales/production of a specific product or service. They are the direct costs to make the item or deliver the service: thus the more we make or do, the more direct costs we incur. The main elements of cost are the actual labour, the materials, and any direct overhead costs that are consumed.

Consider the product example used in learning activity 4.2 above – the rotary mowing machine.

- The direct labour is the time needed to manufacture and assemble the machine, charged at the respective pay rates.
- The materials specified or listed in the bill of materials are the direct material costs.
- The production manager's/supervisor's time allocated to make this item is part of this direct overhead cost.

There are allocation decisions to be made here. For example, if a supervisor is responsible for more than one product, how is the cost of his or her time allocated? We need not go into this in detail; suffice it to say that we are interested in the principle of the main cost centres, and are aware that certain allocated costs need clarification.

The value of this class of information for the measurement of purchasing performance is that, if we are aware of these more detailed costs, then:

- we can make more informed purchasing decisions, and
- manage and measure any price or rate movements over time more accurately for each element of cost.

For example, say you are the buyer of components for the rotary mower considered in learning activity 4.2 above. The engine is made mainly of aluminium alloy and steel. It would be useful for you to solicit the original base price, with cost analysis details, so that when prices or rates move, you can be in a better position to negotiate with a long-term supplier on any selling price review or variation requests.

4

By knowing the cost of sales in terms of labour and materials you can ensure that any price increase negotiations are within benchmark limits, as indicated by analysis of independent government indexes of labour in the industry or published price movements for material base costs.

The measurement opportunity is to maintain and retain prices/costs from suppliers that continue to give you competitive advantage at any point in time.

By having detailed cost price analysis and access to independent comparators, your purchasing 'price paid' performance can be measured more accurately and more fairly.

Learning activity 4.3

Based on the rotary mower example in learning activity 4.2 above, create a pie chart showing the main direct cost elements.

When you have completed this, develop your skill by doing self-assessment question 4.3 below.

Feedback on page 69

Now tackle the following self-assessment question.

Self-assessment question 4.3

You are the buyer at Motor Mowers UK Ltd. You plan to purchase a 9hp petrol mower engine for one of your products, and request a quotation from Alloy Engines UK Ltd.

The engine selling price is quoted at £94.00. You also request a cost analysis breakdown on this price. The details of the cost analysis are as given in table 4.5.

Table 4.5

Cost centre	Amount
Direct labour costs	£42.0
Direct materials	£31.0
Direct overheads	£12.0
Profit	£9.0
Selling price	£94.0

Calculate the four cost centres as percentages of the total selling price, and create a pie chart to illustrate your result.

Feedback on page 70

4

4.4 Using cost analysis and measuring your purchasing performance

Developing cost information, or requesting it, as part of establishing a selling price has several added value opportunities for purchasing managers. The evaluation and awarding of contracts is a complex process of assessment and decision, and cost information is a key part of that process. Depending on the industry, and on the time period of a project or contract, there can be many changes or variations during its life. For example:

- changes in costs/price over time
- changes in specification or quality levels
- redesign over time
- additions or removal of work over time
- variations to the work.

Change and change management are a part of business life. Purchasing managers need to respond to change on an ongoing basis.

The opportunity to manage costs can be measured as part of a purchasing manager's contribution to profit. The principle here is that every pound saved by buyers for the same specification goods or services from suppliers has a direct effect on profit. A £1 reduction in cost can be equal to or greater than a £4 increase in sales turnover. Many organisations recognise this, and treat purchasing departments as profit centres, based on this principle.

Buyers cannot just keep obtaining price reductions; no one is just going to supply on a regular basis at or below their own cost. The measurement criterion is to set an opening or target price, and then aim to achieve or improve on this. Very often these measures are on a portfolio basis rather than a single-item basis; with this methodology a measure for a sector can be compared over time.

Certain industries, such as construction or electrical/mechanical engineering, have had processes linked with variation and change included with their contracts. For example:

- The Institution of Civil Engineers (ICE) Institution of Civil Engineers: http://www.ice.org.uk developed the New Engineering Contract (NEC) in 1993. This has now been updated as the Engineering and Construction Contract (ECC) for the industry. The ICE also offers advice on application and conciliation of contract adjustment issues.
- The British Electrotechnical and Allied Manufacturers' Association (BEAMA) British Electrotechnical and Allied Manufacturers' Association: http://www.beama.org.uk has developed the BEAMA Contract Price Adjustment Clause and Formulae, the BEAMA Labour and Material Cost Indices, and the BEAMA Contract Price Adjustment Advisory Service.

These two industrial examples are excellent best practice processes and methodologies based on the principles of cost price analysis of work.

At a more basic level we can use cost price analysis data to manage and measure performance. Price increases are inevitable over time, but the skill is to manage the changes so that you maintain and retain the competitive position you achieved when you first awarded the order or contract.

In order to achieve this you need base cost information and data on price and rate movements over time. You can then use these to check your position over time for the goods and services in question.

4

Learning activity 4.4

You work for Alloy Engines UK Ltd, and you have been supplying engines to Motor Mowers UK Ltd for one year. This was the first year of a four-year supply contract. You are reviewing the selling price of the 9 hp petrol engine.

The costs a year ago were quoted as shown in table 4.7.

Table 4.7

Cost centre	Amount
Direct labour costs	£42.0
Direct materials	£31.0
Direct overheads	£12.0
Profit	£9.0
Selling price	£94.0

Your agreement with at Motor Mowers UK Ltd is that you can request an increase on direct labour and materials, but your overhead and profit percentages are fixed.

- Labour: During the last 12 months the engineering labour index for your industry has moved up by an increase of 2.8%.
- Materials: The main items have moved over the same period by an average of 3.6%.

Calculate a new selling price for the 9hp petrol engine

Feedback on page 71

Now go on to tackle this self-assessment question.

Self-assessment question 4.4

List the main issues when dealing with price increase requests from suppliers. What and how would you measure in terms of purchasing performance?

Feedback on page 71

4.5 How are fixed costs managed?

In section 4.1 above we listed the main cost elements that make up a commercial selling price.

In this section we focusing on overhead costs.

In business there are certain costs that have to be covered independent of production activity or saleable services. These **overhead costs** include:

- premises costs
- administration costs
- management functions, such as finance, human resources
- health and safety
- security
- facilities management services, such as cleaning and catering.

All these are needed if there is to be production or service provision, but most are not directly related to the cost analysis of specific products or services.

In considering these fixed costs, we need to ask:

- Are the fixed costs completely independent of the cost of sales?
- How are these overheads allocated into the selling price?

Some fixed costs may clearly be shared: for example, there may be a security cost for the premises. However, let us consider the example of security further:

- There may be some aspects of security that are clearly part of the production cost, and so can be allocated as a 'direct overhead' and therefore part of the selling price.
- Some security may be only part of a direct overhead cost, and thus may be described and allocated as a semi-variable cost.
- Other security costs are completely unrelated to the product or service, and so come under general business overheads.

Each of these points links to best practice accounting policy, tax financial rules or accounting processes, and will vary according to the situation.

In basic terms the fixed overheads can be allocated from a single central cost centre and charged back to the selling price costs in a equal spread over all activities. Alternatively the principle of **activity-based costing** (ABC) can be used. This is an approach that recognises that not all activities and processes consume or utilise the same amount of resources. Activity-based costing is an allocation approach that uses multiple cost centres with different cost drivers linked to business activity, rather than a single, central cost centre.

All overhead costs will eventually be reflected in the selling price, but if you are a buyer it is in your interest to be sure that you pick up only those overhead costs that are fair and relevant to your product or service.

Cost price analysis facilitates this information for the key goods and service items you purchase. Thus an understanding of the principles of their allocation is a useful part of measurement and tracking. This clearly links to performance measurement processes.

4

Learning activity 4.5

Using the example of the motor mower manufacturer, identify from the following list of costs which elements are indirect fixed cost items:

- the wages of the production workers
- the head office power costs
- the paint for the machines
- the office cleaning costs
- the maintenance costs for the assembly line
- the canteen costs
- the cost of the outsourced engines for assembly
- the payroll costs
- the health and safety manager's costs
- the sales manager's salary.

Feedback on page 72

Now tackle the final self-assessment question in this session.

Self-assessment question 4.5

Give True or False responses to the following statements.

1 Direct labour costs are fixed costs. TRUE/FALSE
2 Premises costs are fixed costs. TRUE/FALSE
3 ABC overhead apportionment allocates all costs equally. TRUE/FALSE
4 Bill of materials (BOM) components are variable costs. TRUE/FALSE

Feedback on page 72

Revision question

Now try the revision question for this session on page 334.

Summary

Purchasing managers are concerned with the 5 Rs: right price, right place, right time, right quality, and right quantity.

Each element of the 5 Rs can be measured. One of the basic measures is price. In this session you looked at this term, and considered the definitions of price and cost.

Detailed cost analysis is valuable information to a professional buyer. Although price is only one criterion of a purchasing decision, the more information we have on price the better we can use that as part of the evaluation process. Later on we can measure how prices have moved over time and thus ensure that we continue to get value for money over longer-term deals/contracts.

The elements of cost price analysis (CPA) were covered and discussed. CPA puts you, as a buyer, in a position to monitor and use measurement processes to best advantage for your organisation.

Suggested further reading

Useful websites to support references in this session are those of the Institute of Civil Engineers http://www.ice.org.uk, and the British Electro-technical and Allied Manufacturers Association (BEAMA) http://www.beama.org.uk.

Feedback on learning activities and self-assessment questions

Feedback on learning activity 4.1

Many financial and professional publications contain commodity prices and indexed price movements over time.

Thus if you are purchasing, for example, goods containing copper you need to know the London Metal Exchange (LME) published price for copper so that you can 'track and trace' the raw material cost that makes up part of this item's price. Financial newspapers usually publish commodity prices in their business analysis sections.

Similarly, government departments maintain details of labour wage or pay rates in many categories, so if you know the category you can 'track and trace' cost movements of the direct labour costs included in items you are buying.

Based on this data a buyer can set cost and price performance measures that can be compared with agreed independent commodity/labour benchmarks.

For further information see UK National Statistics online at UK National Statistics: http://www.statistics.gov.uk.

Feedback on self-assessment question 4.1

A good working example is a commodity metal, such as copper.

Your answer should be a clear analysis of the data you collected and keyed into a spreadsheet, and should include the visual illustration of a graph of copper price movements over time.

4

Feedback on learning activity 4.2

Consider, for example, an item such as a commercial rotary motor mower selling for £250.00. The analysis of cost data could look like this (see table 4.2, table 4.3 and figure 4.2).

Table 4.2

Cost centre	Cost (£)	(%)
Direct labour	79.00	52.7
Raw materials and components	49.00	32.7
Direct overheads	22.00	14.6
Total cost of sales	**150.00**	**100.0**

Table 4.3

	£	%
Sales price	250.00	100.0
Less costs	150.00	60.0
Operating margin and profit	100.00	40.0

Figure 4.2

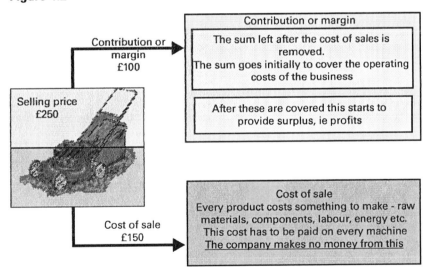

Feedback on self-assessment question 4.2

Direct costs are those costs directly allocated to the cost of production and sales, including labour, materials and any direct overhead costs. These costs are 'variable' in direct proportion to the quantity produced.

Indirect or fixed costs accrue in managing and operating a business and its general overhead costs. These costs are mainly independent of the quantity produced.

Feedback on learning activity 4.3

The cost of sales data in learning activity 4.2 was as shown in table 4.4.

Table 4.4

	£	%
Direct labour	79.00	52.7
Raw materials and components	49.00	32.7
Direct overheads	22.00	14.6

Figure 4.3 shows this data plotted as a pie chart.

Figure 4.3

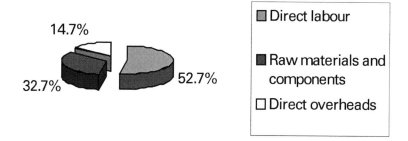

Rotary mower

Feedback on self-assessment question 4.3

On the basis that this type of purchase will be based on a longer-term supply relationship, you may continue to buy engines from Alloy Engines UK for, say, the next two to four years. By requesting a cost analysis, and seeing this in both cost and percentage terms, you have better purchasing information.

You can now measure their costs and percentages at the bid evaluation stage before making a commitment.

On the basis that this supplier was the chosen source, you are now in a position to 'track and trace' the main cost elements over time. In addition you can measure any price increases against independent information sources in the future.

The calculation is given in table 4.6, and the graphical analysis is shown in figure 4.4.

Table 4.6

	£	%
Labour	42.00	44.7
Materials	31.00	33.0
Direct overheads	12.00	12.8
Profit	9.00	9.6
Opening base price	94.00	100.0

Figure 4.4: Cost price analysis, 9 hp petrol engine

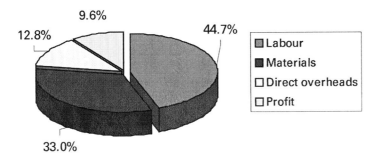

Feedback on learning activity 4.4

The new selling price is now £97.00, based on the opening price 12 months ago, and:

- 2.8% increase in labour costs
- 3.6% increase in materials costs.

The direct overhead and profit margin percentages are fixed at 12.8% and 9.6% of the new selling price respectively.

The calculation is as shown in table 4.8.

Table 4.8

	Index price movement (%)	New cost (£)	(%)
Direct labour	2.8	43.20	44.5
Direct materials	3.6	32.10	33.1
Direct overheads	pro rata	12.40	12.8
Profit	pro rata	9.30	9.6
Total		**97.00**	**100.0**

Feedback on self-assessment question 4.4

- Review purchasing processes in terms of the use and application of cost price analysis.
- Make sure that key suppliers and products have cost price analysis information.
- Calculate the expected increases yourself.
- Challenge and check the suppliers' claims.
- Make sure claims are on variable direct cost elements only.

- Look for alternatives to an increase: order volume discounts, learning curve effect, value analysis reductions, no cost service/quality improvements.
- Aim to negotiate in any event.
- Target at equal or less than the indexed increases you have calculated: that is, maintain competitive advantage.
- Measure your result against the set target.

Feedback on learning activity 4.5

See table 4.9.

Table 4.9

Cost	Comment
The wages of the production workers	A direct variable cost. The more mowers made, the more labour is needed
The head office power costs	An indirect fixed cost overhead, which could be allocated as an evenly spread central cost, or by ABC allocation
The paint for the machines	A direct variable cost. The more mowers made, the more paint is needed
The office cleaning costs	An indirect fixed cost overhead
The maintenance costs for the assembly line	A direct fixed cost overhead for product production
The canteen costs	A fixed cost overhead
The cost of the outsourced engines for assembly	A direct variable cost. The more mowers made, the more engines are needed
The payroll costs	A fixed cost overhead, which could be allocated as an evenly spread central cost or by ABC allocation
The health and safety manager's costs	On the assumption that this person covers other products, a fixed cost overhead, which could be allocated as an evenly spread central cost or by ABC allocation
The sales manager's salary	On the assumption that this person covers other products, a fixed cost overhead, which could be allocated as an evenly spread central cost or by ABC allocation

Feedback on self-assessment question 4.5

1 FALSE. The direct labour time is a function of producing the goods or service. The more made, the more labour is needed.
2 TRUE. They are not directly related to the manufacture of specific goods or services.
3 FALSE. ABC allocates in proportion to the activity related to specific goods or services.
4 TRUE. The BOM items are a list of components necessary to manufacture an item. The more items made, the more components are needed.

Inventory management measures

Introduction

- Stock costs money. How much?
- Is it wrong to hold stock?
- What is the real cost of holding stock?

How do we find out the answers to these and other questions about our business stock?

Stock is a valuable asset, but it can be a sinking liability. The existence of stock is reassuring to those who are relaxed about planning their requirements sufficiently in advance of the need, and to those who take its availability for granted. Unfortunately, the premium for holding stock is too high to be complacent about it. The annual cost is typically between 25p and 40p in the £ of its value, and for some items – of low unit value but relatively bulky – it can work out to be much more.

The ideal would be to hold no stock at all and to be able to call on the supplier to provide items when the end user or customer needs them. In practice this approach is unlikely to be realistic, because administrative and usage level timings will require some stock to be held for operational reasons.

The aim must therefore be to reduce stockholding to the minimum level compatible with operational requirements and cost-effectiveness, and to set our performance indicators accordingly. These indicators are consistent with the other study session topics and include all three factors:

- economy: the added value/value for money (VFM) in holding stock
- efficiency: how well we manage the stock
- effectiveness: the stock availability 'service level' that we offer to users or customers.

In other words, is the cost of operating our stockholding as low as it can be while still providing the level of service that the end user or customer requires and minimising our investment in the goods stored?

Stock is part of business working capital in a balance sheet along with cash and other liquid assets. The more stock we hold, the more working capital is tied up.

In distributive trades we rely on those businesses that hold stock in wholesale and retail operations. However, most manufacturing businesses want to eliminate stock and become just-in-time operations.

In any situation, why are some businesses better than others at managing their stock and providing excellent customer service levels?

Session learning objectives

After completing this session you should be able to:

5.1 Assess the advantages and disadvantages of holding stock in a business operation.

5.2 State the main elements of cost that will accrue in the operation of a stores operation.

5.3 Show diagrammatically how costs are allocated into subgroups of inventory-holding costs.

5.4 Summarise the key performance indicators for a stores operation carrying inventory for a manufacturing operation.

5.5 Evaluate how a manager would review the performance indicators linked to inventory held in terms of economy, efficiency and effectiveness.

Unit content coverage

This study session covers the following topics from the official CIPS unit content document:

Learning outcomes

- Categorise types of performance measures that are available to supply chain managers.
- Use a range of accounting techniques to measure organisational efficiency.
- Interpret and apply statistical data used to measure performance.

Learning objective

1.5 Demonstrate an understanding of how an organisation's purchase and supply function can manage and reduce inventory costs, and outline the methods available to do so.
   - Economy: achieving best value for money. Managing the cost of the supply operation
   - Efficiency: use of appropriate inventory management systems/techniques.
   - Effectiveness: level of service provided by the inventory function to its end users.

Prior knowledge

There are no specific prerequisites other than to understand where stock and inventory fit within a supply chain.

Resources

No specific resources are required for this session.

Timing

You should set aside about 4.25 hours to read and complete this session, including learning activities, self-assessment questions, the suggested further reading (if any) and the revision question.

5

5.1 Stock: its place and value in business operations

Stock is part of most commercial operations, and is listed in the main financial record – the balance sheet. Stock is part of working capital, and is valued as part of the assets.

Once a business buys stock from liquid assets (cash or bank) it remains a semi-liquid asset till it is used or sold. Stock is held for different reasons in various levels of business operation. There are three generic business operation levels, as shown in figure 5.1:

- primary industry: raw materials and resources
- secondary operations: value-adding businesses
- tertiary operations: retail, wholesale and services.

Figure 5.1: The three levels of business operation

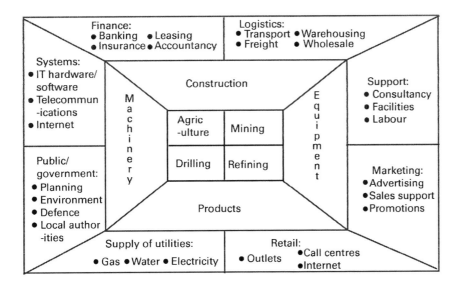

Stock is held in all sectors, but for differing reasons. Table 5.1 provides a brief summary of the sort of stock that would be held or used at each of the three levels.

There are many reasons for holding – or not holding – stock (figure 5.2). The performance measure has to reflect the value to a business that stock offers.

Table 5.1 Types of stockholding

Stock held at each operation	Classification of stock
Primary industry: raw materials and resources	MRO spares, bulk stock for sale
Secondary operations: value-adding businesses	Raw materials and components inbound
	Added value – work in progress stocks, MRO stock
	Finished goods stock for sale
Tertiary operations: retail, wholesale and services	Trading stock inbound, wholesale/retail
	Administrative and service stock
	Stock for service delivery

Figure 5.2: Factors affecting the need to hold stock

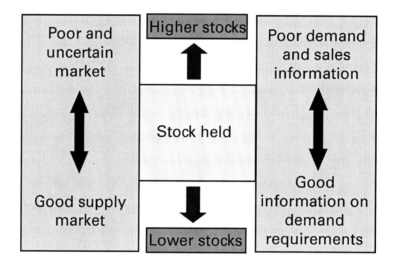

Learning activity 5.1

Using a manufacturing company as an example, design a questionnaire or checklist of information that will be of use in discussing with management how much stock should be held.

Feedback on page 84

Now you have completed this activity, try the following self-assessment question.

Self-assessment question 5.1

Which of the following will be needed to calculate the value of stock used in one year?

1 The part number.
2 The purchase price of the item.

(continued on next page)

Self-assessment question 5.1 (continued)
3   The name of the supplier.
4   The annual consumption.
5   The lead time for delivery.
6   The safety stock level.

Feedback on page 84

5.2   The cost of holding stock

Before we consider the cost of holding stock we need to consider the drivers behind stockholding policy:

- Finance managers want low stockholding to give better utilisation of financial resources.
- Production managers want stock availability to meet production plans.
- Marketing managers want to be able to sell based on low lead times for ex-stock products. Out-of-stock products lose sales too.
- Customers want quick delivery ex-stock.
- Buyers may get better deals for larger quantities.

As you can see, there are many push–pull drivers impinging on the supply chain managers in this sector of the cycle.

The business case for holding stock must take several cost centres into account, but the two main issues are:

- financial opportunity cost
- physical opportunity cost.

We introduced the economics concept of opportunity cost in study session 2. It is the opportunity of having (or not having) something – in this case stock. Before you can measure performance you need to know the basis of this cost.

Figure 5.3 summarises these two cost issues, which aggregate to a **total opportunity cost** – in effect the cost of holding stock for a business operation.

Figure 5.3: The real cost of holding stock

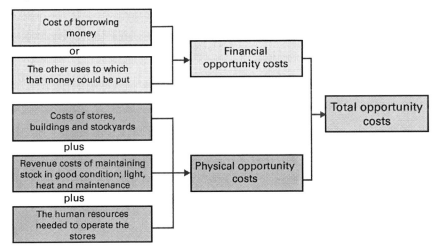

Learning activity 5.2

Reflect on our motor mower manufacturer Rotary Mowers UK Ltd, and the issues noted in figure 5.3.

Where would you obtain the key information that would allow you to calculate the total opportunity cost of stock held in such a business?

Feedback on page 85

Now you have completed this activity, try the following self-assessment question.

Self-assessment question 5.2

Which of the following costs are *not* part of the cost of holding stock?

1   The rent of the stores building.
2   The shareholders' dividend.
3   The cost of a bank loan.
4   The delivery time of goods into stock.
5   The Warehouse manager's salary.
6   The payroll costs.

Feedback on page 85

5.3   Building up the stockholding cost base and identifying links to performance management

We illustrated the concept of total opportunity cost in figure 5.3. You now need to relate these cost centres to your area of operation.

Figure 5.4 summarises the key operational processes involved in stock flow, movement, control and management. Stockholding costs aggregate along the process flow: each stage of the process can be measured and then its performance can be managed.

Figure 5.4: Stock flow

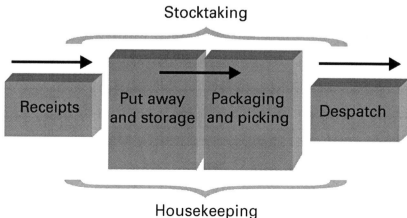

Learning activity 5.3

Develop a cost model for an area of business activity with which you are familiar. List the main costs of operating and managing inventory.

Feedback on page 85

Now you have completed this activity, try the following self-assessment question.

Self-assessment question 5.3

A business had a stock turnover of £350,000 in its last financial year. The bank loan allocated to fund the average stock value was £1,000 per month. The physical/service operating costs for the stores were £21,000. The HR costs were £43,000.

What is the gross percentage cost of stockholding for this business?

Feedback on page 85

5.4 Stores and inventory key performance indicators

On the basis that appropriate stock is essential for selective business needs, how will the stores and stock availability service be measured?

A stores/inventory manager would develop a set of operating indicators based on cost and customer service.

These key performance indicators (KPIs) would be equally useful to both internal and external customers, and could form part of staff incentive productivity bonus payments.

The KPIs would reflect the operational issues in running the stores, in holding stock, and the service offered.

In the introduction to this study session we referred to three factors linked to stockholding costs and measures:

*   economy
*   efficiency
*   effectiveness.

Using this introductory framework, how would more detailed KPIs be set and managed?

Financial KPIs (linked to economy issues)

- Purchasing costs.
- Stores holding on-cost percentage calculated, then tracked over time.
- Sub-analysis of stores on-costs, split between operations and HR staffing.
- Stock turnover rate.
- Average stock value amount.
- Stock losses: depreciation, obsolescence etc.

Operational KPIs (linked to efficiency issues)

- How much stock to hold (range and depth of stock).
- The methods and management of the stock.
- Pareto, 80:20 or ABC analysis.

Stores/stock service delivery (linked to effectiveness issues)

Service level is based on the percentage of orders fulfilled on first request.

- Benchmark:
    - High range: 95–98% service level
    - Medium range: 91–95% service level
    - Low range: < 90% service level.
- Stock damage/obsolescence rates.
- Staff pick/put away rates.
- Maintenance percentages.
- The cost–benefit analysis of improving service levels.

Choosing your measures: converting the theory into best practice

The above headers are not mutually exclusive, and will vary from sector to sector, but they do form the basis for applied development to your organisation.

The principle here is to identify what measures are useful and then to track and trace them over time in order to effect continuous improvement in this part of the supply chain.

Practical examples

In large warehouse operations, where the number of individual items stored may run into many thousands, it is impractical to consider each item individually. There are various techniques that can be used to make the task more manageable. For example, the **Pareto rule** or 80:20 analysis can be a useful tool. The Pareto rule suggests that 80% of the value of the stockholding will be in the top 20% of the individual items.

Using this technique, individual stock items should be analysed to establish their total value over a 12-month period (ie annual usage × purchase price) and ranked according to the highest value. See figure 5.5.

Figure 5.5: The Pareto curve

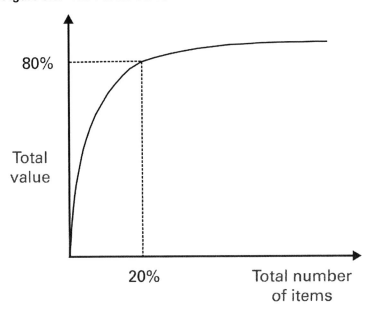

Focus should then be given to the top 20% of items, as they will account for approximately 80% of the total value of the stock during a year.

Another technique widely used is called **ABC analysis**. ABC is calculated in a similar way to Pareto but uses three or more categories of stock based on an item's turnover/usage in the stores rather than its value. See the example in table 5.5.

Table 5.5 ABC tabulation

Item	Movement	Turnover p.a.	Issues
Class A	Fast	7–10	70%
Class B	Medium	2–6	20%
Class C	Slow	< 2	10%
Class D	No movement		Scrap?

Stock turnover (which is generally calculated by dividing the total turnover - usually for a year - by the average stock value – for example, £100m turnover divided by average stock value of £7m equals 14.2 stock turn) is an important indicator, and is often used to describe stores performance. Increases in stores turnover rates indicate an improvement throughout the whole of the inventory management process

Learning activity 5.4

Create a customer survey questionnaire designed to rate the service performance of stock availability from a stores.

Feedback on page 86

Now you have completed this activity, try the following self-assessment question.

5

Self-assessment question 5.4

1 Which of the following would be the best measure of a stores' service level?
   A the percentage of items that are damaged in a period
   B the percentage of days' absence of staff
   C the percentage of items picked on first request
   D the percentage of interest charged on stock.

2 Which of the following is the best definition of a stores' stock range?
   A the lead time taken to deliver goods
   B the variety of stock items available
   C the level of safety stock held
   D the brand name list of stock items.

3 Rotary Mowers UK Ltd has classified its stock based on the usage of items in the stores. This technique and measure is known as:
   A Pareto analysis.
   B ABC analysis.
   C stocktaking analysis.
   D pick time analysis.

Feedback on page 86

5.5 Managing inventory KPIs within the wider supply chain

This section turns theory into continuous improvement practice by managing the outputs in terms of cost and service indicators.

The key issue is how the KPIs are used to manage cost and service stores and stock indicators.

As in other aspects of performance measurement it is important to select the measures and targets carefully.

In this highly transactional part of the supply, where there is a large volume of data, managers need to identify the best KPIs to manage cost and service if they are to maintain and retain competitive edge via continuous improvement.

In this section you need to focus on the management of this objective: the service provision of stock to users.

The performance management process is thus customer driven, first in establishing both targets and KPIs, and then in reporting the results in a clear and practical format for all those persons concerned:

- Senior managers will be looking at longer-term trends in order to develop strategic planning decisions and/or stock investment plans based on the data.
- Operational managers need KPI information to plan workload and service delivery outputs in the medium term.

- Operative/workforce staff need to be aware of their operational efficiency and effectiveness outputs at the transactional, week-to-week level.

5

Learning activity 5.5

Taking a work example within your own experience, complete a template that will track a set of stores and inventory management KPIs at operational management level over time.

Feedback on page 86

Now tackle the final self-assessment question in this session.

Self-assessment question 5.5

Draft a report to management to communicate the performance of inventory management in the business.

Feedback on page 87

Revision question

Now try the revision question for this session on page 334.

Summary

The inventory management process and measures are an important element of the supply chain. Stock is an important part of the chain but the fundamental question is: how much stock do we need, and when do we need it. The traditional answer was to have stock in a store, but this is only one solution. In manufacturing and many service-based organisations just-in-time logistics solutions offer better solutions. In either case the 'just too late' outcome is to be avoided.

This session looked at the need for stock, at what it costs to hold stock, and at how we measure how well supply chain managers are delivering stock needs.

On the basis that many industries need stock we reviewed how best to measure the inventory management process to ensure that the lowest cost option consistent with service needs is achieved.

This balance is achieved in a variety of ways, and the session closed with suggestions as to how managers at all levels can simultaneously deliver the targets of low costs and high service levels .

5

Feedback on learning activities and self-assessment questions

Feedback on learning activity 5.1

Taking the example from study session 4 of a rotary mower manufactured by Rotary Mowers UK Ltd, we can use a single bought-in component such as a spark plug to develop a typical list. See table 5.2.

Table 5.2 Stockholding review data sheet

Component	Volume, value or data
Spark plug: 1 per machine	
Usage:	
• original equipment needs (OE)	
• spares sales (aftermarket)	
• consumption history	
• production plan	
• forecast production/sales needs	
Product:	
• pack size	
• price	
• lead time	
Supplier:	
• current supplier	
• alternative suppliers	
Stock history:	
• turnover	
• value	
• forecasts	
• service level indicator	
Stock levels:	
• EOQ	
• minimum stock	
• maximum stock	
• average stock	
• safety stock	
Other business issues	

Feedback on self-assessment question 5.1

See table 5.3.

Table 5.3

1	The part number	Nominal information only for identification
2	The purchase price of the item	Yes. This is the basic unit cost
3	The name of the supplier	No. Not relevant to this answer
4	The annual consumption	Yes. Annual consumption × purchase price gives annual turnover value of a stock item
5	The lead time for delivery	No. This is the time it takes to deliver the goods from placing an order with a supplier
6	The safety stock level	No. This is a stock level minimum, which is set as a safety against stock-out

Feedback on learning activity 5.2

See table 5.4.

Table 5.4 Rotary Mowers UK Ltd: cost of holding stock

Financial opportunity costs	
Cost of borrowing money	The rate of borrowing money to buy stock. This percentage is a function of bank rate and business creditworthiness
or The other uses to which the money could have been put	What could the same money be invested in that would give a better return?
Physical opportunity costs	
Cost of stores buildings and stockyards	The rent, rates, costs, capital equipment, maintenance etc of and within the stores building
plus Revenue costs of maintaining stock in good condition. stores operating costs	The revenue costs light, heat, admin, IT costs of the stores building
plus The human resources costs to operate the stores	Staffing costs: management, supervision, workforce. Direct pay and employment costs.

Feedback on self-assessment question 5.2

1   Yes. Part of physical opportunity costs.
2   No. Not part of the cost of holding stock.
3   Yes. Part of the financial opportunity costs.
4   No. Not part of the cost of holding stock.
5   Yes. Part of the HR physical opportunity costs.
6   No. Not part of the cost of holding stock, although there is an indirect overhead chargeback cost for this service.

Feedback on learning activity 5.3

Your list will vary depending on which business sector you operate in. The three main sectors are:

- Primary industry. Mining/agriculture: raw materials and resources.
- Secondary operations. Manufacturing/assembly: value-adding businesses.
- Tertiary operations. Retail, wholesale and services.

Your list must include cost centres for both financial and physical opportunity costs. In order to calculate the percentage on costs you need to aggregate these costs and calculate them as a percentage of annual stock turnover value to get a figure for your industry.

Feedback on self-assessment question 5.3

The total costs are:

5

Bank interest	£12,000
Operational costs	£21,000
HR costs	£43,000
Total costs	£76,000

$$\text{Stores gross stockholding percentage} = \frac{\text{Total costs}}{\text{Stock turnover}}$$

$$= \frac{76,000}{350,000}$$

$$= 21.7\%$$

(Note that we have used the term 'gross stockholding' here. In reality there may be other amounts and adjustments, such as damaged stock, obsolescent stock, or stock adjustments, which may be used in a more detailed analysis.)

Feedback on learning activity 5.4

A customer survey needs to be industry/service specific for the customers in question. However, the following checklist is a basis for development for your industry.

- Range: Does the stores carry an adequate range of items?
- Depth: Does the stores carry sufficient stock to meet your needs?
- Service: Is the service adequate for your needs?
- Cost: In your view, is the cost of stock as charged out within your expectation/budget?
- Continuous improvement: How could range, depth or service be improved for you?

Your survey should remind customers that although range, depth and service can always be increased or improved there is a cost for this. What we are looking for in the responses is thus a customer/service balance of real needs at an acceptable cost.

Feedback on self-assessment question 5.4

Answers

1 C
2 B
3 B

Feedback on learning activity 5.5

Such a template will vary with the selected industry and management level.

This activity focuses on mid managers/supervisors, and a suggested template is shown in table 5.6. However, you should be able to develop similar templates at any level or for any industrial sector.

Table 5.6 Stores KPIs for operation managers

Broad category	General header example	Action/continuous improvement
Economy	Stores on-cost percentage	Identify variances, and manage within target budget
		Liaise with other supply chain managers/stakeholders
Efficiency	Stores pick rates	Identify variances and manage process
	Stores space utilisation	Review process as required
		Train as necessary
		Review technology
Effectiveness	Stores service level to customers	Identify variances and trace negative factors

Feedback on self-assessment question 5.5

Your management report would be based on a template process, as illustrated in learning activity 5.5. It would include most of the following headers:

- Current results
- Track of results over time
- Analysis of trend
- Actions on variance
- Opportunities for improvement
- Any review of process
- Actions taken.

5

IT and data management

Introduction

'Information is power.'

How can you use the wide range of information available to measure purchasing performance and demonstrate continuous improvement to others?

You will recall from the unit content and the course introduction that this unit, *Measuring Purchasing Performance*, is based on three distinct categories of supply chain management:

- measuring and evaluating the performance of the purchasing and supply function (40% course content)
- measuring and evaluating the performance of the supplier (30% course content)
- measuring and evaluating the performance of the buyer (30% course content).

This study session introduces the way in which IT systems and information processes collect and subsequently report management information that can be used to measure performance in each of these three categories. In later study sessions these principles will enable you to add value to the opportunities to measure the various aspects of performance in all three categories.

Session learning objectives

After completing this session you should be able to:

6.1 State how IT systems are used in business operations in general, and where purchasing and supply systems support the process in particular.
6.2 Define the main elements of a purchasing and supply IT system.
6.3 Summarise the issues that, if measured, would add value to the management of purchasing and supply.
6.4 Summarise the issues that, if measured, would add value to the management of suppliers within an organisation.
6.5 Appraise how developments in IT technology can assist purchasing and supply managers in both current performance and future continuous improvement issues.
6.6 Formulate a set of performance indicators that would help a purchasing manager to reduce costs and/or improve service delivery.

Unit content coverage

This study session covers the following topics from the official CIPS unit content document:

Learning outcomes

- Categorise types of performance measures that are available to supply chain managers.
- Appraise measures that can be used to improve supplier performance.
- Interpret and apply statistical data used to measure performance.

Learning objective

1.6 Suggest how the use of information technology may help in the acquisition of purchase and supply performance data.
  - Use of appropriate management information systems to capture and record information relating to all related costs re: stock/inventory levels and use; and overall costs relating to the purchasing function
  - Databases for recording/storing supplier/vendor information
  - Stock movement/monitoring systems, including point-of-sale data capture and delivery details

Prior knowledge

You will need a general knowledge of generic and certain bespoke IT systems and applications.

Resources

No specific resources are required for this session.

Timing

You should set aside about 5.25 hours to read and complete this session, including learning activities, self-assessment questions, the suggested further reading (if any) and the revision question.

6.1 Information systems in business, and the links with supply chain systems used to measure performance

Information is a key tool in achieving stated business goals and objectives. CEOs and strategic managers in most organisations see information as power, and thus as a valuable business asset. In the context of this study session you need to understand how information can support and develop the various links within the supply chain in particular, and the wider business goals and objectives in general.

Most managers want their enterprises to be more 'intelligent', meaning that they are able to react and plan by using information effectively. However, it is a challenge to define and characterise what an **intelligent enterprise** looks like.

Opinions vary widely on this, because all companies and organisations use information technology (IT) and use information systems (IS) differently. Organisations are at varying levels of IT/IS evolution and maturity, and at the same time the technology continues to move forward. The key to using information successfully is not necessarily how far the organisation has *evolved*, but how it is *evolving*.

The intelligent enterprise shows sound judgement and rationality in planning a practical approach to delivering solutions that meet the long-term information needs of the organisation.

This does not mean that the intelligent enterprise has all the latest and greatest technology; rather it means that it exploits information to establish and maintain the strategic vision, and then applies it in an effective manner.

The intelligent enterprise achieves its strategic and tactical objectives through information use. In private sector businesses this is to done to attain financial targets and maintain sustainable competitive advantage. In NPO and service sector organisations the mission is to attain service delivery within budget and VFM criteria. This can be achieved with simple or complex technology, from an SME to a corporate organisation.

As an organisation moves along the evolutionary process, it expands its capability for delivering increased business value via information. Understanding how to evolve to an intelligent enterprise means the organisation has to comprehend the steps along the way.

Organisations need to recognise where they are and why, and then understand how to move to the next level. These steps are best classified into the following five levels:

- Level 1: Operate.
- Level 2: Consolidate.
- Level 3: Integrate.
- Level 4: Optimise.
- Level 5: Innovate.

These five steps along the IT/IS evolutionary road, and some milestone issues, are illustrated in figure 6.1.

Figure 6.1: Evolving information systems

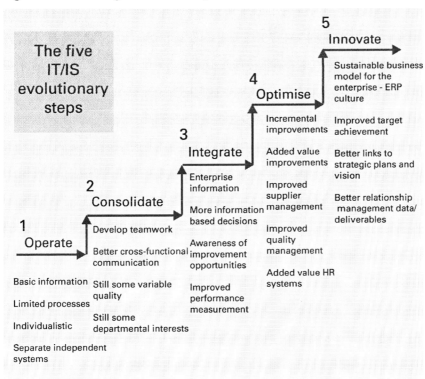

Having discussed the wider issues of IT/IS within an organisation, we now need to reflect on how to use information for the purposes of performance management in a variety of business and service sectors.

One of the first issues is to differentiate between data and information. Recall the old saying 'We can't see the wood for the trees.' Managers are often in this position: surrounded with data but having little information to work with.

In basic terms data is a set of facts or transactions. The skill of information reporting is to select the data for sorting and aggregation into meaningful sets and reports.

Selecting the data from robust sources/transactions is the basis of analysis. The aim should be to use existing data and then report selected trends, milestones, results from this. One common error is to create new data input to achieve this; best practice reporting relies on using existing transactional sources entered as part of daily operational transactions and then utilising that for information purposes.

Within supply chains there are several typical data sources. Figure 6.2 illustrates the main groupings that can be identified in most systems. These facilitate supply chain information and report sets that are the basis for performance measurement, and will also interface with corporate information needs.

Figure 6.2: Typical supply chain databases and outputs

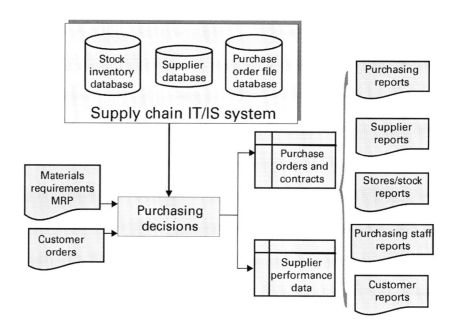

Learning activity 6.1

Describe the main elements of a corporate business IT system and the links to the supply chain process and systems.

Feedback on page 102

Now go on to tackle the following self-assessment question.

6

Self-assessment question 6.1

1   In the supply chain system, purchasing transactional data is input:
     A by finance in entering a budget cost centre value.
     B by buyers in raising purchase orders.
     C by buyers in entering quotation information.
     D by production in recording volume produced.
2   In a manufacturing company, the transactions on which a stores parts stock report is based are:
     A the volume and value of sales to customers.
     B the volume and value of supply chain distribution costs.
     C the volume and value of production stock items.
     D the volume and value of finished goods.
3   An information system that integrates with other corporate systems is known as:
     A a materials requirements planning (MRP) system.
     B a distribution requirements planning (DRP) system.
     C a purchasing management system.
     D An enterprise resource planning (ERP) system.

Feedback on page 102

6.2   The key elements of a purchasing IT system

Purchasing and supply systems can be either stand-alone or part of a corporate package. In either case, how do managers get the most from the system?

At this point we are not concerned what business sector is being served or whether or not the system should be stand-alone. For information, most larger systems now operate in a 'procure to pay' environment linked to e-procurement and web links.

The basic purposes of a purchasing system are to:

* receive or identify and log customer demands or requirements
* identify a source of supply to specification
* ensure audit processes and authority
* enable a buyer to agree a price and terms for supply

- raise an order or contract for delivery from a supplier
- ensure that goods are delivered to that order requirement
- generate the order or contract as a prime document in the payment process
- produce procurement reports.

The assessment and evaluation of existing or planned purchasing systems should relate to these basic purposes. However, if a buyer is involved in specifying an upgrade or a new system, there are several other costs and measures that should be considered:

- IT software licence fees
- database integration costs – set-up and or integration with existing systems
- installation costs
- training costs, both at set-up and ongoing
- usage costs, including software maintenance and upgrade time and costs.

In terms of the above processes, what outputs should be measured from a purchasing system in addition to ensuring good process control?

- the management of a rationalised supplier base
- the opportunities from using leveraged buying power
- the opportunity to reduce purchasing transactional costs.

These three headers are intentionally broad. The operational details will vary according to the business sector in which a buyer works, and the IT environment of the organisation. However, the purchasing performance measures and targets can be related to these three key headers in most situations. You will develop the added value and purchasing measurement opportunities offered via IT systems in more detail later in this session.

Learning activity 6.2

Create a process/flow diagram of a purchasing and supply IT system, and note the corporate interfaces.

Feedback on page 102

Having completed this, now try the following self-assessment question.

Self-assessment question 6.2

List at least five reports that a buyer could generate and use at the transactional level as a basis for measuring aspects of purchasing performance over time.

Feedback on page 103

6.3 The added value issues and linked performance indicators for managing the purchasing function

In any IT system there is a high volume of data. Managers must be able to select, classify and create useful reports to support their professional or management skills.

In section 6.2 above we reviewed the added value of an IT system in purchasing management, and the self-assessment question required you to elaborate on how purchasing performance measures can be identified from data available.

In these next three sections of this session you will categorise those opportunities in line with the unit content, setting the scene for their further development later in this course book:

- performance management of purchasing
- performance management of suppliers
- performance management of buyers.

The final section will review the specific opportunities for saving costs and adding value that are offered to purchasing by IT/IS systems.

6

Learning activity 6.3

In self-assessment question 6.2 above you developed a list of basic transactional reports concerned with the management of purchasing.

Based on your own experience, rank the top five in order of priority, and briefly explain your reasoning.

Feedback on page 103

In any business, each department has to perform efficiently and effectively. The purchasing function is a cost to the business in providing the service of obtaining goods and services required. You therefore need to manage this cost as part of purchasing performance management.

The cost of purchasing is an element in the concept of the total cost of acquisition (TCA) and/or the wider concept, the total cost of ownership (TCO), which we introduced in study session 2.

In some organisations purchasing is set up as a cost centre or profit centre linked to production costs or business profit margins. In other organisations the purchasing department staff and operating budgets are just part of a departmental, operational or corporate budget, and are not specifically identified. But however the cost accountants set up the details, purchasing managers need to be able to manage their 'business'.

In managing the purchasing business there are various aspects to be considered: process and procedures, professional practice and methods, and

6

HR costs. The application and operation of IT systems form part of that management process.

Performance measurement of the purchasing function can be either objective or subjective:

Objective measures involve measurable quantity or values, such as money, time, or rates.

Subjective measures involve more qualitative or service value measurements, such as customer surveys, personal assessment or value judgement opinions.

In the measurement process both formats can be used independently or jointly. You will see examples of both in this course book, and will no doubt be aware of specific examples in your own organisation or experience.

To summarise, purchasing performance management will draw on a wide range of facts, opinions and information in assessing its effectiveness and efficiency as a service provider within a commercial, service or manufacturing operation. IT systems can support, facilitate, log, track, trace and collate such information, but success is not guaranteed by merely having the latest state-of-the-art system.

Self-assessment question 6.3

Give True or False responses to the following statements.

1   The measurement of a category of spend by purchasing is a subjective measure. TRUE/FALSE
2   Purchasing can have a direct effect on the gross profit of a business. TRUE/FALSE
3   The cost of the purchasing function is part of the total cost of acquisition for an organisation. TRUE/FALSE
4   A purchasing department can operate as a profit centre in a business. TRUE/FALSE

Feedback on page 104

6.4   The added value issues and processes in managing the performance of suppliers

Most organisations have too many suppliers. How do we manage the supplier base for best performance?

Consider the following questions, which purchasing managers should review on a regular basis:

*   How many suppliers does our business organisation have?
*   How many suppliers does our business organisation need?
*   How do we manage the selection of potential new suppliers?

The management of the supplier base is just as important as the management of the performance of suppliers currently being used.

In most organisations there are too many suppliers. The purchase ledger is full of suppliers who are seldom used. Suppliers who supply the same goods or services are listed, and others are left on the lists with minimal annual spend amounts. There are of course some positive reasons for having more than one supplier for some goods or services, but the issue in this section is how well we manage our supplier base.

Learning activity 6.4

Undertake a review of your own organisation's list of suppliers. Categorise them by annual spend value.

Feedback on page 104

Having considered the supplier base, it is equally important to consider how we manage those suppliers with whom we have current agreements or contracts to supply goods and services.

Purchasing managers can use their IT/IS systems to facilitate the management of the performance of current suppliers:

- How do we manage the relationship with current suppliers of goods and services?
- How do we manage the performance of these existing suppliers?

Later sessions of this course book cover the detail of these and other processes. In this session we are looking at the way in which IT/IS systems can collect data and consolidate information into performance management reports for transactional, operational and strategic management purposes.

The important word here is 'manage'. On the basis that we must manage business resources, our suppliers and their performance are key to success or failure. Therefore the management of suppliers must be a proactive role for purchasing managers.

As in all aspects of management there are different priorities of need and action: short-term transactional matters, medium-term operational/tactical issues and long-term strategic policy.

Self-assessment question 6.4

Draft a management report on the current supplier base list in a commercial or service operation.

Feedback on page 105

6.5 The added value issues and processes in managing the performance of buyers

Having considered how purchasing IT systems can assist in managing the purchasing function and the supplier base, we now move forward to issues concerned with the purchasing people.

The people who work in purchasing and the associated supply chain functions are the key human resource of the service. Therefore performance management of these human resources is a vital link in the chain of purchasing performance management.

In considering this aspect of performance management there are several criteria to take into account. There are many possible headers, but the following list covers most general areas that can be measured in the context of purchasing performance management:

- the purchasing/supply management competence requirement
- the person
- the post
- the customer service.

The general term 'competence' is used in many aspects of commercial and academic assessment. Competence is generally a measure of several factors, including skill, experience, knowledge, qualifications and attitude.

Competence attributes are acquired over time, and can be assessed and graded according to the needs of a job or certain standards. The elements of competence are not necessarily equal or mutually exclusive.

In terms of purchasing, for example, there are a set of national competence standards aligned to NVQ qualifications. However, not having a qualification, skills or certain knowledge does not necessarily mean that a person does not have competence to do a job. It is all a matter of judgement, linked to the other criterion of needs.

The needs of a purchasing job will be based on a person specification and a job description, written to meet the needs of the job and service required.

In terms of service, our purchasing customers are those people who use the purchasing or supply chain service. Later sessions of this course book will develop these assessment processes and measurement opportunities. In this session we need to focus on how purchasing IT systems will facilitate the purchasing HR measurement process.

Data records will link with corporate HR information, but the purchasing manager needs to provide and have access to this resource in order to undertake performance measurement processes.

The prime documents are the person specification and job description. Based on this, the purchasing manager can measure a person according to the criteria for and needs of the job. This can be by formal assessment or by informal interview. Many organisations undertake an annual review with managers and staff, and this can form part of that process.

A positive review will identify aspects of competence or gaps, with actions to support staff in whatever needs are identified, such as training, mentoring, coaching, or customer service advice. In some cases formal competence assessment is linked to grades and pay, and is seen to be progressive. IT systems can be used to track and trace HR information and link this with performance measurement targets.

Staff development of IT skills, in particular, is part of the general purchasing competence assessment process. Figure 6.1 highlighted the continuous development of IT systems. As purchasing systems evolve there is a specific need to ensure continuous professional development (CPD) in this area of purchasing management.

Staff may need to develop their skills on generic systems, such as Microsoft Office, or in using bespoke software. In both cases there is also a need to interface to web developments such as e-commerce, e-tendering, e-auctions, business interfaces (eg business to government, B2G), and ERP systems. Part of the process of competence review and measurement is clearly linked to the performance of these tasks too.

Learning activity 6.5

List four recent developments that you have researched on IT/IS systems or web information opportunities.

Feedback on page 105

Now go straight on to the following self-assessment question.

Self-assessment question 6.5

Rank the list in learning activity 6.5 above in order of importance as it would apply to your business.

Feedback on page 105

6.6 Best practice: which KPIs will help supply chain managers reduce cost and improve service?

Having considered how IT systems can support the management of the purchasing function, its suppliers and the purchasing staff, we move on to business values and outline how IT systems can reduce cost or improve service – or preferably both.

All supply chain managers must manage costs, manage the supplier base, and deliver measurable contributions and business benefits.

In terms of the issues in this course book we can review cost reduction and service improvement under various supply chain headers, as follows.

Purchasing:

1　interactive cost price analysis (CPA) for goods and services
2　a proactive approach to market knowledge and supplier source management
3　a strategic approach to supplier management of goods and services
4　negotiation at every stage in supply chain and contract management – the contribution to the bottom line
5　improving purchasing customer service, both perceived and actual.

Inventory, warehouse and distribution management:

6　managing the flow of goods in the supply chain via IT systems
7　standardisation and variety reduction in the supply chain
8　improving stores/inventory users customer service, both perceived and actual.

On this basis, how can IT systems support the purchasing performance measurement process?

There is usually an abundance of data and information to draw from. In selecting which ones to use, the keys are relevance and value. Setting KPIs and targets is an important task, and will involve time and effort, so their selection is critical.

The first step is to refer back to the issues introduced in study session 1 – the links to an organisation's mission and values – and ensure that the main performance indicators are in line with these.

Having thus ensured that the corporate strategic issues are addressed, purchasing managers can then focus on both the subjective and the objective measures of the purchasing business.

The task here is to choose a lead KPI for each issue. Use the eight-point list above to identify the most effective measures that relate to these tactical supply chain operations.

In order to support these main KPIs the manager should select the transactional KPIs that feed upwards to the main KPIs.

The IT issue here is to select data and consolidate information that, wherever possible, already exists in the system. Special entries or searches are often valuable, but performance management measures that arise from regular process transactions and analysis are more robust and reasonably accessible on a long-term basis.

Learning activity 6.6

Develop a list of important purchasing and supply KPIs for your business.

Feedback on page 105

Now go on to tackle the final self-assessment question in this session.

Self-assessment question 6.6

Complete a purchasing and supply department questionnaire ready to be issued to a management meeting that will discuss and choose the KPIs for the next 12 months.

Feedback on page 106

Revision question

Now try the revision question for this session on page 334.

Summary

This session has focused on two main issues:

* the use of IT/IS systems in purchasing and supply chain management as applicable to all business and service sectors
* how purchasing managers use information covered in this subject area in relation to:
    * the purchasing function
    * supplier performance
    * buyer performance.

The session reviewed the IT links with corporate systems, and considered how these systems evolve within organisations large and small. It then reviewed the nature of data and information available to purchasing managers in order to undertake the process of measuring each of the above aspects of performance.

The final section considered the business case performance indicators for a purchasing manager, namely cost reduction and service improvement. These performance indicators are equally valid in private or public sector organisations.

These issues are all developed as session titles in the course book and students need to keep this IT information session in mind throughout their studies of each of the respective topics to follow.

Feedback on learning activities and self-assessment questions

Feedback on learning activity 6.1

A corporate IT/IS system will integrate data from all management and operational areas of action, including finance, marketing, production, HR, supply chain, R&D, administration/services and other special interests.

A totally integrated system will be based on the principles of an enterprise resource planning (ERP) system, and will interface with both inbound suppliers and outbound customers. A corporate IT system integrates with the movement of goods and information flows, as illustrated in figure 6.3.

Figure 6.3: Controlling and tracking the flow of information and materials

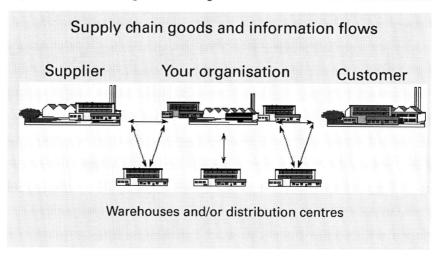

Within a supply chain process and system there will be interfaces with various other subsystems, such as the purchasing system, the materials requirements planning (MRP) system, stores and stock systems, distribution planning systems (DRP), HR systems, and finance systems.

Feedback on self-assessment question 6.1

Answers

1 B
2 C
3 D

Feedback on learning activity 6.2

Figure 6.4 is a generic diagram of IT relationships. It shows the supply chain IT system at the centre, surrounded by the possible departmental interfaces.

Figure 6.4: Supply chain IT relationships

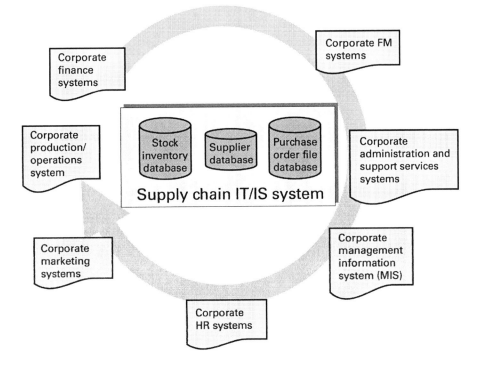

Feedback on self-assessment question 6.2

There is a wide cross-section of possible areas, including:

- purchase order details: supplier, volume and value
- back orders awaiting delivery
- details of contracts for call-off of goods and services
- cost per order raised
- spend per buyer
- spend per category
- saving or added value reports
- cost of purchasing: corporate turnover and/or corporate HR cost
- links to suppliers' prices, catalogues, discount structures
- supplier database details
- EDI, e-commerce links
- delivery schedules, planned and actual
- expediting progress data
- goods received records
- basic quality records: goods rejected/returned to suppliers
- vendor rating database
- invoice links to finance (linked to payment-days reports).

Feedback on learning activity 6.3

Your ranking will depend on the business sector you operate in, and on the nature of the goods or services you are involved with.

You could apply the reports you have listed to reviewing and reporting on the efficiency and effectiveness of the purchasing function. Such reports will lead to:

- an analysis of the volume and value of goods and services purchased

- an analysis of the number of transactions
- an 80:20 analysis of purchasing spend
- an analysis of the cost of the purchasing function, as a proportion of business turnover in the last full financial year
- an analysis of the cost savings targets achieved.

This is a broad, general list. You should develop this activity by considering an area of operation with which you are familiar and grouping your priority list into objective measures or subjective measures.

Consider how you would collect the data, and how you would report the information to others.

Reporting would be delivered upward to senior managers for operational, tactical and longer-term strategic use. Reporting across and down the hierarchy would be used to track workflows and productivity on a shorter-term basis.

This methodology can thus be applied to any aspect of supply chain management performance measurement, as required.

Feedback on self-assessment question 6.3

1   FALSE. The summation of a category spend is an objective measurable value.
2   TRUE. Savings made on direct/indirect costs will have a direct positive impact on gross profit.
3   TRUE. The TCA includes the actual cost of procuring goods and services.
4   TRUE. In many manufacturing and retail sectors purchasing departments operate as profit centres.

Feedback on learning activity 6.4

This activity leads to some basic information on the spend analysis of your active supplier base.

You can collect the data from the purchase ledger database, and start by listing the spend by supplier for a selected period in descending order, from highest to lowest values. From this data you can identify the total spend for the time period, and then calculate the percentage spend with each supplier. From this you will be able to undertake sub-analysis. The most useful first step is to identify your top 20% of suppliers by value.

The general principle of the 80:20 rule is that around 80% of the money you spend is typically with the top 20% of suppliers. From this basic data analysis you are in a position to identify your top 20% suppliers and thereby apply your skills to this group.

There are many other, more detailed techniques and analysis methods for the supplier base. However, the principle here is to illustrate how purchasing/business IT systems can facilitate data analysis.

Feedback on self-assessment question 6.4

This question takes you to the next step of using information. In learning activity 6.4 you gathered information and produced a basic 80:20 supplier base analysis. You now need to use this information to manage and/or report to others.

A management report would include the results of the supplier base analysis and the actions that a purchasing manager could take, including some or all of the following points:

- actions planned to use the information for purchasing leverage
- actions planned to undertake negotiations with suppliers
- actions planned to realign the supplier base
- actions planned to manage the supplier base more closely.

Feedback on learning activity 6.5

There are many examples. They include:

- web pages with interactive catalogues
- web supplier/product search facilities
- e-commerce applications
- e-government applications
- e-bidding/tendering facilities
- intranet developments
- supplier registration packages
- specialist professional trade body links
- interactive subscription services, such as the British Standards Institution (BSI)
- certain remaining or specialist electronic data interchange (EDI) applications
- conferencing and communications packages.

Feedback on self-assessment question 6.5

Your answer to this question will vary depending on the nature of your business or organisation and the evolutionary stage it is at.

Most organisations have benefited from basic web searches for products, suppliers and technical information.

You may also have considered some of the competences and competence development issues in working with these processes and systems.

Your answer should develop a response of a specific example.

Feedback on learning activity 6.6

Your list should include cost reduction and service improvement KPIs at each level:

- Strategic/corporate KPIs: linked to the longer-term mission and values of the organisation.

6

- Tactical/middle management KPIs: linked to delivering the current annual business plan.
- Operational/transactional KPIs: linked to managing the shorter-term transactions and operational processes.

Feedback on self-assessment question 6.6

Memo to Heads of:

Finance, IT, Production, Marketing, Human Resources, R&D, Administration

Management Team meeting with the CEO

Each management team has submitted its annual departmental business plan to the Board. Each manager is requested to enter the most important KPI with respect to the service that purchasing/supply management provides and interfaces with their respective department. From the responses to this questionnaire the purchasing manager will report back on the set of KPIs most relevant to the organisational aims and departmental customer needs.

Selection of key performance indicators	Customer requests	Issue/target to be measured
Strategic/corporate KPIs		
Tactical/middle management KPIs		
Operational/transactional KPIs		
Special KPIs		

Why measure suppliers?

Introduction

They may not be friends, but your key suppliers can be respected and developed, and they can provide support in bad times. It is estimated that the average business spends about 50–60% of its total operating costs on bought-in goods, works and services, although this percentage is often lower in public services such as healthcare and local government. It is clear that the performance of these external suppliers will have a significant effect on both the real and the perceived performance of the business or organisation. This therefore presents the purchasing department with a real challenge.

> 'What matters is working with a few close friends, people you respect, knowing that if times turn bad these people would hold together.'
>
> **Richard Branson**

7

Session learning objectives

After completing this session you should be able to:

7.1 Explain the link between supplier performance and business success.
7.2 Summarise the measurement of suppliers within the procurement function.
7.3 Define the contribution of measurement in 'quality management'.
7.4 Argue that the measurement process contributes to the building of relationships.
7.5 Distinguish between the measurement processes of supplier selection and supplier evaluation.
7.6 Describe a situation where both business stakeholders cooperate in performance measures for mutual advantage.

Unit content coverage

This study session covers the following topics from the official CIPS unit content document:

Learning outcome

- Determine how measuring performance in the supply chain activities fits into the overall management process of an organisation.

Learning objective

2.2 Explain the importance of measuring a supplier's performance and distinguish from supplier appraisal.
   - Supplier appraisal: assessment of supplier capability to control quality, quantity and price
   - Supplier performance: comparison against a standard, performance on previous orders and against other supplier's performances

Prior knowledge

A general understanding of the concept of the supply chain and the benefit to a business of good key suppliers.

Resources

No specific resources are required, but it will be useful to be or to have been involved in the measurement or monitoring of suppliers. If you have not, you may find it useful to discuss this issue with other students or colleagues, or a manager.

Timing

You should set aside about 4.75 hours to read and complete this session, including learning activities, self-assessment questions, the suggested further reading (if any) and the revision question.

7.1 Supplier performance and business success.

The purchasing challenge is to secure the best suppliers, in terms of value for money, to supply goods and services to the organisation. This can only really be achieved if:

- The supplier's abilities and performance are measured.
- The measurement uses sensible and appropriate **tools** (a generic term for management techniques, ideas and ways of working for undertaking a particular task).
- The measurement takes place over time to show trends.
- The results are compared with past performance, and other benchmarks if available, such as your competitors, or published indices.

The impact of success on the organisation may be considered in terms of the traditional five rights of purchasing (see table 7.1).

Table 7.1 Impact of supplier performance

The right *price*	Reductions in price by purchasing impact directly on the **bottom line** of the organisation (management-speak for the profitability of a business: the profit is usually the bottom line of a profit and loss account). Typically savings by purchasing can equate to increased sales of between 5% and 10%, often hard to achieve in many markets. This is why there is increased focus on purchasing in many organisations.
The right *quality*	Quality improvements help with branding and satisfy consumer demand for reliability and service. Quality can save money when designed in from the start: hence the importance of **early purchasing involvement** (ensuring that purchasing are involved early in a deal, and not brought in at the last minute) and good specifications.

(continued on next page)

7

Table 7.1 *(continued)*

Reduced product failure helps with warranty claims and consumer perceptions.

Fixing quality problems is more expensive than preventing them.

The right *quantity*	It is a key objective of many organisations to reduce **inventory** (also known as stock), and this has direct benefits in efficiency and cost reduction.
	In manufacturing and retail the move to JIT and lean manufacturing is dependent on suppliers' abilities to deliver the needed quantities as and when required.
The right *place*	Failure to deliver to the correct location becomes critical as inventory reduces.
The right *time*	Failure to deliver at the right time becomes critical as inventory reduces and JIT-type systems are introduced. Late delivery can cause severe production or service problems.

Clearly, if all the above are effective then the impact on the business is significant.

Learning activity 7.1

Identify a supplier who you consider has performed successfully for your business. In a table like the one below, write down between three and five positive success features that you attribute to this supplier, and which you have been able to measure. Then rank them in order of importance to your business, showing what you have gained from each feature, and how it was measured.

Table 7.2

Success feature	Description	How measured
1		
2		
3		
4		
5		

Feedback on page 121

'Good' suppliers allow an organisation to perform efficiently and effectively, and to focus on its core activities. The organisation does not need to worry about supplier performance and quality, which are – as far as possible – 'right first time'. As we have seen, this leads to lower costs of operation. Conversely, if suppliers perform badly, then service to customers suffers, along with product or service image. Also, management time and resources are required to improve the situation.

Although it is purchasing's overall responsibility to acquire good suppliers, the actual result will depend on the performance of the suppliers they choose. Also, and depending on the importance to the organisation of the type of purchase involved, purchasing may be interested not only in the **primary supplier** – the one responsible for supplying to them – but also in their supplier's supplier(s) (the second-level suppliers). Increasingly this is leading to purchasing being involved in the whole supply chain, rather than merely focusing on the primary suppliers.

Whatever the industry, supplier performance is increasingly being seen as critical, and there is increased pressure on purchasing to select suppliers who can perform to these standards, and to monitor delivery to ensure that they do!

7

Self-assessment question 7.1

Give True or False responses to the following statements.

1 Measuring supplier performance is only effective if done over a period of time. TRUE/FALSE
2 It is cheaper to fix quality problems as they occur. TRUE/FALSE
3 Purchasing staff are increasingly measuring the performance of suppliers further up the supply chain. TRUE/FALSE
4 Our product image may suffer if our suppliers have problems. TRUE/FALSE

Feedback on page 121

7.2 Supplier performance measures within the procurement function

We can see from the above that purchasing management is increasingly expected to measure the performance of suppliers, and in study session 8 we shall look in more depth at how this is done. The amount of direct effort that the buying organisation will need to put into the scope of the measurement system will depend on the importance of the purchase to the organisation in terms of:

- the criticality of the order(s) to the buying organisation
- the value of orders likely to be placed
- the time and resources available to continually review and update the measurements
- whether the purchase is a one-off or an ongoing requirement
- factors outside the supplier's control.

Learning activity 7.2

Identify a 'key supplier' in your business and write down four points that illustrate which aspect of the supplier's performance contributes most to your organisation's success, brand image or reputation.

Feedback on page 121

Any issue can be measured, but realistically most issues relate to cost and performance. Table 7.3 shows typical areas for analysis using supplier performance measurement ratings.

Table 7.3 Supplier performance: basic measures

Delivery	Often measured as percentage received, in a stipulated acceptable condition, at the agreed time. Sometimes more complex to calculate on service contracts
Quality	On manufactured items failure or reject rates are often used, while service contracts measure the recorded fails in service. Increasingly performance is related to quality standards such as ISO 9000 or management systems such as total quality management (TQM)
Service	Often more subjective, but tries to measure acceptable performance in areas such as after-sales service, response to problems, dealing with emergencies, and so on.
Pricing and costing	How do they price, and where are they in the market? Will they provide information on costs breakdowns?

For even the most basic system to be effective, measurement must be ongoing, not just a snapshot at one time. The aim is to measure real performance over time, and to improve it through dialogue, communication and development.

In addition to these basic areas of performance we may also wish to consider those in table 7.4.

Table 7.4 Supplier performance: advanced measures

Overall ability	This is a holistic view of the supplier's performance as a business. Have they the ability to deliver the required service or product over the period of the working relationship? This may include opportunities to benchmark against other suppliers. (See also study session 13.)
Financial stability	What is the supplier's stability for the period in question, and do they meet the necessary financial tests? (See also study session 12.)
Ability to contribute	Does the supplier see the need for and have the ability to make a positive contribution to our business, perhaps through design or innovation ideas or by contributing to cost reduction programmes?

Because both supplier status and market conditions change, these factors need to be reviewed regularly.

Self-assessment question 7.2

Read the following mini case study, and then rank the factors in what you feel is the appropriate order, giving your reasons for doing so. Put the most important first.

(continued on next page)

7

Self-assessment question 7.2 *(continued)*

ABC Trading plc supplies rear-light clusters to several car and caravan manufacturers. The smallest and cheapest components used are threaded steel bolts, moulded into the assembly and used to lock the unit in place. ABC uses one supplier, but there are many for this item. ABC is running at full capacity and is doing well in sales and profit terms, but is in a JIT delivery environment with most of its customers. What does ABC most need from its bolt supplier, and why?

1 Good prices
2 Good delivery
3 Innovative input
4 Financial strength
5 Good quality

Feedback on page 122

7.3 Performance measurement and 'quality management'

Although all the performance areas in table 7.3 and table 7.4 are significant, quality is becoming increasingly important in supplier performance measurement. This is because the issue of quality has moved on from the basic 'does it work' principle, and now embraces many aspects of a supplier's business performance.

In addition, quality control and management have been 'pushed' up the supply chain as companies, trying to improve their own quality, pass their philosophy to suppliers in their supply chain. Figure 7.1 shows how the view of quality has changed.

Figure 7.1: The changing view of quality

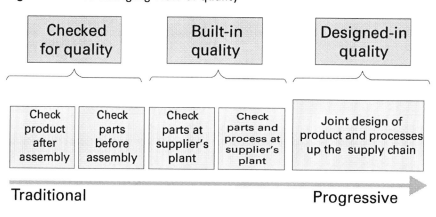

This change has required different and better relationships to be successful, but the intention is that every stage in the business process is inherently high quality, even on products and services that are of quite low value. In addition, a different philosophy now applies: it is less the quality of the product that matters, and more the overall quality of design, and the business process that produces it.

Learning activity 7.3

Consider one of your important suppliers. Give two examples of business activities you would like to measure for this supplier, and give reasons why you feel this is important to your organisation. You may wish to discuss this with your line manager, or quality manager.

Feedback on page 122

7

This change process now requires purchasing to find and hold on to suppliers that are capable of meeting these increasingly challenging requirements. Measurement plays a key part in this process, and purchasing will now consider measuring quality aspects in areas they would not have looked at previously. These might include:

- supplier's testing capability and facilities
- supplier's workforce training and skills
- supplier's equipment and machinery
- supplier's investment in technology
- supplier's production or process management methods
- supplier's organisation and management of quality systems, such as TQM or specialised mechanisms such as 'six sigma'
- supplier's quality certifications, such as ISO 9000
- supplier's general management structures and overall quality 'feel'.

It will be obvious from this that the move away from simple product or service checks has made the process of supplier performance measurement much more difficult, and has set purchasing departments a real challenge.

Self-assessment question 7.3

Answer the following multiple-choice questions.

1 Which of the following is an aspect of a supplier's business you would *not* measure for quality purposes?
   A supplier's workforce training and skills
   B supplier's salesforce training and skills
   C supplier's equipment and machinery
   D supplier's investment in technology.
2 In quality thinking we are now focusing on:
   A checking quality more rigorously
   B assuming quality is right

(continued on next page)

Self-assessment question 7.3 *(continued)*

    C designing in quality
    D building in quality.
3   Quality issues have been pushed up the supply chain because:
    A it is the responsibility of suppliers in the supply chain
    B it is cheaper to let suppliers do the checking at source
    C it is required by modern production processes
    D companies push their quality philosophy up the supply chain.
4   Moving to designed-in quality has created a need for:
    A better training
    B better relationships
    C better facilities
    D better quality checks.

Feedback on page 122

7

7.4 Supplier measurement and the building of relationships

For effective measurement to happen, purchasing must be successfully managing a triangle of complex relationships with both suppliers and internal customers. A large part of the service provision will depend upon the relationships between those involved, and these relationships need to be established early (during the procurement process), and then constantly reviewed and actively managed.

We have seen that the more progressive approach to quality has required relationships that are less adversarial. Relationships can be flexible and open, while maintaining proper businesslike and professional conduct. Good procedures help to establish this balance, and encourage mutual trust and open measurement between the parties.

There are two policies or strategic approaches to developing the necessary relationships: the traditional approach and the partnership approach. The players are the same, but the discussion and communication varies, as we shall see: the intention is to create a more focused approach.

Learning activity 7.4

Consider a major supplier to your organisation. Draw a diagram to illustrate the measurement processes involved in managing this supplier and the three-way relationships that are needed.

Feedback on page 122

In general, adversarial relationships are less likely to be productive, and very often we find that customers and suppliers are working together, while purchasing is under pressure and failing to drive the relationship, as figure 7.3 shows.

Figure 7.3: Traditional sourcing

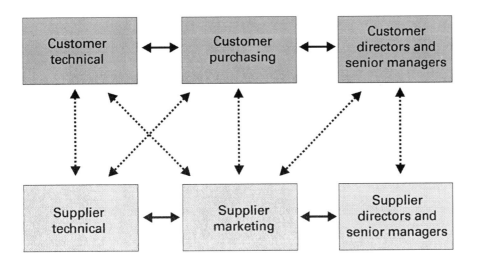

Figure 7.4 shows how the need to develop a more coordinated approach to suppliers has led to a team-based strategy, which aims to deliver much more focus in the developing of relationships. Often this will be led by purchasing, and measurement is a key component in the success of this type of relationship.

Figure 7.4: Partnership sourcing

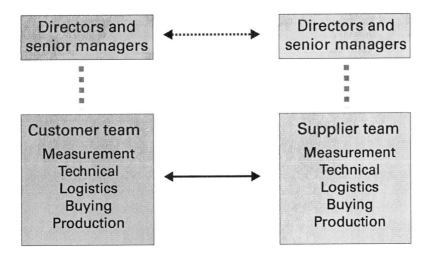

Although true partnerships are still rare, the principles are now well established between buyer and supplier. Partnership sourcing is a commitment by purchasing, customers and suppliers to a long-term relationship based on agreed objectives. Typically there are three key objectives:

* To minimise the total value cost chain, not just unit cost, and improve quality, through **partner development** (working to develop a partnered supplier to jointly improve cost, quality etc) and joint problem-solving.

7

- To ensure continuous improvement, through equal sharing of technical and cost information.
- To ensure information exchange and efficiency through long-term commitment, inter-organisational exchanges and frequent communication.

Such relationships will generally be longer-term, and can sometimes be more difficult to create in the tender-led public service environment. Figure 7.5 shows how these relationships develop and how the management of the relationship becomes increasingly important.

Figure 7.5: Development of the partnership sourcing relationship

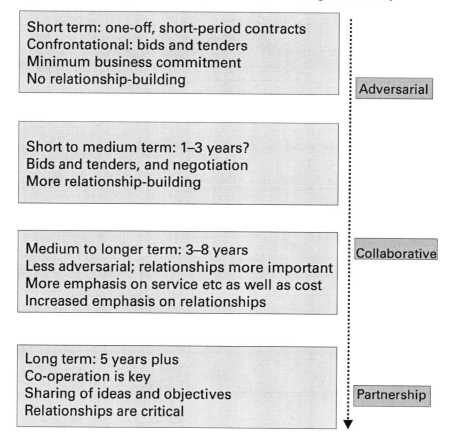

Note also that the use of large numbers of key performance indicators (KPIs) in a relationship can be a sign of insecurity, and it decreases as business strategies are aligned. It is possible that in very long-term partnerships measurement becomes less important, and performance is 'built in' to the relationship.

Self-assessment question 7.4

Complete the following statements:

1 True partnerships between buyers and suppliers are still _____.
2 Supplier and buyer relationships are often considered as a _____ that also includes _____ _____.

(continued on next page)

Self-assessment question 7.4 (continued)

3   Today many organisations are seeking a less _____ style of supplier measurement.
4   Measurement is easier in a partnership style of relationship because there is more _____ between the parties.
5   In long-term partnerships performance may require less measurement and is _____ _____ to the relationship.

Feedback on page 123

7.5 Measurement in supplier selection and supplier evaluation

So far in this session we have considered various issues in regard to *why* we should measure supplier's performance. However, it is equally important to consider *when* we measure performance. In practice, supplier measurement takes place at two points in a typical purchasing process, as shown in figure 7.6. As you can see from the figure, different terms are sometimes used.

Figure 7.6: Stages in the purchasing process

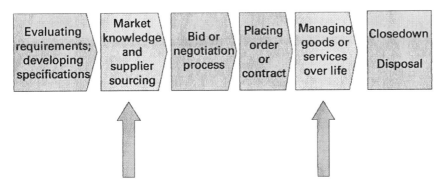

Measuring supplier's potential ability   Measuring supplier's actual performance
(Supplier appraisal)   (Supplier evaluation)
(Supplier assessment)   (Vendor rating)
(Supplier certification)

Learning activity 7.5

Based on your level of study so far write down a definition of each main measurement stage:

1   pre-award
2   post-award.

Which (if any) is the most important, and why? Give examples of each type as used in your organisation.

Feedback on page 123

At the sourcing stage we need to assess or appraise suppliers to see which ones are able to perform to the standards required, and we may also wish to certify or categorise suppliers based on the outcomes of this measurement.

When we have awarded a contract to a supplier (who has already been appraised), we then need to evaluate (measure) their actual performance. This is often called vendor rating, and it requires the cooperation of both the supplier and the internal customer if it is to be done effectively.

7

Self-assessment question 7.5

Write a report on your own experiences of pre- and post-award measurement, bringing out:

- the good and bad points
- any specific difficulties or problems
- how the suppliers and customers contributed.

Aim for around 1 page of A4.

Feedback on page 123

7.6 Performance measurement for mutual advantage

So far in this study session we have seen that it is in the interest of both the organisation and the purchasing and supply function that suppliers perform well. This also has major benefits in terms of improved quality and relationships. However, an important question is whether this feeling is shared by the supplier(s) involved. Is this a mutually beneficial approach?

Learning activity 7.6

Consider one of your major suppliers, and identify three measures that characterise the relationship you have with them. Given these, how would you think that the *supplier* sees the business relationship?

Feedback on page 124

To some extent, whether or not the relationship is mutually beneficial will depend on how the supplier views the buyer's company. Buyers often assume that their order, especially if high value, means the supplier automatically sees them as important.

This is not necessarily so. The four-box matrix in figure 7.7 shows that a supplier may see business relationships in various ways, as explained in table 7.5.

Figure 7.7: Supplier motivation and preferences

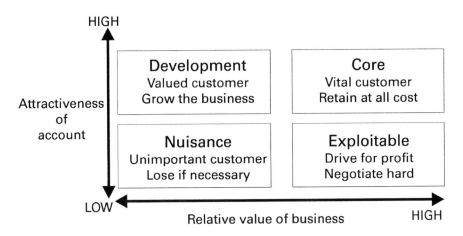

Table 7.5 How a supplier views relationships

Core	I see the buyer as my core business.
	Developing a relationship is highly desirable, and I see development and measurement as essential to the process.
	I may take the lead in proposing this.
Development	I wish to grow the business. The order is valuable, and so is the relationship.
	I am likely to want to work on developing the relationship, and will react well to development and measurement proposals.
Exploitable	I do not see a relationship as other than a way to get business.
	Attempts by the buyer to develop and monitor my performance are likely to be met with resistance or little real effort.
Nuisance	Frankly, the business is not of great interest, and you get transaction service at best.

Buyers who wish to implement performance management with suppliers must try to understand the nature of the relationship, or their effort may be wasted. Also, it is worth noting that this is not a question of the size of the order, but is a complex mix of factors, including:

- the volume of business
- the proportion of the supplier's business the buyer represents
- the supplier's business circumstances at the time, eg full order book, capacity problems etc
- any business history
- the supplier's view of the purchasing organisation
- the supplier's longer-term strategies and tactics.

When the relationship is in the core or development boxes in figure 7.7 the supplier may well be interested in developing the relationship, and be

7

comfortable with enhanced performance measurement. There are several benefits for suppliers that move this to being a mutually advantageous process. These include:

- The opportunity to prove how good their performance is in an 'open' environment.
- The opportunity to discuss problems they are experiencing with the buying organisation.
- The opportunity to submit ideas on design, cost reduction, inventory controls, new technologies and other issues of mutual benefit.
- The creation of an environment in which the concept that the supplier is in business to make a profit can be discussed.

Self-assessment question 7.6

The loner

Mrs Jones is Chair of Goody Foods plc, and has to lead a board-level discussion on developing supplier relationships over the next ten years. She is aware of the trend for a partnership style of relationship with suppliers, but prefers a more aggressive approach, and is a firm believer that quality must be measured on the production line to maintain Goody's product quality. Her purchasing director disagrees, and is proposing that for four of their 20 key suppliers they attempt to enter into longer-term agreements with a different style of relationship. He is a believer in measuring service, but believes that this should be undertaken further up the supply chain, and is less necessary if the relationship is better.

Also, there are major supply market problems that affect products supplied by two of the companies, which he believes this new approach could alleviate.

Provide five comments on this mini case study

Feedback on page 124

Revision question

Now try the revision question for this session on page 335.

Summary

In this session we have tried to see the benefits of measuring performance for the organisation, and look at some of the broad areas that may be measured. We have also considered the major contribution made by measurement in the changing field of quality management and relationship-building, and have understood the difference between pre-award assessment and post-award measurement and vendor rating.

In the next three study sessions we shall consider some of these points in more detail.

Suggested further reading

For study sessions 7 to 14 students will find that chapter 9 of Neely et al (2002) provides a useful view of supplier, alliance and partner relationship measures, though without specific reference to procurement. Students should also look at Lysons and Farrington (2006), chapters 7, 11, and 17 which are also relevant to these eight sessions.

A useful website to support references for this session in particular is that of the official International Standards Organisation (ISO) http://www.iso.org.

Students who wish to read further on the quality management concept 'six sigma' should check Lysons and Farrington (2006), chapter 9, page 288.

Feedback on learning activities and self-assessment questions

Feedback on learning activity 7.1

Your should have a table that shows the success features you have chosen. Your chosen features should have some fit with the five basic rights in the study session, but you must have derived this information through a measurement process.

Feedback on self-assessment question 7.1

1   TRUE. A 'one-off' exercise provides no information on trends or real-time performance.
2   FALSE. Fixing quality problems is usually more expensive than preventing them.
3   TRUE. The focus is no longer just on the primary supplier.
4   TRUE. Quality or delivery failures can have adverse and long-lasting effects on the image of a product.

Feedback on learning activity 7.2

There is no one right answer, but you may have identified some of the following criteria in your list:

- delivery performance
- quality performance
- service performance
- pricing performance
- overall capabilities

- financial performance
- innovation performance.

Feedback on self-assessment question 7.2

There is no absolutely correct answer, but your ranking could look like this:

2 Any delivery problems will put production at risk. Stock can be held, but even on low-priced items this should be avoided.
5 Even on a small component, failure can result in assembly rejection or warranty claims.
1 This is not a high priority, but costs will add up, because large numbers of components are used.
3 There is no real need for innovation in this area.
4 There are plenty of other suppliers if the current one fails.

Feedback on learning activity 7.3

There is no one correct answer, because what should be measured depends on the nature of the businesses involved. The areas you may have considered could include:

- testing capability and facilities
- workforce training and skills
- equipment and machinery
- production or process management
- quality systems such as TQM and 'six sigma'
- quality certifications (eg ISO 9000)
- management structures and overall quality 'feel'.

TQM is total quality management – a philosophy of quality management in which quality is seen as everyone's responsibility, and one that affects all aspects of business.

'Six sigma' is a high-level quality system used in industries where absolute quality is essential; it aims at a failure rate as low as 3–4 parts per million.

Feedback on self-assessment question 7.3

Answers

1 B
2 C
3 D
4 B.

Feedback on learning activity 7.4

There is no one correct answer. Your diagram might look something like figure 7.2 to show the role of the supplier and the customer.

Figure 7.2

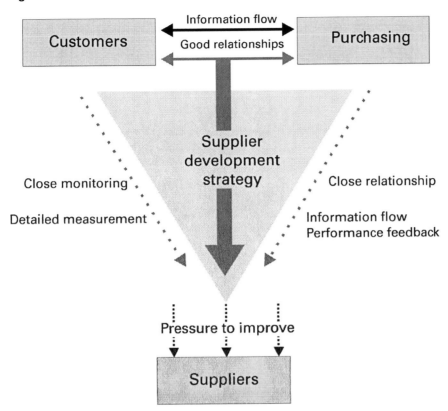

Feedback on self-assessment question 7.4

1 rare
2 triangle – internal customers
3 adversarial
4 trust
5 built in

Feedback on learning activity 7.5

There is no one right answer.

1 Pre-award (supplier assessment) is concerned with the process of choosing the right supplier, and measurements are aimed at ensuring that the supplier can perform well.
2 Post-award (vendor rating) is concerned with making sure the supplier is performing, and with helping to develop that performance.

Both are equally important activities; however, pre-award measurement can help to eliminate many problems, whereas even the best vendor rating system can struggle to improve a bad supplier.

Feedback on self-assessment question 7.5

There is no specific feedback, but your report must cover each of the three points of discussion.

Feedback on learning activity 7.6

There is no specific answer, but you may include such measures as:

- value or volume of business
- relationships
- dependence
- trading history.

Do not forget to see this from the supplier's point of view.

Feedback on self-assessment question 7.6

Your comments could include:

1 Mrs Jones may be right about the benefit of aggressive relationships: theory tends to swing from one to the other. The good buyer sees the relationship style as a tool to be used as appropriate.
2 Mrs Jones is wrong over the best place to measure quality; the current view is to prevent rather than correct.
3 The purchasing director is therefore right over quality: going further up the supply chain is often more cost-effective too!
4 In going for four of 20 suppliers the purchasing director is being sensible, at least in the short term; partnerships take a lot of time and resources to develop.
5 The purchasing director is right: if there are supply market problems, then a partner should give you better service if the relationship is working well.

Steps in the supplier measurement process

Introduction

As with many good management practices, supplier performance works best when it is the outcome of a process that has been well planned and organised, and has been implemented at the appropriate stages in the purchasing process.

Sometimes you can make things up as you go along; try this in performance management and you will not get the results you want.

Session learning objectives

After completing this session you should be able to:

8.1 Define the key stages in the buying process.
8.2 Describe the key steps in a pre-award assessment process.
8.3 Describe the key steps in a pre assessment process – supplier evaluation.
8.4 Analyse the importance of internal and external supplier feedback and corrective action.
8.5 Formulate a process to undertake a continuous review of the supplier measurement process.

Unit content coverage

This study session covers the following topics from the official CIPS unit content document:

Learning outcome

Discuss the benefits of implementing a well structured approach to measuring organisational, functional and individual performance.

Learning objective

2.1 Demonstrate an understanding of the key areas associated with supplier selection and evaluation:
   • The key stages in the buying process
   • The variables considered when making the purchasing decision

Prior knowledge

You should have a general understanding of the concept of the supply chain and the benefit to a business of good key suppliers. You should have read study session 7.

Resources

No specific resources are required, but it will be useful to be or to have been involved in the measurement or monitoring of suppliers. If you have not, you may find it useful to discuss this topic with other students or colleagues, or a manager.

Timing

You should set aside about 5.75 hours to read and complete this session, including learning activities, self-assessment questions, the suggested further reading (if any) and the revision question.

8.1 The key stages in the buying process

As we have seen in study session 7 there is a flow process to much purchasing activity, especially when we move away from basic transactional activity. Figure 8.1 shows this in a more detailed form as it might apply in public sector contracting. A similar process will apply in the private sector, but usually with less emphasis on tendering.

Figure 8.1: The flow of purchasing activity in public sector contracting

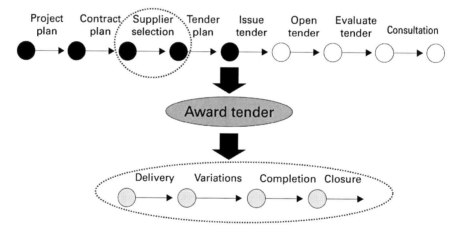

Basically, supplier measurement happens either as part of supplier selection or after a contract has been awarded. This is shown in figure 8.1 by the black circles. Of course, we may measure suppliers at other times if there is a specific requirement. For example, if a public sector organisation is particularly concerned with poor responses to bids or tenders, it may measure the quality of suppliers' responses in this activity.

Learning activity 8.1

Match figure 8.1 to the process typically followed in your organisation, and cross-reference the action points in table 8.1 with comments where appropriate.

(continued on next page)

8

Learning activity 8.1 *(continued)*

Highlight where you find the most supplier performance measurement.

Table 8.1

Stage	Common to my organisation	Comment
Project planning		
Contract planning		
Supplier selection		
Tender planning		
Negotiation planning		
Tender planning		
Negotiation process		
Award		
Delivery		
Variations		
Completion		
Closure		

Feedback on page 138

8

Although we can see two principal stages where performance measurement occurs, we should also recognise that the 'tools' can be applied at different degrees or levels of complexity, depending on what we want to achieve. This is shown in table 8.2.

Table 8.2 Levels of supplier measurement

Level	Purpose
Pre-award measurement	
Basic supplier selection	In order to narrow down a field of prospective suppliers, we undertake a series of limited measurements aimed at ensuring a basic level of supplier acceptability.
	• Applies to lower-value, less complex purchases and one-off arrangements.
	• Likely to require little resource input, and be desk based.
	• Likely to be based on basic quality and delivery functions.
Supplier categorisation	Many organisations have developed the above process and have divided suppliers into various categories. For example:
	Approved supplier: a supplier who has passed certain basic technical and quality requirements.
	Preferred supplier: an approved supplier who offers some additional value or who has some track record of performance.
	• Allows other users to buy from these suppliers without checking.
	• Allows suppliers to see where they stand, and move up the 'list'.
	• Allows for special measurements and process controls to be put in place.
	• Helps to distinguish between suppliers.

(continued on next page)

Table 8.2 *(continued)*

Advanced supplier selection	For key suppliers, or for high-value or high-risk purchases, a more advanced measurement process may be introduced. • Will extend beyond the basic into areas of business competence (see also table 7.3). • Will require sophisticated measurement tools and resources. • Could include third-party involvement. • Could require international accreditation, such as ISO 9000 series.

Post-award measurement

Basic vendor rating	Simple service monitoring to ensure compliance with the five rights. • Mostly reactive. • Some customer inputs. • Little feedback or review. • Only limited information.
Advanced vendor rating	A much more sophisticated approach, planned in advance and with supplier and customer active participation. • Proactive. • Can lead to better relationships. • More information led. • Much more review and feedback.
Supplier development	Can spin out of the above as good suppliers are identified and the buyer wishes to work more closely with the supplier to take the relationships towards the 'partnership' style. • Supplier will have demonstrated acceptance of measurement and have contributed to business improvement. • Measurement is still important. but is moving from basic transactions towards processes, design and management issues.
Partner suppliers	• Suppliers have a different status. • Measurement of performance will continue, but is now less important.

Vendor rating is a systematic process of measuring supplier performance; it applies to suppliers with whom you are doing business. It is a particularly useful technique. It is often employed when dealing with suppliers that exist in a competitive market with many sources of supply. It is perhaps not such a useful tool if the supplier is a monopoly, and may have little interest in improvement. As with all purchasing tools, buyers must ensure they use vendor rating only to the degree necessary to achieve results for their organisation.

Supplier development is the process of identifying and working with a supplier to 'develop' the supplier's performance for the benefit of your organisation.

Self-assessment question 8.1

Give True or False responses to the following statements.

1 Vendor rating is extremely useful, and should be used with all our suppliers. TRUE/FALSE
2 In the private sector there is less emphasis on bids and tenders, so supplier performance measurement is less important. TRUE/FALSE
3 Performance measurement and vendor rating are capable of being introduced with different levels of complexity. TRUE/FALSE
4 Advanced vendor rating techniques can identify potential 'partner' suppliers for our business. TRUE/FALSE
5 Assessing suppliers' potential must be done by in-house staff. TRUE/FALSE

Feedback on page 138

8

8.2 Steps in a pre-award assessment

The requirement to select suppliers is a key function of purchasing. Sometimes the selection of suppliers is guided by an organisation's financial or procurement policies, and also to some extent by location and market conditions. The policy may be in the organisation's strategic documentation, and will then be governed by many factors, including legislation, business practice in a country or region, the management board, financial accountability and audit, best practice and organisational culture.

In some cases buyers and contract managers have limited choice as to supplier selection – for example on spares from an original equipment manufacturer (OEM). In many other cases the buyer, usually in cooperation with the customer, can influence supplier selection to good effect. In the public sector, tendering requirements and EU legislation are designed to encourage suppliers to bid for business; measurement of supplier ability is still very important.

Learning activity 8.2

You are the buyer for an engineering manufacturer. You have been asked to develop a new supplier assessment process, and have to prepare a checklist of the steps needed to undertake such work. Provide this checklist.

Feedback on page 139

In most cases, purchasing managers will need to establish a process for assessing new suppliers. Figure 8.2 shows some key steps to be followed, and these are described in more detail below.

Figure 8.2: Steps in a pre-award assessment

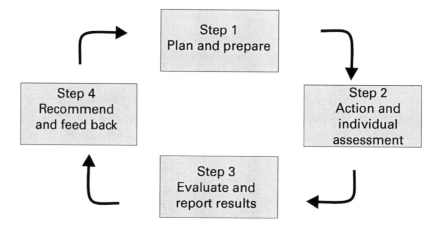

Step 1: Plan and prepare

As in most aspects of business, good planning will help to achieve good results, and adequate time should be allowed in the procurement process for the necessary measurement activity. Planning can include:

- checking rules and policies
- checking feedback from existing vendor-rating schemes
- choosing a field- or desk-based approach
- certified or informal requirement
- the degree and coverage of the assessments
- communications strategy
- briefing and administration.

Step 2: Action and individual assessment

It is important that the assessments are carried out efficiently and effectively. Remember that at this stage the supplier is cooperating in the hope of gaining business; do not forget this process is also costing the supplier time and money.

- Undertake the assessments (see also study session 7).

Step 3: Evaluate and report results

After the assessments are completed, it is important that time is made available to study the results, undertake calculations, and analyse all collected data.

- Arrange review meetings if required.
- Appoint a 'secretary' to record details.
- Match assessments with other data, such as existing performance information or market research.
- Prepare a report if required and recommendations on supplier's status and areas of concern.

Step 4: Recommend and feed back

It is important that clear recommendations are produced from what will have been a complex process. In addition, the supplier should be properly debriefed on both their strengths and weaknesses. This is especially important if the supplier's performance is not acceptable, because:

- It is good practice.
- The supplier should be allowed to respond.
- The supplier may be able to correct faults, and can be reviewed again in future.

Self-assessment question 8.2

This self-assessment question has been combined with self-assessment question 8.3 below, and you should complete it when you have read learning section 8.3 below.

Feedback on page 139

8.3 Steps in a post-award evaluation

Post-award supplier performance measurement is commonly known as vendor rating. It is intended to be a positive process that:

- Evaluates the supplier's performance against set performance criteria (sometimes known as key performance indicators or KPIs) that are built into the agreement between the parties.
- Collects performance data from reports and/or IT systems for use by the organisation in the future.
- Uses the information in positive discussion with the supplier to assist in improving performance.
- Allows the buyer to determine whether to develop the relationship or abandon it completely.

As we shall see in later study sessions, vendor rating can be a very complex and sophisticated tool. It has several special characteristics:

- the need to blend **quantitative** data (based more on measurements and figures) and **qualitative** data (based more on perception and opinion)
- the need for good data collection systems
- the need for good internal and external relationships
- the need to understand statistical tools.

Also, it may take place off the buyer's site.

Learning activity 8.3

You are the buyer for a public service organisation. You have been asked to develop a new supplier vendor rating process, and have to prepare a checklist of the steps needed to undertake such work. Provide this checklist.

Feedback on page 139

The nature of vendor rating will vary from supplier to supplier, depending on the value of the purchase and the degree of purchasing risk involved. Generally, however, the planning stages are similar to those for pre-award assessment.

Step 1: Planning

- Needs to be early in the development of the deal, and planned into the process, so that all parties are aware of the system and their own input.
- What style of vendor rating is to be used, and which vendor rating 'tools' will be applied?
- Who will be involved, and what is the definition of their role? This may need internal consultation and negotiation to resolve, as it may require the commitment of resources.
- What will be the required information flows, and do the systems (IT and manual) exist to collect and process the data?
- How will feedback and development take place?

Step 2: Introduction

- There may be a need to formally launch the proposed system.
- Introduce on a pilot basis if required.
- Implement the full system (amended as a result of the introduction and pilot if required).

Step 3: Action, monitoring and feedback

This is the working stage, and may last for a long period.

- Monitor information supplied by the system.
- Feedback to suppliers and users on a regular basis, with review meetings as required.
- Make minor changes and improvements to reflect information received.
- Identify scope for major changes and developments.

Step 4: Re-engineering

- Use output from step 3 to propose major changes (re-engineering) to the system.
- Review and agree these changes with the parties.
- Introduce amended system.

(The term **re-engineering** is management-speak for the act of looking at a business system or process and making changes and improvements to it.)

Step 5: Action, monitoring and feedback

This repeats step 3 using the re-engineered process and performance requirement. This cycle of review and improvement can continue, and may run several times.

Step 6: Closedown

At the end of the relationship the system is closed down. In a positive relationship both parties will wish to review what has been achieved, and for the buyer it is important that feedback goes as an input into the creation of new schemes. In this way the process constantly improves. Figure 8.3 shows this in diagram form.

Figure 8.3: Closedown

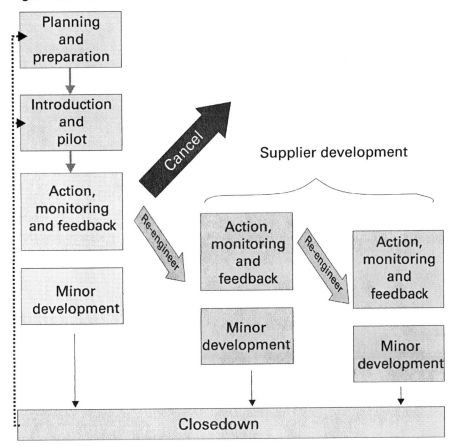

Self-assessment question 8.3

Complete the missing words in the following paragraphs relating to sections 8.2 and 8.3 above.

Miss M is senior buyer for Toytown plc, a major toy company. She has been asked to implement a supplier _____ programme as her company is about to begin _____ product from Thailand and China. Miss M is not constrained by her company's financial or procurement _____, but has never done this before. She understands how this differs from the _____ _____ used to measure the existing supplier base, and wonders whether the process steps are similar. Given her inexperience she feels a _____ approach might be useful, and has wondered whether there is scope for _____ _____ to be involved.

So far she can see four possible stages: planning, action, _____ and _____.

Toytown's current suppliers are subject to rigorous _____ measurement using a range of _____, and the process has been _____ several times as part of the company's attempts practice continuous _____. The company also places great emphasis on good _____ to suppliers. As a result, several

(continued on next page)

8

Self-assessment question 8.3 *(continued)*

suppliers now work in close _____, although one supplier failed to improve, and the contract was _____.

Feedback on page 139

8.4 Internal and external supplier feedback and corrective action

We have already seen that, as part of both pre-award assessment and post-award vendor rating, we need to build in feedback and corrective action. But what do we really mean by these terms?

What is feedback?

In an acoustic sense feedback occurs when a sound passes through a microphone, is amplified through a loudspeaker system and is picked up again by the microphone. This creates a howl or whistle that you may have heard at concerts. Feedback in a management process of this type occurs when information is fed into the process, (in this case supplier measurement) and the outputs are analysed by the responsible manager and passed back to the originator.

Learning activity 8.4

Consider a contract or purchase in which you have participated. Try to draw a cycle/flow diagram illustrating the process used to provide feedback, and comment on how well you feel it worked. Try to identify the main flows, rather than every possible piece of feedback. You may wish to discuss this with your line manager if you have only limited experience in this area.

Feedback on page 139

Figure 8.4 shows a typical feedback arrangement.

Figure 8.4: A typical feedback arrangement

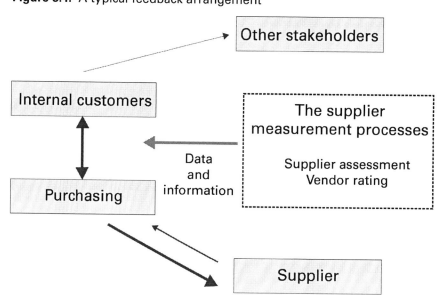

The principle of feedback is as follows:

1 Data flows out from the process to the performance measurement manager (often purchasing).
2 Processed data, conclusions and recommendations flow between purchasing and their internal customers.
3 Data, recommendations and suggestions are fed back to the supplier to allow for change and improvement.

There will also be some minor feedback, as internal customers (and purchasing) may share information and opinions with other stakeholders (including senior management) on the effectiveness of the process. Also, suppliers develop perceptions as to how the process is working, which they feed back to the relevant manager.

But why is this process really necessary? Unlike acoustic feedback this type of management feedback is desirable because:

The supplier needs to know what the problems are if he is to correct them. This may sound obvious, but not all companies do in fact do this. (Lysons and Farrington (2006) refer to surprise by Jaguar suppliers when this was introduced in the 1980s.)

A more formal process involves people in the supplier's organisation who may be more concerned with problem-solving than the sales and customer services staff who are the usual point of contact.

The intention of performance measurement is usually to jointly improve, *not* to penalise and complain. This is hard to do without good feedback. Corrective action is easier with accurate feedback and good data.

The feedback process helps to build team and personal relationships.

Internal feedback helps to show the purchasing function as proactive in performance improvement.

The feedback and corrective action process is likely to involve most of the departments involved in the measurement process itself, because the two elements are interconnected. It is essential at the planning stage to ensure that provision is made for such feedback to take place, and that systems exist for handling the data.

However, in terms of the actual communication of feedback it will often be found best to establish more formal channels, and this is discussed in section 8.5 below.

Self-assessment question 8.4

You have been asked to draft a new page for the purchasing procedures manual, providing advice on performance measurement feedback. Produce the first draft of this document, using the ideas in this section plus thoughts of your own. Write no more than one page of A4.

Feedback on page 139

8.5 Continuous review and the supplier measurement process

Given the emphasis placed on the importance of feedback, it is also important to note that neither vendor rating nor the feedback process can normally be a one-off exercise. Supplier measurement can be really effective only if the initiative is sustained, and in this section we shall consider some of the issues around a regular review process.

A review may take place in various ways, which can be adapted to the particular circumstances of the deal. Some of these different ways may also form steps in an escalating process on long-term contracts. This could be as shown in table 8.3, although few organisations will use every stage. The timescales are only examples, and in practice will be designed to suit the particular business environment.

Table 8.3 Schedule for performance review

Level 1 (say daily or weekly)	• Low-level contact and routine comment • Regular data exchange • Electronic or paper-based, with telephone or email support • Exceptions noted and flagged to next level with comment • Could be a short, low-level meeting, especially if suppliers have an on-site representative
Level 2 (say monthly)	• Summary data from Level 1 • Exceptions are reviewed to look for patterns • Recommendations for change/improvement (and termination of bad suppliers) are passed forward • Previous changes are reviewed • Meetings with key managers and staff • Notes are kept
Level 4 (say quarterly)	• Recommendations for change are made • Previous changes are reviewed and accepted/rejected • Key decisions on supplier terminations are made • Meetings with key managers and staff • Notes and minutes are kept
Level 5 (say yearly)	• High-level review • Key managers plus senior management • Formal meeting • Conformation of business position and future relationships
Special issues/emergencies	• An ad hoc session will be held if necessary • Attendees as required

Learning activity 8.5

Develop a second page for the procedural manual you wrote in self-assessment question 8.4 above. This time add a section that recommends how to ensure that there is a proper review mechanism in place for all performance measurement arrangements.

Feedback on page 140

Attendance at review meetings will vary, and it will be useful to plan this in at the beginning, because the time commitment can be significant – especially if there are several suppliers being measured. There is no set list of who should be involved, but it is likely that the following departments will be asked for an input:

- Purchasing – who may well be leading the initiative.
- The internal customer(s) – note that when the supplier services many internal customers it may not be practical to involve them all!
- IT or data support – to provide and interpret information.
- Finance – a management accountant can often provide useful support.
- Specialist support – as required.
- The supplier's staff.

This process is intended to be constructive, and most meetings should be informal and positive. An aggressive approach is inappropriate, especially if the supplier is in a minority. The optimum location of meetings will depend on the nature of the contract, but buyers should be aware that there are benefits from visiting suppliers' premises from time to time; they should not assume all meetings are on their own premises.

This type of review process can be aided on large contracts by one of the parties placing a representative on the other party's site. This is common in the car industry on JIT contracts, and can help to share responsibility and improve communication and relationships.

8

Self-assessment question 8.5

Answer the following multiple-choice questions.

1   Review in post-award supplier performance management is never:
A quarterly
B yearly
C infrequent
D one-off.

2   Because all purchases and organisations are different, the review process tends to:
A escalate
B be the same
C be adaptable to circumstances
D be different every time.

3   On large or complex contracts what type of review process may be used?
A escalating
B manual
C IT-based
D third party.

4   Senior management is likely to attend:
A every meeting
B occasional meetings
C high-level reviews
D never on performance management.

(continued on next page)

Revision question

Now try the revision question for this session on page 335.

Summary

Supplier performance measurement can be a complex process, which needs to be fitted into the right place in the procurement process. For best results it is essential that it is implemented well and that good feedback and review processes are in place, creating an environment in which results become the main objective.

We shall now move on to consider in more detail some of the tools that may be used.

Suggested further reading

Students will find the reference to the surprise of the Jaguar workers in Lysons and Farrington (2005).

Feedback on learning activities and self-assessment questions

Feedback on learning activity 8.1

There is no specific feedback for this activity, but your response should show where your organisation differs from this model, and where most supplier measurement takes place.

Typically, most supplier measurement will occur either as part of supplier selection or after the award stage.

Feedback on self-assessment question 8.1

1   FALSE. Buyers must ensure they only use it to the degree necessary to achieve results for their organisation.
2   FALSE. Supplier performance measurement is equally important in the public and private sectors.
3   TRUE. The complexity can be tailored to the purchase and to the available organisational resources.
4   TRUE. This can spin out of the above as good suppliers are identified and the buyer wishes to work more closely with the supplier.

5   FALSE. Although this is often true, third-party consultants may make a contribution if in-house skills or resources are not available.

Feedback on learning activity 8.2

There is no one correct definition, but your checklist is likely to pick up on at least four main steps:

1   preparation
2   action and assessment
3   evaluation
4   recommendation and feedback.

Feedback on self-assessment question 8.2

See self-assessment question 8.3

Feedback on learning activity 8.3

There is no one correct definition, but your checklist is likely to pick up on some of the following steps:

1   planning
2   introduction or pilot
3   action, monitoring and feedback
4   alteration or re-engineering
5   closedown.

You should also pick up on the fact that steps 3 and 4 tend to cycle as improvements are required: this may happen several times over the life of the process.

Feedback on self-assessment question 8.3

You should have words similar to:

assessment – sourcing – policies – vendor rating – team – third parties – evaluation – recommendation – performance – tools – re-engineered – improvement – feedback – partnership – cancelled.

Feedback on learning activity 8.4

There is no right answer or diagram here. Your model may look similar to that in figure 8.4, or it may be much more complicated.

Feedback on self-assessment question 8.4

There is no one correct answer. As with all tasks of this type you may find it useful to consider the five Ws: Who, What, When, Where, Why (and How!).

8

A good order might be:

1   What is feedback?
2   Why is feedback necessary?
3   How do we feed back?
4   Who does the feedback?
5   When and where do we feed back?

Feedback on learning activity 8.5

There is no one correct answer.

You may wish to use the same methodology as in self-assessment question 8.4, but don't forget to add your own views based on your experience.

You should now have a two-page policy draft on the feedback and review process.

Feedback on self-assessment question 8.5

1   D
2   C
3   A
4   C
5   D

Study session 9
About measurement tools

'A bad workman blames his tools.'

Proverb. If your supplier performance measurement system isn't working, you may have chosen the wrong tools for the job!

Introduction

So far we have discussed some issues surrounding the concept of supplier performance measurement, both pre- and post-award of business. However, in reality, performance measurement is more a series of 'tools' that can be used in different ways, and in this study session we shall look in more detail at the concept of the 'performance measurement toolbox'. In study session 10 we shall then examine some of these tools in more detail.

Session learning objectives

After completing this session you should be able to:

9.1 Demonstrate the different performance measurement 'tools' for various categories of supplier and activity.
9.2 Distinguish between qualitative and quantitative measurements.
9.3 Appraise the issues involved in designing measurement systems and ensuring data availability.
9.4 Propose the involvement of other stakeholders in the measurement process.
9.5 Compare the benefits of a desk-based and a visit-based approach.

9

Unit content coverage

This study session covers the following topics from the official CIPS unit content document:

Learning outcomes

- Appraise measures that can be used to improve supplier performance.
- Use a range of accounting techniques to measure organisational efficiency.

Learning objective

2.4 Apply and evaluate appropriate measures to develop sustained improvement of supplier performance.

Prior knowledge

You should have a general understanding of the concept of management tools, the way in which they can be used, and some of the factors in their design.

You should have read study sessions 7 and 8.

Resources

No specific resources are required, but it will be useful to be, or to have been involved in, the design of a supplier measurement system. If you have not, you may find it useful to discuss this topic with other students or colleagues, or a manager.

Timing

You should set aside about 4.5 hours to read and complete this session, including learning activities, self-assessment questions, the suggested further reading (if any) and the revision question.

9.1 Using the right performance measurement 'tools'

In purchasing we can liken the various techniques we have available to the toolbox a mechanic may use to fix your car. Sometimes there is just one tool for the job (say an oil filter remover); sometimes there are several tools that could do the job (spanners, sockets etc), and the mechanic uses the one that seems most appropriate to the job in question. Sometimes the tools relate only to servicing a car, and sometimes they are common tools that can be used in many different applications.

The same principle applies in performance management. There are some dedicated tools for vendor rating, or for financial appraisal, and we have to decide how best to apply these. Equally, there are other more general management tools that can help us as well. This section does not provide detailed explanations of each tool or technique, but shows only how it might be useful in performance management.

Learning activity 9.1

Consider a supplier whose performance you are currently measuring or are about to measure. List the tools and techniques that you are using, or will use, and indicate some of the reasons why you have chosen them.

Feedback on page 154

Figure 9.1 shows our toolbox in graphic form.

Figure 9.1: Performance measurement toolbox

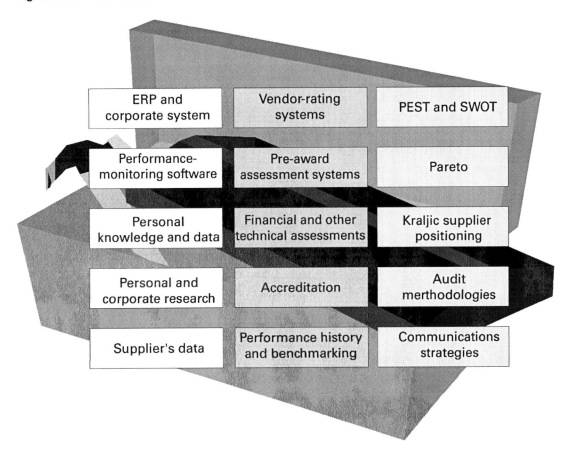

We can identify three main categories of tool (in this context tools may also be information and research):

- systems and information tools
- performance measurement and accreditation tools
- management, theoretical and support tools.

Systems and information tools

This includes a wide range of data and information tools that may be available to support performance measurement, and which may be particularly useful at the pre-award assessment stage. They may include:

- ERP, DRP and MRP systems and other corporate software tools. These can provide data to support performance management, and sometimes include a performance measurement software module.
- A dedicated supplier performance measurement software tool.
- Data from suppliers, either as part of a performance management agreement or from straightforward information-gathering. This may include financial, sales, general management and company information.
- Personal knowledge and data that you have acquired in your job.
- Personal or corporate research undertaken to assist supplier performance measurement projects.

Performance measurement and accreditation tools

These are specific tools and techniques designed to measure a supplier's performance, and the buyer needs to understand them well enough to decide which one is appropriate, and to what degree it should be applied.

- Supplier assessment tools. These are specifically designed to assess suppliers before business is awarded, and we have already discussed them in some detail. They may be internally designed, or based on established models.
- Vendor rating tools. There are many different models, and we shall discuss these in more detail in study session 10.
- Self-assessment tools, in which the suppliers check their own performance. The buyer may accept the supplier's measurements, or jointly devise the tools with the supplier.
- Technical assessments, which may take place particularly at the pre-award stage. This could include financial, personnel, plant, quality systems, customer service arrangements, general management and any other aspect of the supplier's business considered important.
- Quality or performance accreditation tools such as ISO 9000 (business process) or ISO 14000 (environment).
- Performance history. This may be a particularly useful benchmarking tool if the supplier has been used before.

Management, theoretical and support tools

These tools are not specific to performance management, but can be particularly helpful to buyers in helping to decide which suppliers to assess and how to manage data.

- There are a couple of 'quick' analytical tools that can help decision making and understanding. They are referred to by their acronyms, and you will probably have heard of SWOT (Strengths, Weaknesses, Opportunities and Threats) which is very useful in analysing relationships. PESTLE is a tool for analysing risk and relationships, and stands for Political, Economic, Social, Technological, Legal and Environmental. Lysons and Farrington (2006) give more details on these tools.
- Pareto analysis (also known as ABC analysis or the 80:20 rule) is a logistics technique often used in stock control, in which it is usually found that 80% of the value of stock is in 20% of the lines. It can equally be applied to the selection of suppliers, or to data supplied from performance management systems. Its main function is to help you concentrate on the important areas.
- Kraljic's 'four box' matrix is helpful in the classification of suppliers, and suggests that suppliers fall into four categories. (Lysons gives more details on this tool.)
  - Strategic items: high profit impact and supply risk to us. Performance measurement would be important in pointing to possible partner organisations.
  - Bottleneck items: little profit impact, but failure could be disruptive. Performance measurement would be important.

- • Leverage items: high profit impact but little supply risk. The buyer has the upper hand here. Performance data is less important as supplier substitution is easier.
    - • Non-critical: less need for performance measurement.
- • Audit methodologies will help to ensure that performance measurement stays on track, and that there is no scope for fraud (see study session 10).
- • **Communications strategies** will help to ensure smooth operations and effective problem-solving. (There are many types of communication, but the process works best when a plan or 'strategy' is developed.)

Self-assessment question 9.1

Read this mini case study and then provide answers, with comments, to the questions below.

Jacob's ladders

Jacob is the buyer responsible for a range of aluminium ladders produced by his company, Easy Ladders plc. There are shortages and supply difficulties in the world aluminium market, and Jacob has decided to introduce vendor rating on his two key suppliers of castings. Easy Ladders has an ERP system in place with an (unused) supplier performance measurement module, but there are extensive archived performance records sheets on quality and delivery.

Easy Ladders is a small company, with a tight management structure and budget. Historically, relationships with the two suppliers have been poor, and each party has repeatedly blamed the other for problems. Jacob believes he has improved this recently.

1 Is Jacob right to introduce vendor rating to deal with the shortage and supply difficulties?
2 Would there be any reason to involve external support in developing the scheme?
3 Should Jacob rely on the currently unused module in the ERP system?
4 Would the historical archive be a useful tool for Jacob?

Feedback on page 154

9.2 Qualitative and quantitative measures of performance

The criteria and factors listed above are capable of being measured either subjectively or objectively, and this difference will be a recurring theme in all aspects of performance management and measurement.

Table 9.1 shows some of the key characteristics of both types of measure.

Table 9.1 Quantitative and qualitative measures

Quantitative (objective) measures	Qualitative (subjective) measures
Based more around numbers and values	Based more around quality or service issues
More measurable and comparable over time	Less easy to measure
More easily turned into targets	More complex to turn into targets
Often more task-oriented	Designed more to measure processes and service than efficiency at tasks
Focus on efficiency and improvement (in the numbers) over time	Focus on improved perception, effectiveness and contribution over time
Particularly suitable for: • leverage and non-critical items • transactional arrangements • post-award vendor rating systems • product-based purchasing	Particularly suitable for: • pre-award assessment • where purchasing is seen as a key or strategic contributor • service contracts and purchases • gaining a 'feel' for a supplier • perception issues such as attitude, contribution
Examples • Component quality • Delivery performance • Prices • Response times to call-outs • Financial performance • Equipment used	**Examples** • Business contribution • Attitude to technology • Management strengths • Staffing issues • Market conditions • Overall financial strength

Learning activity 9.2

Draw up a table similar to table 9.2.

Table 9.2

Quantitative	Qualitative

From your experience and knowledge to date, set down some advantages and disadvantages of each type of measurement.

Feedback on page 154

Quantitative measures tend to be easier to define and to track, because they relate to actual performance, and 'real' data will exist. They also help to eliminate any bias in the reporting. Disadvantages can include:

- the cost of setting up recording systems and actually analysing all the data
- difficulty in interpreting the data
- ensuring all participants are working to the same guidelines.

Qualitative measures are more difficult, because they rely on the expertise of the individual(s) making value judgements on the supplier's performance. Care should be taken to ensure that bias is not allowed to enter the decision-making process when using qualitative measures. Often qualitative measures are turned into a 'numbers approach', as we shall see in study session 10. Disadvantages can include:

- ensuring a common basis for judgements
- holding too much data in the heads of individuals (who may then leave)
- too much emphasis on one success or failure (no matter how problematic).

In practice, many buyers will try to ensure that, when serious performance measurement is being introduced, a mix of different measures is used. Care should also be taken to ensure that issues are within the scope of the supplier to resolve.

9

Self-assessment question 9.2

Answer these multiple-choice questions.

1   Biased opinion can be a problem when dealing with:
    A qualitative measurements
    B vendor rating
    C quantitative measurements
    D customer service performance.
2   Which of the following would be best suited to qualitative measurement?
    A leverage and non-critical items
    B perception issues
    C transactional arrangements
    D post-award vendor rating systems.
3   Quantitative measurements rely on:
    A the buyer's systems
    B actual performance and 'real' data
    C the supplier's systems
    D ERP systems.
4   Which of the following is *least* likely to be a quantitative measurement?
    A component quality
    B delivery performance
    C prices
    D management strengths.

Feedback on page 155

9.3 Planning measurement systems and ensuring data availability

We have seen that there is a range of tools and techniques that we may wish to use to measure a supplier. We may be able to tap straight into an existing system or methodology, but often this is not the case, and the buyer will need to consider shaping a 'new' approach. In this section we shall look at some of the issues to be considered when choosing which tools to use.

Learning activity 9.3

Choose a supplier whose performance you would like to measure, and prepare a list of key issues you need to consider in planning the measurement system to be used. Why are these particularly important for you?

You may wish to discuss this with your line manager.

Feedback on page 155

We have already discussed the importance of planning when developing performance measurement, and table 9.4 provides a basic checklist of points to consider when undertaking this planning. (In this table, the term **IT capability** is usually applied to a group or organisation: it encompasses an audit of all aspects of IT, including hardware, software and user skills.)

Table 9.4 Performance measurement planning checklist

Key issue	Questions
What do we have already?	• Is there a system in existence? • What history and data do we have? • Do we have expertise in the organisation?
Who will be using the tools?	• Have they done this before? • Do they have the necessary skills? • Will they need training? • What are our relationships like at present? • Can the system be automatic?
What is the nature of the application?	• What is the detail of the job in question? • Do we know the key areas we need to measure? • Do we know the measurements we need in these areas? • Are we sure having these measurements will be helpful?
What is the optimum amount of data needed?	• We should measure only what is really necessary to obtain a result – but what is this optimum?
What are our available resources?	• Can we do this in-house? • Have we the overall skills and data-handling capability? • Do we need external guidance? • Do we need a third party to undertake the work? • Do we have a budget constraint? • What are the supplier's resources?

(continued on next page)

Table 9.4 *(continued)*

Key issue	Questions
Do we have to follow procedures or organisational policies?	• What are they? • Do they help or hinder the process?
What is our IT capability?	• Does the plan envisage a large IT requirement? • Do we have the IT capability? • Do existing systems have performance measurement modules or tools that could help? • Do we have the IT staff resource? • Do our people need training or re-skilling in this area?
How long will the process run for?	If short-term, is it really necessary, or can it be kept simple? If long-term, is it worth a real resource investment to get right? Do we need to develop a project plan or management proposal?
What is the audit, review and feedback required?	• How will we check that it is operating effectively? • What will the meeting time commitment be? • What degree of administration will be needed? • Who will be involved?

9

Self-assessment question 9.3

Fill in the gaps in this paragraph of text:

Brian is planning a vendor rating system for a supplier. He is concerned over the size of the project, and realises the need to obtain the _____ amount of data, thus putting the least strain on _____ _____. He also feels that some staff lack the necessary _____, and that some _____ input might be beneficial.

This is the first time the company has done this, and there is no _____ information available as a starting point. However, the deal runs for 5 years, so some _____ of time and resources can be justified. However, if this happens it will be necessary to have proper _____ and _____ mechanisms built into the system to monitor results.

Feedback on page 155

9.4   Involving others in the measurement process

Sometimes performance measurement will be led by, and carried out by, the purchasing and supply function alone. This is not a problem, but there are stakeholders and others who may be able to make a contribution to the measurement process once they are involved. (**Stakeholders** are those people or bodies with an interest or 'stake' in the issue of buyer or supplier performance.)

Why involve others?

• To share responsibility on major projects.
• To widen the range of skills available, particularly in pre-award assessments.

- To spread the burden of providing time and/or financial resources across the organisation.
- To provide access to skills or resources that the buyer's organisation does not possess.
- To help build a team and break down communication barriers.
- To allow faster assessment or vendor rating implementation.
- There is an organisational requirement to do so.

Learning activity 9.4

Draw a diagram with purchasing at the centre, and name the main links to others who could be involved in the performance measurement process (see figure 9.2). Do not just think of internal departments.

Figure 9.2

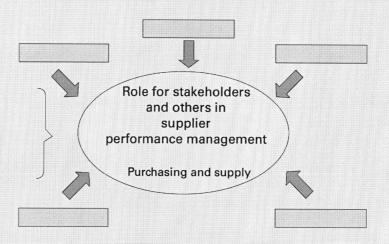

Feedback on page 155

Given that there are almost always some benefits from involving others in the process, figure 9. shows some of those most commonly involved, and table 9.3 provides more detail.

Figure 9.3: Involving others in the measurement process

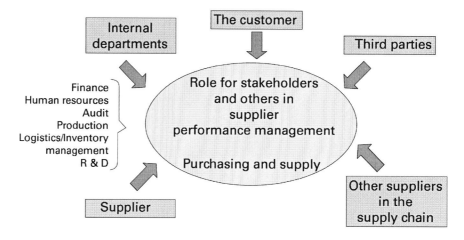

Table 9.5 Role for stakeholders and others in supplier performance management

Department or function	Role
Purchasing and supply	• Leadership and management • Coordination and implementation • Review and feedback • Overall responsibility
The internal customer	• Supplier monitoring • Determining quality and service requirements • Technical input
Other organisational functions	• Finance – assist in financial appraisal and budget issues • Human resources – assist with people and structural issues • Quality management – assist with quality issues • Audit – help devise review processes • Production – help assess supplier's capability to perform • Logistics/inventory management – assist with delivery and service capability • Research and development – advise on supplier's innovative abilities
The supplier	• Provides data and access • May undertake self-assessment or have existing internal measurements that can be utilised • Provides ideas for improvement • Provides feedback on the performance of the buyer's organisation • Provides data on other suppliers
Other suppliers in the supply chain	• There may be occasional benefits from involving others in the supply chain if there are areas of common interest or concern, eg rising oil prices, or shortage of steel
Third parties	• External consultants can provide advice and guidance, and draw up schemes if required • External testing houses can act for the buyer's organisation
	(See also study session 10)

9

Self-assessment question 9.4

Draft a short management report commenting on the possible benefits to your organisation of involving some other stakeholders in supplier measurement.

Feedback on page 155

9.5 A desk-based or visit-based approach?

It will be clear from all of the above that effective performance measurement requires a significant amount of work. Some of this work can be undertaken from the buyer's desk, some of it will require meetings, discussion and consultation, and some may require visits to suppliers' premises.

Learning activity 9.5

Draft out three checklists showing some key benefits of

- desk-based activity
- meetings, discussions and consultations
- supplier visits.

Feedback on page 156

Let us look at these in more detail.

At the desk

Desk-based work has several benefits for the buyer, not the least of which is that it is cheaper and maximises the use of time, which is not wasted in travel. Desk-based activity underpins the whole process, and should include:

- the detailed planning and administration
- reading or internet-based research (company information, annual reports etc)
- using internal data such as performance history
- studying and analysing data collected once a performance measurement scheme is operational
- recommendations and report writing.

Meetings, discussion and consultation

Inevitably there will be a need for consultation and meetings, often on a regular basis. Much of this may be internal, but there is a cost and time factor attached, as well as the usual diary-scheduling difficulties. Meetings and consultations do help to build up the team, and are a good communications opportunity. They may include:

- initial planning meetings
- implementation or project team meetings
- one-to-one sessions with key or difficult players
- regular review and feedback meetings
- pre-visit planning meetings.

Visits

Visits can be complex and hard to arrange, especially with overseas suppliers, but are essential for developing more qualitative measures about a supplier and the way the supplier operates. Of course the supplier will normally

9

make a special effort during these visits – what you see may not be actual practice all of the time!

- Although supplier visits incur expenditure they are well worth doing because they help build knowledge and develop relationships.
- Visits by individuals are generally far less useful than those by a team from different functions: however those taking part must have a useful role to play and not be on a 'day out'.
- Visits should only take place when something useful can be gained. Visiting to an agreed programme can be less effective as it allows for preparation by the supplier. Remember that the timing of your visit is especially important if the supplier has any kind of cyclical aspect to their business.
- Visits should not just be to see the 'sales team' but should look at all aspects of the supplier's business. Remember to try and look at less obvious issues such as management capability, employee relationships and so on, and consider the general feel and appearance as well (often known as the 'housekeeping').
- A standard approach is alright as a starting point but suppliers should be visited as individual companies, and untried suppliers will need a different approach to existing suppliers.

9

Self-assessment question 9.5

Give True or False responses to the following statements.

1   Supplier visits can be expensive, but are essential for developing more qualitative measures. TRUE/FALSE
2   Regular review and feedback meetings help build a 'team'. TRUE/FALSE
3   It is best for the buyer to visit a supplier on his/her own to ensure that all aspects are covered. TRUE/FALSE
4   Desk-based work is little use once a system begins to operate. TRUE/FALSE
5   It is important to visit suppliers at regular intervals. TRUE/FALSE

Feedback on page 156

Revision question

Now try the revision question for this session on page 336.

Summary

In this study session we have looked various aspects of supplier measurement tools:

- using the right tools
- quantitative and qualitative measures
- planning the use of measurement tools

- involving other stakeholders
- desk-based and visit-based activity.

In study session 10 we shall examine some specific tools in detail.

Suggested further reading

More details of SWOT analysis, PESTLE analysis and Kraljic's 'four box' matrix can be found in Lysons and Farrington (2006), chapter 2, pages 49–64. Pareto analysis (also know as ABC analysis or the 80:20 rule) is also used extensively in inventory management and details can be found in Lysons and Farrington (2006), chapter 10, page 319.

Students will find Neely et al (2002) especially relevant for this session as it particularly emphasises the role and input which stakeholders can make.

Feedback on learning activities and self-assessment questions

Feedback on learning activity 9.1

There is no one correct answer. You should have identified a list of tools and techniques, and should be able to match them to some of those identified in this section. At the least you should have identified:

- systems and information tools
- performance measurement and accreditation tools
- management, theoretical and support tools.

Feedback on self-assessment question 9.1

Your answer could read like this:

1   Jacob is right to introduce a rating system on these two suppliers, because they are key to business success. However, rating the suppliers will not in itself cure problems in the world market, although it may help develop partnership relationships, which should help him achieve better service.
2   External consultants might provide Easy Ladders with some good ideas on how to take the concept forward. They might also provide manpower resources that Easy cannot, which could help speed up the development process.
3   He should consider using this module. However, many such modules have limitations because they are generic in design, and he must also consider whether the company has the necessary IT resources to use the module effectively.
4   Yes, it would. History can show useful trends on performance, which can form the basis for discussions with suppliers. It will, however, be less useful in predicting what happens in the future.

Feedback on learning activity 9.2

Your table could include the answers shown in table 9.3.

Table 9.3

Quantitative	Qualitative
Expensive to set up and operate	Ensure a common basis for judgements
Difficult to interpret the data	Data is in people's heads
Standardising guidelines	Too much emphasis on one success or failure
Uses real data	Possible bias
Easy to track and trace	

Feedback on self-assessment question 9.2

1   A. Qualitative measurements can be affected by biased opinions.
2   B. Perceptions are best measured with qualitative measures.
3   B.
4   D. Management strengths would be a qualitative measurement.

Feedback on learning activity 9.3

There is no one right answer, but your list could include:

- current position
- who will be involved
- the detail of the application
- the minimum data needed
- available resources
- IT capability
- timescale
- audit and review required.

Feedback on self-assessment question 9.3

You should have some or all of the following:

optimum – available resources – skills – external – historical – investment – audit – review

Feedback on learning activity 9.4

Your diagram could have included:

- the internal customer
- other organisational functions
- the supplier
- other suppliers in the supply chain
- third parties.

Feedback on self-assessment question 9.4

You should feed back in report form on the benefits you feel are important, which should include some of those mentioned above. Your criticism should be balanced to show good and bad points, with suggestions for

9

improvement and for widening stakeholder involvement if – on balance – you feel this would be useful.

Feedback on learning activity 9.5

There is no one right answer, but you should have identified at least some points from the text that follows.

Feedback on self-assessment question 9.5

1 TRUE. Visits are an essential part of much supplier measurement.
2 TRUE. Review and feedback help to develop the team.
3 FALSE. Team approach will provide a better mix of skills and trained observation.
4 FALSE. Desk-based work underpins the success of a measurement project.
5 FALSE. Suppliers should be visited when necessary, not to a timetable.

9

Study session 10
Performance measurement

Introduction

To get good results from performance measurement you need to understand the basic principles. In this study session we shall look in more depth at how performance measurement can be undertaken, using some simple examples. Generally, the measurement of a supplier's performance may be compared with:

- an agreed standard
- performance on a previous order
- another supplier's performance
- other criteria appropriate to your organisation.

'It ain't what you do it's the way that you do it – that's what gets results.'
Bananarama song lyric

Session learning objectives

After completing this session you should be able to:

10.1 Summarise some generic methodologies for performance measurement.
10.2 Explain and give examples of the basic process of vendor rating.
10.3 Explain and give examples of the category approach to supplier performance measurement.
10.4 Summarise the benefits of using weighted measurements.
10.5 Explain the advantages of third-party involvement and testing procedures.
10.6 Plan audit processes to avoid financial or performance fraud.

Unit content coverage

This study session covers the following topics from the official CIPS unit content document:

Learning outcomes

- Categorise types of performance measures that are available to supply chain managers.
- Interpret and apply statistical data used to measure performance.

Learning objectives

2.4 Apply and evaluate appropriate measures to develop sustained improvement of supplier performance including:
  - Carter's model of performance measures (9Cs)
  - Simple vendor rating calculations
2.9 Determine ways of measuring supplier achievement of service levels. Use of evaluation reports relating to:

10

157

- Ongoing levels of performance in carrying out the service: quality, after-sales service, price, consistency of performance

Prior knowledge

You should have a general understanding of the concept of vendor rating and supplier measurement. There is some basic maths in this session.

You should have read study sessions 7, 8 and 9.

Resources

No specific resources are required, but it will be useful to be, or to have been involved in, the design of a suppler measurement system. If you have not, you may find it useful to discuss this topic with other students or colleagues, or a manager.

You may find a calculator useful, and access to the internet will allow you to check on testing houses and vendor rating in general.

Timing

You should set aside about 5.5 hours to read and complete this session, including learning activities, self-assessment questions, the suggested further reading (if any) and the revision question.

10.1 Generic methodologies for post-award performance measurement

Measurement will identify weaknesses on the part of the supplier. It will allow the supplier the opportunity to improve their performance (assuming of course that the cause of the weakness lies with the supplier). It will also allow the buying organisation to seek concessions and/or compensation for poor performance.

Feedback obtained during the measurement process may also be used to develop staff and organisational measurement skills, helping to ensure continuous improvement in overall supplier performance.

Learning activity 10.1

Draft a checklist of ways you could choose to assess one of your key suppliers.

Feedback on page 171

In table 10.1 we can see that there are several different methods we can use to measure suppliers. Variations in *italic* are discussed later in this study session. Some of the terms in the table merit a fuller explanation:

- **Cost ratio rating** is a measurement system for supplier performance, which applies a cost to a performance failure: for example, 'a late delivery costs us £125 per occasion'. These costs are then totalled for each supplier
- **Categorical rating** is a measurement system for supplier performance that identifies a series of measurement categories and then rates suppliers against them using subjective criteria.
- **Standard** is a commonly used term that usually means an agreed company, national or international standard such as ISO 9000.

Table 10.1 Generic methods of measuring supplier performance

Type	Description	Variations
Statistics-based	Relies heavily on the availability of statistics, and is therefore orientated to measurable or transactional activities. There can be different levels of complexity in terms of content and statistical analysis.	• *Simple rating – a few selected categories are measured.* • Complex rating – a wide range of categories are measured. • *Weighted rating – a weighting is applied to the selected categories.* • Cost ratio rating – attempts to convert the performance failures into an actual cash cost to the organisation.
Perception-based	Is concerned with perceptions and opinions. Can be an easy way to undertake a simple review of a supplier's performance. In a more complex form it is used when a more 'rounded' view of the supplier is required. Opinions are often converted to figures for positioning purposes.	• *Simple rating – opinion is sought on a few selected categories.* • Categorical rating – a more complex approach with a wide range of categories and functions involved. • *The 7 Cs – a set of statements that can be used to assess suppliers.*
Research-based	Checking out a supplier's performance through research.	• Financial analysis • References • Historical performance • Reputation
Standards and accreditations	Using supplier's accreditations as a basis for performance. ISO standards are recognised worldwide, but there may be company or national schemes that could be used.	• ISO 9000 (series) • ISO 14000 • Supplier's total quality management systems • Others by discussion
Self-assessment	Using supplier's existing or proposed self-assessment of performance	Supplier's existing systems of measurement are utilised.

(continued on next page)

10

Table 10.1 *(continued)*

Type	Description	Variations
	to avoid introducing a new performance measurement system in the buyer's organisation.	A new system of self-measurement is agreed with the supplier for this job.

Self-assessment question 10.1

Consider a supplier you believe is performing badly. Write a short report indicating the nature of the problems experienced, and recommending a method or model best suited to correct the situation.

Feedback on page 171

10.2 Simple vendor rating

Vendor rating is the process of measuring the performance of a vendor (supplier): it usually implies the use of a process or system. It is a tool that will act as a control on performance. Problems will be highlighted, allowing corrective action to be taken by either or both parties as appropriate.

At a simplistic level, supplier performance is typically measured by:

- Quality – could be the number of acceptable deliveries in relation to the total number of deliveries received. 'Acceptable' in this case is often defined as 'complete'.
- Delivery – could be the number of deliveries delivered on time in relation to the total number of deliveries received.
- After-sales service – could be the time taken in hours or days for queries to be resolved, measured against a target.
- Price – could be measured as the delivered price quoted by the supplier against the lowest delivered price for the same article by any one supplier.

However, other calculations can be used. This information would be received in purchasing, and simple calculations undertaken. Figure 10.1 shows an example in which:

- Quality is good: 15 out of 15 deliveries are acceptable.
- Delivery is less good: only 13 of the 15 deliveries were on time.
- Service: was poor, averaging 20 days to resolve a query instead of the target of 10.
- Price: is close to the lowest at £300 instead of £290.

Figure 10.1: Simple vendor rating

Factor	Score	Target	Score
Quality (by delivery)	15	15	1.00
Delivery timing (by delivery)	13	15	0.87
After-sales service (by days)	20	10	0.50
Price (by £s)	£300	£290	0.97
Total			3.33
	Target		4.00
	Actual		3.33
	Overall assessment		83%

The calculations

1. Express each factor as a proportion of 1. (For example, after-sales service is half of the desired performance, so it rates only 0.5)

2. Add up the scores (in this case 3.33).

3. Calculate the target (the maximum achievable – in this case 4).

4. Compare the actual with the target and express as a percentage – in this case 3.33 as a percentage of 4.

Note that in this type of rating system we do not normally 'add' anything for better performance. For example, if the after-sales service provided was 8 days against our target of 10, the answer would still be 1.

From this we can say that that this supplier's performance over the measured period of time was 83% of that required. Clearly, this information, supported by the raw data, can form the basis for serious discussion with the supplier on service improvements.

Learning activity 10.2

Examine this given data from a simple vendor rating system.

- Quality – 70 out of 75 deliveries are correct.
- Delivery – 13 of the 75 deliveries were late.
- Service – 4 days actual against 5 days target.
- Price – actual £250; best £250.

Create a matrix similar to figure 10.1 and calculate the supplier's overall rating

Feedback on page 171

There is no separate self-assessment question for this section. These topics are covered in self-assessment question 10.2 below.

10.3 Perception-based rating

A more comprehensive approach will need to be taken to vendor rating when a supplier is more critical to the ongoing success of the organisation, or when more complex factors and factors that require subjective opinions need to be assessed.

An alternative to basic vendor rating is the category model, in which (often through a team exercise) the buyer can assess the supplier in some depth. Very often this will be centred around a checklist, which might look similar to that shown in table 10.3.

Table 10.3 Category rating form

Supplier:		Date:	
Performance category – typical examples		**Rating**	
	Good	**Acceptable**	**Poor**
Delivery performance (correct quantities)			
Delivery performance (on time)			
Price (performance over time)			
Quality and compliance to specification			
Invoicing and financial performance			
Service from representative and after sales team			
Good accurate documentation			
Problem solving when difficulties occur			
Emergency backup if needed			
Plus other categories as appropriate to the supplier goods or service being evaluated			

In this example a *good – acceptable – poor* rating has been used. Another common method is to allocate a numerical position: for example, '1 equals poor – 5 equals excellent'. This then allows some basic calculations to be made, which makes it easier to compare suppliers. Note that a standard form will be less useful than one devised for each evaluation.

Learning activity 10.3

Examine all supplier assessment you are aware of in your organisation, and look for an example of a simple form used in the measurement process.

(continued on next page)

Learning activity 10.3 (continued)

List the categories of rating that the form covers. Is this a good list, in your view, and what if anything would you add, based on your reading so far? How does this compare with the example in table 10.3?

You may wish to discuss this with your line manager or supervisor.

Feedback on page 171

A more sophisticated approach uses the '7Cs' shown in table 10.4. This approach is equally useful in pre- and post-award assessment situations. A checklist is used to identify all the key categories in which the supplier is expected to perform. This is very useful when beginning the measurement planning, but the buyer must then determine in detail what mix of measurement tools and techniques will be used in each category.

Table 10.4 The 7Cs of supplier performance measurement

Category	Description
Competency	The ability of the relevant key personnel within the supplier's organisation: for example, management, technical, administrative and professional staff.
Capacity	The ability of the supplier, in terms of physical, intellectual and financial resources, to meet the buyer's total requirements. For example, has the supplier the production and financial capacity to meet the requirement?
Commitment	Evidence available to the organisation in the form of statistical data on such items as process control, failures, or quality. Quality control records are a good example of this.
Control	Evidence available to the organisation of the existence of effective management controls and information systems. Quality management systems such as ISO 9000 are a good example.
Cash	The supplier's cash resources and financial stability over the previous five years or so. More details of this aspect are given later in this unit.
Cost	A measure of the total cost of acquisition rather than just the price.
Consistency	The ability of the supplier to demonstrate a high standard of delivery reliability and quality, preferably with evidence of improvement over time

Self-assessment question 10.2

Study this mini case study.

Benjamin's Blocks

Benjamin's Blocks plc are involved in producing block paving for local councils, and feel they need to introduce a more sophisticated supplier performance measurement system for one of their key suppliers. They hope this will create a better relationship with the supplier. They already have lots of performance 'numbers' and a basic numerical vendor rating system, but feel that this does not give a true 'feel' for the relationship.

The lead buyer at Benjamin's has been shown the 7Cs by a CIPS-qualified member of staff, and feels they provide all that is needed to begin the

(continued on next page)

Self-assessment question 10.2 *(continued)*

process. At the first planning meeting he meets objections from his deputy, who believes they should look for a simpler approach. This should continue to utilise the basic rating system, but bring in references to the more subjective issues needed for a wider perspective.

Identify four points that you feel can be drawn from this scenario.

Feedback on page 171

10.4 The benefits of using weighted measurements

The rating systems that we have discussed so far can be either simple or complex, but they have the characteristic of treating each category or rating factor as equal. However, in practice this is not usually the case, and we therefore need to weight factors in relation to their perceived importance to the organisation.

Weighting simply means giving a higher priority (or weight) to one characteristic over another, but its effect on a rating system can be quite significant.

Figure 10.2 shows the same vendor rating calculation we used earlier. However, in this example we have made a judgement to emphasise quality and delivery and de-emphasise after-sales service. The weighting column shows how this is done. Note that, when using weighting, the total of the weight is always 1 or 100%

Figure 10.2: Weighted vendor rating

Factor	Score	Target	Score	Weighting	Weighted score	The calculations
Quality (by delivery)	15	15	1.00	30%	0.300	1. Work out the score as before.
Delivery timing (by delivery)	13	15	0.87	35%	0.303	2. Apply the weighting (for example, delivery timing = 0.87 × 35% = 0.30).
After-sales service (by days)	20	10	0.50	10%	0.050	
Price (by £s)	£300	£290	0.97	25%	0.242	
Total				100%(1)	0.895	3. Add up the weighted scores.
Target					1.000	4. Compare the actual with the target score (1 or 100%).
Actual					0.895	
Overall assessment					90%	

So we can see that using the weighted score the same supplier providing the same service scores 90% as against 83% from simple rating – an increase of 7 points. In real terms this may mean a substantial change in our view of the supplier, and weighted systems, though more complex, are generally more useful.

10

There are, however, several factors that can distort this type of calculation. The most common ones are:

- Data is either inaccurate or taken from an inappropriate source.
- Weighting is inappropriate and data is therefore 'biased' towards an inappropriate performance measure.
- Qualitative data based on opinion can be either biased or inaccurate compared to quantitative data.
- Over time new systems and personnel can provide different data resulting in an apparent change of performance. Also over time systems often degrade unless regular management audits are carried out on their effectiveness.

Learning activity 10.4

Take the vendor rating matrix you prepared in learning activity 10.2 above. Weight it as follows:

- Quality: 30%
- Delivery: 35%
- Service: 10%
- Price: 25%

Create a matrix similar to figure 10.2 and calculate the supplier's overall rating

Feedback on page 172

10

Now go on to tackle the following self-assessment question.

Self-assessment question 10.3

These questions also cover section 10.2 above.

Give True or False responses to the following statements.

1   In basic vendor rating there are only four factors that can be used. TRUE/FALSE
2   In basic vendor rating the maximum a supplier can score on any given factor is 1 or 100%. TRUE/FALSE
3   Quality will always be the number of acceptable deliveries in relation to the total number of deliveries received. TRUE/FALSE
4   The reason for weighting is that suppliers cannot be expected to perform equally well in all areas. TRUE/FALSE
5   In weighted vendor rating the weighting applied must always add up to 1 (or 100%). TRUE/FALSE
6   The weighting factors applied should come from the user. TRUE/FALSE

Feedback on page 172

10.5 Third party involvement and testing procedures

In study session 9 we touched briefly on the potential role for **third parties** in the supplier measurement process. This involves the inclusion of another party in what is usually a two-party relationship: for example, in third party quality testing the work is undertaken by someone who is *not* the buyer or seller

But why would we wish to use a third party at all?

Learning activity 10.5

Investigate whether your organisation is using any third parties or testing bodies in any current supplier measurement activities. Why was this role given to the third party?

What are the advantages and disadvantages of third party input?

You may need to discuss this with your colleagues or line manager.

Feedback on page 172

10

Ultimately, the success of any measurement system depends on the skills of the people who operate and use it. Purchasing personnel should be familiar with the various applications discussed, but they may well lack experience in using them, especially if the systems are being introduced for the first time. Additional support and training may be needed, which may be available from either internal or external sources. Purchasing and supply management must decide this, based on their estimate of in-house capabilities and resources. This will include an assessment of:

- available finance
- available time
- staffing levels and staffing skills
- organisational policy and procedures
- quality of internal relationships
- size and technical content of the project or purchase.

Following this assessment, a decision can be made on the potential for involving third-party organisations. Typical areas of involvement include the following:

- The provision of skilled labour or a project manager for a period of time.
- Specialist consultants can provide advice and guidance on how to implement a supplier measurement project.
- The provision of related IT services.
- Market and supplier research.
- Specialist financial assessments.
- External testing houses can test specific components, assess a supplier's total capability, or assess for compliance with international standards

such as ISO 9000. Some of these houses are members of the Association of British Certification Bodies (ABCB), and a well-known name internationally is the Norwegian firm DNV (Det Norske Veritas).
- On building projects a whole range of performance measurement can be carried out via architects and surveyors.
- For some service contracts, third-party suppliers will provide 'mystery shoppers', who will test service performance.

The principal disadvantages of using third parties include:

- Cost, especially over long periods.
- Regular changes of the contractor's personnel which often make continuity different.
- Loss of interest by the contractor. Consultants often offer high-level personnel at the beginning, but gradually change this over the life of the contract.
- The need to monitor the contractor's services.

Self-assessment question 10.4

Answer the following multiple-choice questions.

1 Which of the following is *not* a reason for using third parties?
A availability of time
B lack of skills
C poor-quality internal relationships
D the supplier requests it.
2 External testing houses can test:
I products and components.
II compliance with international standards.
Which of the above statements is true?
A I
B I and II
C II
D Neither
3 Responsibility for involving third parties will lie with:
A senior management
B purchasing and supply management
C quality management
D the internal customer.
4 A big disadvantage of third-party involvement is:
A the time to award the contract
B cost over time
C lack of suitable contractors
D difficulty in specifying what is needed.
5 third-party contractors:
I sometimes substitute lower grade personnel.
II often fail to follow the required specifications.
Which of the above statements is true?
A I
B I and II

(continued on next page)

Self-assessment question 10.4 *(continued)*

C II

D Neither

Feedback on page 173

10.6 Audit and the planning of an audit trail

When considering the planning and implementation of a supplier measurement process, it is important that sufficient thought is given to the role of audit and the need for a good **audit trail** (documents or records that allow a process or action to be tracked back to its origin – a trail that an auditor can follow).

Learning activity 10.6

Draft a checklist to your head of audit that suggest issues or points of action that can give the audit team a useful role or roles in your supplier performance measurement activities.

You may wish to discuss this with your audit team manager.

Feedback on page 173

Although many occurrences of supplier measurement will be relatively simple and basic, a few will relate to large or complex projects that involve many people and last for significant periods of time. For these projects good audit practice is essential.

The terms can be defined as follows:

- Traditional financial audit, to ensure that all systems are compliant with good practice and organisational regulations
- Process audit, to ensure that the systems and process are working properly and that the desired information is being provided.
- Value for money audit, to check whether the organisation is gaining more from the measurement than it is costing to undertake it.
- Audit trail: is there a sufficiently clear specification, supported by records, notes minutes etc, to allow audit to do their job?

Traditional audit

If the supplier measurement process involves the significant commitment of staff or financial resources it may be part of the normal organisational audit process, either of itself, or as part of the purchasing and supply audit. It may therefore take place through either internal or external auditors, and will typically focus on the following issues:

- Have all organisational policies and procedures been complied with?
- Are all expenditures being made in accordance with financial procedures?

10

- Are supplier visits being administered properly, for example fares and expenses?
- Is required documentation up to date?

This aspect of audit is often a necessary part of organisational life, but it is more a 'policing' function, and makes little positive contribution. However, some of the auditor's skills may be very useful in the other types of audit.

Process audit

On any measurement process that runs for a long time it is useful to check that the systems are working as intended. Typically this might be done once, as the system becomes live, and at regular intervals thereafter during its life. This type of audit would typically focus on compliance:

- Are all the required data flows working as intended?
- Are systems (IT and paper) working as intended?
- Are review meetings taking place as agreed?
- Are recommendations and actions being taken, once agreed?
- Is the supplier complying with its obligations (particularly in self-assessment)?
- Is the buying organisation complying with its obligations?

This type of audit should provide feedback, which can help correct mistakes that are being made, and ideas for improvement.

Value for money audit

Both of the above audits set out to check that the processes are working as intended, and that the organisation does not lose money through process or compliance failure. Value for money (VFM) audit sets out to establish whether the organisation is gaining value from the processes, and would typically focus on benefits:

- Can we show what we have saved relative to what we have spent?
- Are there cash savings?
- If there are no cash savings, have we gained in other areas, such as better quality of product or service?
- Can we put a value to intangible issues such as better relationships?

Audit trail

The audit trail is an important part of any management process of this kind. Much of it will be documentation, but the key principle should be transparency and openness.

- It should start with a well-documented 'project plan' that sets out what is to be achieved and how it is to be carried out. This is helpful, because it allows better planning, facilitates audit, and acts as a benchmark for assessing progress.
- It will include all necessary documents, files, records, data and minutes generated by activity as the process is running. This is particularly important, because the intention is to continuously improve, and this cannot be measured without data.

10

- It will include records of all significant decisions, such as the upgrading or downgrading of a supplier, and will be helpful should there be enquiries or protests.
- It will include regular reports to senior management as required.
- It will act as a valuable training 'library' for other projects, and for inducting new team members.

Self-assessment question 10.5

Provide the missing words in the following paragraph of text.

Simon has been reviewing the role of audit in one of his larger supplier performance measurement schemes. He is fairly satisfied that the _____ _____ is well documented, and that the various documents, records and notes provide a good _____ _____ for others to follow, but is concerned that other audit input has been more _____, focusing on procedures.

In discussions with the head of audit he has identified a need for a _____ _____ _____ audit to ensure that his company is really _____ from the measurement process. In addition, because the scheme has been running for a long period, he feels that a _____ audit would help to ensure _____ with the requirements of the scheme.

Feedback on page 173

Revision question

Now try the revision question for this session on page 336.

Summary

In this study session you have looked at generic methodologies for assessing suppliers and have undertaken some basic calculations as well as looking at how to incorporate more perception-based activities.

In addition we have looked at the roles for third parties and for audit, both of whom can make useful contributions.

In study session 11 we shall look at some issues relating to communications.

Suggested further reading

Students can find more detail on the 7 Cs in Lysons and Farrington (2006), chapter 11, page 389.

Useful websites to support references in this session are those of the Association of British Certification Bodies (ABCB) http://www.abcb.demon.co.uk and Det Norske Veritas (DNV) http://www.dnv.com/.

Feedback on learning activities and self-assessment questions

Feedback on learning activity 10.1

There is no one correct answer. Your checklist should include some of the variations covered in table 10.1, and you may also have been able to identify some of the main types of measurement.

Feedback on self-assessment question 10.1

There is no one correct answer, but your report will probably cover:

- Introduction
- The supplier, and the problem you believe exists
- Your recommended model
- Why this would be appropriate in your organisation.

Feedback on learning activity 10.2

Your matrix should look like table 10.2.

Table 10.2

Factor	Score	Target	Score
Quality (by delivery)	70	75	0.93
Delivery timing (by delivery)	62	75	0.83
After-sales service (by days)	4	5	1.00
Price (by £)	£250	£250	1.00
Total			3.76
		Target	4.00
		Actual	3.76
		Overall assessment	94%

Feedback on learning activity 10.3

You should have a sample form or checklist that you can compare with table 10.3. How many matches do you have?

You should have commented on your own form, and have a list of any suggested additional measures.

Feedback on self-assessment question 10.2

1 Benjamin's are right to hope that better relationships can come from introducing a more sophisticated measurement system, but only if this is done well and with the supplier's cooperation.
2 They are also right in their view that basic numerical rating systems show performance measurements well, but give no indications of

thinking, strategy, attitude or commitment issues, which are important in long-term relationships.

3 The lead buyer is wrong: the 7Cs are a comprehensive high-level checklist for aspects of a supplier's business approach and activity. They then need considerable time, effort and planning to work into specific actions.

4 The buyer and his deputy need to resolve this. The correct action depends on the pressures they are under. However, because the 7Cs route would take time to implement, one solution would be to add a category-based assessment process to the current vendor rating, and use this with the aim of moving to a more comprehensive approach in the future.

Feedback on learning activity 10.4

Your matrix should look like table 10.5. Note that the supplier's performance is now lower as a result of his poor delivery, which you weighted at 35%.

Table 10.5

Factor	Score	Target	Score	Weighting	Weighted score
Quality (by delivery)	70	75	0.93	30%	0.280
Delivery timing (by delivery)	62	75	0.83	35%	0.289
After-sales service (by days)	4	5	1.00	10%	0.100
Price (by £)	£250	£250	1.00	25%	0.250
Total				100%	0.919
				Target	1.000
				Actual	0.919
				Overall assessment	92%

Feedback on self-assessment question 10.3

1 FALSE. You may use as many as you can handle; the principle remains the same.
2 TRUE. The maximum a supplier can score on any given factor is 1 or 100%, and the overall maximum is (1 × the number of factors).
3 FALSE. This is one basic measure, but there could be others.
4 FALSE. Weighting allows the buyer to bias the scoring in favour of those things that are important to his or her organisation.
5 TRUE. The weighting applied must always add up to 1.
6 FALSE. The weighting factors applied must accurately reflect the values of the organisation; usually some consensus will be needed.

Feedback on learning activity 10.5

There is no one right answer. Your response should match with some of the issues raised in this section.

Feedback on self-assessment question 10.4

1   D
2   B
3   B
4   B
5   A

Feedback on learning activity 10.6

There is no one correct answer. The quality of input from audit teams will vary according to how they see their brief, and according to the experience of the team. However, you should find some input opportunities under the following headings, which are developed in this section.

- Financial audit – good practice and organisational regulations.
- Process audit – of systems and processes.
- Value for money audit – checks the organisation is gaining from the measurement.
- Audit trail – ensuring there is one.

Feedback on self-assessment question 10.5

project plan – audit trail – traditional – value for money – benefiting – process – compliance

10

10

Communication

Introduction

Most organisations have a high awareness of the need to communicate, and have some sophisticated systems for doing so. Yet all too often people at all levels lack the real basic data they need to participate and do a job well. This applies just as much when measuring purchasing performance as it does to management in general.

'I've not got a first in philosophy without being able to muddy things pretty satisfactorily.'
John Banham, ex Director General CBI

Session learning objectives

After completing this session you should be able to:

11.1 Determine how different types of communication can support business relationships at all levels: strategic, tactical and operational.
11.2 Explain the link between communication, performance measurement and relationship-building.
11.3 Analyse the importance of good communication mechanisms within performance measurement systems.
11.4 Argue the importance of good communications in resolving disputes and managing conflict.
11.5 Describe some of the different types of communication mechanism available.

Unit content coverage

This study session covers the following topics from the official CIPS unit content document:

Learning outcomes

- Argue the reasons for measuring a suppliers performance.
- Discuss the benefits of implementing a well structured approach to measuring organisational, functional and individual performance.

Learning objective

2.5 Discuss the importance of close and frequent buyer–supplier communication and of its importance within supply contracts.
  - Demand–supply chain relationships

Prior knowledge

You should have a general understanding of the concept of communications in business and some of the methods used.

You should have read from study sessions 7 to 10.

Resources

No specific resources are required, but it will be useful to be, or to have been involved in, some aspects of communication with a supplier over performance measurement. If you have not, you may find it useful to discuss this topic with other students or colleagues, or a manager.

Timing

You should set aside about 4 hours to read and complete this session, including learning activities, self-assessment questions, the suggested further reading (if any) and the revision question.

11.1 Communication and business relationships at strategic, tactical and operational levels

In previous study sessions we have seen that introducing supplier performance measures will alter the nature of the relationships between the parties. When this is done well, the relationship will improve, and may eventually move from an adversarial to a partnership style of relationship.

Learning activity 11.1

Take a supplier with whom you are familiar. Use the template below to review who is involved in communication at present, and how you would ideally like to see this in the future.

Table 11.1

Function involved	Current involvement	Ideal involvement

Feedback on page 189

A large part of this change in relationship will be due to the improved communications that performance measurement should bring about.

Figure 11.1 shows some of the communications links and relationships that can be established.

Figure 11.1: Communication links and relationships

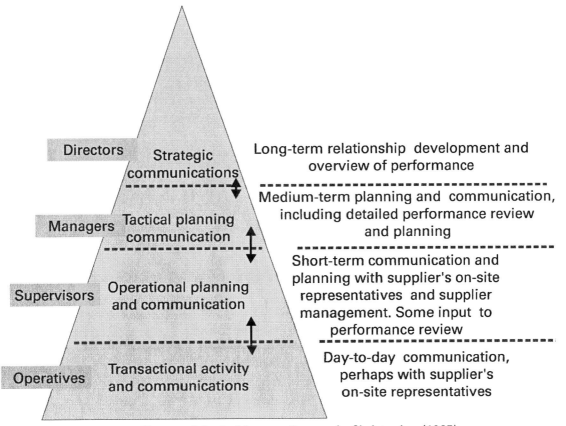

Source: Adapted from a diagram in Christopher (1985)

Director level

- Directors will not generally be meeting frequently, and when they do these may be quite formal sessions, usually with an agenda and notes or minutes. There will be an overview of performance to date, concentrating on the main issues that have emerged from the detailed reviews undertaken at other levels.
- Directors will concentrate on the health of the relationship, and the direction it will take in the future, but they are likely to be working on advice from the managerial level.
- A report may go into company newsletters or annual reports.
- This could be a level for **dispute resolution** (the solving of disputes through a process, or by having a policy, rather than just hoping things will sort themselves out).

Management level

- More frequent meetings, some of which may be informal, and some of which are likely to be formal performance review sessions. There is also likely to be one-to-one dialogue on issues. Managers will take a much more detailed look at performance management issues, because they will be making recommendations to their directors.

- Visits may take place.
- Outputs may go into company newsletters or general circulation and notice boards.
- Could be a level for dispute resolution.

Supervisor level

- There will be fewer formal meetings and much more informal contact, also via telephone and email etc. At this level investigative and corrective action is important, and much of the statistical data will be analysed at this level. Unless the supplier has an on-site presence there is likely to be less supplier contact.
- Outputs may go to management, general circulation and notice boards.
- Disputes are likely to be flagged at this level.

Operative level

- Day-to-day activity regarding performance management but especially important in identifying areas of poor performance. This is often the level responsible for generating many statistics. Little supplier contact
- Problems are flagged at this level.
- An area where perceptions can easily be generated, for example 'very unfriendly to deal with on the phone'.

The key point is that, when measuring suppliers' performance effectively, each part of the organisation has a part to play, and can contribute to the impression one organisation has of the other. It is important that, when planning a supplier performance measurement system, this aspect of communication and relationship-building is taken into account early in the planning stages. Ideally, a communications plan should be part of the system design: relationships and communications need to be managed, and this is not always easy to do.

Self-assessment question 11.1

Take the ideal situation you identified in learning activity 11.1 above and create a communication model diagram that graphically explains what you would like to see happening.

Feedback on page 190

11.2 Communication, performance measurement and relationship-building

Perhaps one of the most significant benefits that performance measurement provides is that it should allow each party to gain a better understanding of the constraints, deadlines and problems that affect the relationship. This higher level of understanding should provide significant opportunities for improvement within both organisations, and therefore opportunities to strengthen the relationship.

Learning activity 11.2

Involvement with suppliers can often lead to a better understanding of supply market conditions or a supplier's problems. Consider a supplier who, through discussion, visit or research, you have come to understand better.

Write a short report (300 words) explaining what you learned, the awareness this gave you, and how it helped in the job.

Feedback on page 190

Essentially, performance measurement should create a business relationship that has much more mutual dialogue and problem-solving than an ordinary business relationship. This in turn leads to altered levels of awareness, as table 11.3 shows.

Table 11.3 Altered awareness in performance management

Party	Awareness
The buyer	Gains better awareness of the supplier's business.
	Gains better understanding of the market and the supplier's supply chains.
	Gains awareness of what effects his/her actions have on the ability of the supplier to manufacture or produce a product.
	Gains awareness of problems within his/her organisation as seen by the supplier.
The supplier	• Begins to understand the customer's business problems • Begins to see how he/she can help the customer better • Begins to understand the buyer's downstream supply issues and his/her involvement in them. • Understands the buyer's use of the product, which may create opportunities to suggest ways in which it could be improved. • Begins to see problems in his/her organisation as seen by the buyer.
Both parties	• Begin to see opportunities for joint business improvement. • Begin to take a wider view of the supply chain. • Begin to recognise common problems elsewhere in each other's upstream and downstream supply chains. • Begin to see opportunities to cooperate outside the immediate business area.

11

If used correctly, performance measurement will provide an objectivity that would not otherwise be possible. Problems in both organisations will be highlighted, but in a positive way, where they are capable of being analysed and corrected. In many cases emotive issues such as the personal relationships between buyer and seller will become less important, to the benefit of both parties.

Interestingly, there can be a significant spin-off from a relationship of this kind as other parties see what is happening and feel it would be a better way to work:

- Other suppliers may wish to see a similar relationship established.
- Other internal customers see the benefits the new relationship is providing, and wish to participate.

This can often enhance the position of purchasing and supply within its own organisation.

Self-assessment question 11.2

Complete the following multiple-choice questions

1   Performance measurement should help a supplier gain awareness of all the following except:
    A the customer's business
    B the buyer's downstream supply issues
    C problems in the buying organisation
    D problems in his/her own organisation.

2   Performance measurement will always help to:
    A create more dialogue
    B design a better product
    C improve quality
    D reduce prices.

3   Performance measurement should be:
    I subjective
    II positive
    Which of the above statements is true?
    A I
    B I and II
    C Neither
    D II

4   Other suppliers may become involved in performance measurement because:
    I they observe the benefits.
    II they are part of the joint supply chains.
    Which of the above statements is true?
    A I
    B I and II
    C Neither
    D II

5   An unexpected benefit of performance measurement can be that:
    A purchasing procedures can be simplified

(continued on next page)

Self-assessment question 11.2 *(continued)*

B less board-level reporting is required
C purchasing position is enhanced
D risk management is simplified.

Feedback on page 190

11.3 The importance of good communication mechanisms within performance measurement systems

Performance measurement is an important tool in the contract management process, as we have seen earlier, but of course it is just one of several tools that may be used, and there are many activities within good contract management that provide opportunities for communications and relationship-building between the supplier and the buying organisation.

Learning activity 11.3

Consider a contract or buying agreement with which you are familiar.
Using the checklist in table 11.4, comment critically on each aspect of your selected contract.

Table 11.4

Checklist	Comment
Description of contract	
Relationships need to be established early	
Relationships need to be actively managed	
Relationships are flexible and open	
Procedures are good	
Style (adversarial to partnership)	
Level of resource commitment needed	
Supplier's view of contract	

Feedback on page 190

Figure 11.3 summarises some of the most important activities of contract management in graphic form, and table 11.6 provides further clarification of the relationships involved. In the table, the term **risk management** is used to denote a formalised process – increasingly common in many organisations – of analysing all aspects of 'risk' to the success of the business, and seeking solutions in advance.

Figure 11.3: Contract management activities

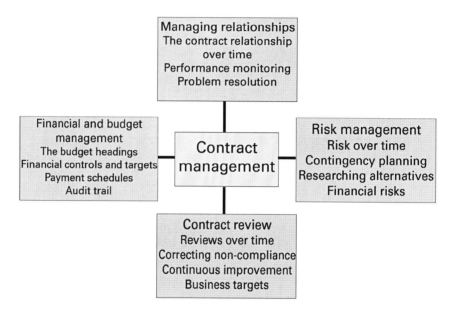

Table 11.6 Contract management relationships

Activity	Description	Key players
Contract review	The basic day-to-day process of making the contract work, changing amending and improving as appropriate	• Contract management • Users • Supplier's representatives
Financial and budget management	The basic process of ensuring that the financial aspects of the contract work, that payments take place as required, and that a financial audit trail is in place	• Accounts/finance • Audit • Contract management • Supplier's accounts
Risk management	A more sophisticated process, looking at 'what if?' in terms of the contract and possible failures	• Contract management • Finance (or risk management team) • Supplier (on occasion)
Managing relationships	A key role, making sure that all the complex relationships needed are working and, by definition, solving problems, networking and dealing with relationship difficulties	• Contract management • General management • Supplier's management

No matter how good the contract and the definition of the roles, effective performance measurement will depend upon the relationships between those involved. So what are some of the key requirements for good relationships?

- Relationships need to be established as early as possible, constantly reviewed, and actively managed.
- Relationships can be flexible and open, while maintaining proper businesslike and professional conduct.

- Good procedures help to establish a balance and encourage mutual trust between the parties.
- Adversarial relationships are less likely to be productive.
- Relationships will be based on the respective roles agreed between the parties, and care should be taken to avoid the generation of a performance measurement 'industry' whose costs exceed its benefits.
- Strategic contracts will place a greater emphasis on these relationships.
- The supplier must see the contract as important (see study session 7).

One difficulty on large contracts with many users is: who should be involved in the measurement process? Does one user act as a representative, or is a team of users put together? Communication plans and mechanisms must be considered, as for example must the extent to which local user/supplier communication is encouraged or permitted on measurement issues.

Self-assessment question 11.3

Consider the example of the agency staffing contract provided in the feedback from learning activity 11.3 above (reproduced here).

1   This contract arrangement is for the supply of agency staff. Our organisation needs to use these staff quite regularly and at short notice.
2   We let this contract by electronic tender, and there was little attempt to establish relationships at the beginning. This caused problems at first, as it was not clear who was really responsible for handling communications. It is now agreed that the contract manager leads on business issues and the lead customer on operational issues.
3   Relationships are still guarded, but improving. Procedures are good, and agreed by both parties.
4   We wish this to be adversarial at first, while the contract beds down, but our strategy is to move to a partnership style if the measurement system indicates good results. Resource commitment has been significant; it has reduced, but still takes too much time.
5   We have had some difficulty getting the supplier's view of the contract. We want to be a 'development' customer but at present we may be 'exploitable'.

Make at least five significant comments (good and bad) on what was said.

Feedback on page 191

11.4 Good communications and the resolution of disputes and management of conflict

As we have seen, good communications will help to build relationships, and performance measurement is a valuable communication tool. However, as we have also seen, measurement will on occasions raise issues that may be contentious or which may become the focus of disagreement between the parties. This is to be expected, and should not of itself be seen as a problem, because both the buyer and supplier organisations are trying to derive benefit from the measurement exercise.

Learning activity 11.4

Draft a procedure note for your purchasing manual on the correct process and procedure to be adopted in the event of dispute or conflict occurring in a performance measurement system for which you are responsible. Use a diagram if you feel it helps. (Maximum 1 page A4.)

Use the style of your own manuals or policy documents.

Feedback on page 191

A performance measurement system will raise issues that may cause disputes, but it should also create an environment in which these issues can be positively resolved. Disputes and conflict are different, and table 11.7 provides some simple definitions of the two terms.

Table 11.7 Definitions of disputes and conflict

Disputes	A dispute occurs when the parties fail to agree over something, but there is not necessarily any bad feeling. Very often this will be a technical or contractual issue.	For example, the performance measurement system calls for delivery information to be submitted monthly. The supplier has interpreted this as the calendar month, and has changed software to do this, but the buyer wanted it to be every four weeks. The supplier does not now want to change back, and a dispute exists. If this cannot be resolved at the operational level it will have to be escalated in some way until a decision can be reached.
Conflict	Conflict occurs when there is a clash between one person or organisation and the other. It is often due to different personalities or cultures. Disputes can become conflicts if they fail to be resolved. Conflict is often down to human relationships, and can be hard to resolve.	For example, the end customer and the supplier's production manager fail to get on, and are always arguing about quality issues, even though the data suggests there is not a problem. This must be resolved, but cannot really be escalated in the same way as a dispute can, because there is often an absence of 'willingness' to reach a result.

In order to manage disputes and conflict several points need to be considered:

- Disputes between businesses are rarely the result of deliberate actions but usually occur because of poor communications, changing circumstances, third party actions or unforeseen circumstances. This should be remembered when trying to solve them.

- Minor items should be dealt with directly at the lowest possible level, but more fundamental issues need to involve the contract manager or performance manager.
- It is more beneficial to solve problems jointly rather than have one party impose a solution on the other, and the continuous dialogue should help to identify problems early.
- A performance measurement system agreement may specify the system of arbitration or arbiter to be used in case of unresolved disputes.
- The purchasing manager has a responsibility to both parties and sometimes has to take the supplier's side as well as his or her own.
- When using overseas suppliers watch for disputes arising through differences in language, understanding or common practice.
- Where conflict is personality-based then changing the personalities may be the only solution.
- Conflicts can be resolved through the courts, but it is usually expensive and often the contract has already failed by this stage.

Although a good performance measurement system should allow the resolution of most problems, it is important at the planning stage to ensure that mechanisms exist to resolve disputes if they cannot be resolved in the normal course of business. Table 11.8 shows some alternatives for dispute and conflict resolution. In the table, both mediation and arbitration denote stages in a disputes procedure. **Mediation** is less formal, and simply involves a third party to try to help; **arbitration** is more formal, and the results are usually binding.

Table 11.8 Resolving disputes and conflicts

Method	Description
Normal course of business	• By far the best and easiest way. • Disputes and conflicts are settled by the parties in the course of performance measurement activities.
Internal escalation	• An escalation process is written into the performance measurement process. • May be to senior manager or director level. • May draw attention to failure at operational level.
Mediation	• The parties enlist the aid of a mediator (internal or external), who will listen to and question each side in an attempt to lead them to settlement. • Not usually binding.
Arbitration	• The parties present their cases to one or more arbitrators, who decide how the case should be settled. • Usually binding, and enforceable through the courts. • Has a cost and a visibility, and suggests a failure in the organisations.
Renegotiation	• The parties agree to renegotiate the contract, or at least the performance management aspects.
Litigation	• If unable to resolve the matter through the means listed above, the matter can be decided in the courts.

11

11.5 Types of communication mechanism

There are many types of communication mechanism that can be applied to performance measurement at both the pre- and post-award stages, and in this section we shall take a brief overview of some of these.

However, it will also be useful to consider what is meant by communication, because many organisations are almost obsessive about it (or about the lack of it!).

Learning activity 11.5

Consider the following situation.

Your vendor rating systems have thrown up quality blemishes in the skins of uPVC doors you are buying. This has been traced to airborne dust and debris at the moulding stage, and can be eliminated if the operators make a slight change to the way they work.

Comment on each of the following as an effective way for the supplier to advise employees of the required changes.

- Company newsletter.
- Internal memo.
- Memo on noticeboard.
- Issue new procedure notice.
- Change IT-based procedural manual.
- Email to all operators.
- Staff meetings.
- Phone calls to operators.
- Management walkabout.
- Quality meetings.

Feedback on page 192

In general terms, communication is an implied willingness to pass on or exchange information or data from one group to another. For this to work effectively there are three important criteria, and these are shown in figure 11.4.

Figure 11.4: Criteria for communication to work

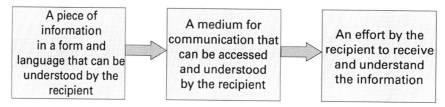

The third point (the right-hand box) is especially important: much communication is wasted because the intended recipients do not attempt to receive it.

Communication channels are formal or informal routes that are *regularly* used for communication, and which can be identified and used. Once communication channels have been established, they need to be kept open and used regularly. Occasional submission of data in a performance measurement system is unlikely to meet requirements, but is also going to be very easy to miss. In terms of performance measurement there are several types of information that may be shared, and different ways of doing it. Table 11.9 shows some of the main types of communication, and table 11.10 the most common methods of communicating, in relation to performance measurement.

Table 11.9 Types of communication

High-level plans	As a relationship moves towards partnership status there needs to be communication on longer-term matters and strategic issues.	• Strategic plans • Business plans • Procurement plans
Operational plans	Ensures that each of the parties is aware of how the others business is performing.	• Market prospects • Customer requirements • Procurement targets • New initiatives, eg e-business
Business performance statistics	The basic data that drives the performance measurement system. Especially important for ongoing vendor rating and other types of evaluation.	Examples would include: • delivery • quality • service price • responsiveness • initiatives
Change control proposals	As performance management develops, there will be a regular process of change, based on the review and feedback from the data.	Will potentially cover any aspect of the product or service that can be highlighted from the data acquired and from the improved relationships created.

Table 11.10 Methods of communication

Library and internet research	All manner of information can be accessed or supplied to help build up a profile of a supplier.	Particularly useful pre-award
Published documents	• Sales information • Company documents (eg environmental policies) • Annual reports Useful but obviously written with a positive spin by the supplier.	Particularly useful pre-award
Exhibitions, conferences and open days	Useful for research and for understanding of markets and supplier-based issues.	Particularly useful pre-award
Correspondence	Essential for major issues, and often helps to provide part of the audit trail on decision-making, provided proper records are kept.	Useful at all times
Telephone and email	Essential for day-to-day operations.	Useful at all times

(continued on next page)

11

Table 11.10 *(continued)*

	Essential that records are kept if major decisions are made via these mechanisms.	
Meetings	Useful for building relationships.	Useful at all times
	Good for reviewing progress and developing new ideas and recommendations.	
Notes and minutes	Essential for record keeping and audit trails.	Useful at all times
	May also function as action planning tools.	
Visits	Particularly useful for • assessing suppliers pre-award • evaluating new ideas or processes post-award • building relationships.	Useful at all times
Electronic data exchange	Essential where vendor rating systems require regular and detailed transfers of information between the parties.	Particularly useful post-award
Trade and professional publications	Useful for providing data and statistics that can be used to monitor markets and innovations (such as CIPS guide to market prices).	Particularly useful post-award
Newsletters	Company newsletters provide a high-level overview of what is happening inside the buyer's and the supplier's organisations.	Particularly useful post-award
Supplier awards	Award schemes are designed to give a high profile to suppliers who achieve targets for service or innovation. They help to build goodwill and cooperation between the parties.	Particularly useful post-award

Having completed this, now try the following self-assessment question.

Self-assessment question 11.4

Give True or False responses to the following statements.

1 Proposals for change and improvement will be very important communications during pre-award assessment. TRUE/FALSE

(continued on next page)

11

2   Internal escalation is by far the best and easiest way of solving disputes.
    TRUE/FALSE
3   If used irregularly, communication channels may not be effective.
    TRUE/FALSE
4   Serious performance measurement disputes are best resolved through
    the courts. TRUE/FALSE
5   Supplier award schemes are an important part of an audit trail.
    TRUE/FALSE
6   Communication planning is best undertaken early in the planning stage
    of performance measurement. TRUE/FALSE
7   An essential element of good communications is choosing the
    appropriate medium to use. TRUE/FALSE
8   In a good performance measurement system the system manager should
    be seen as fair by both parties. TRUE/FALSE

Feedback on page 192

Revision question

Now try the revision question for this session on page 336.

Summary

In this study session we have looked at various aspects of communication
and its effect on performance measurement systems and relationships. We
have also looked at some media that can be used, and have considered what
might happen in the event that we are in dispute with our supplier.

We now move on in study session 12 to consider another particularly useful
tool to use when measuring purchasing performance – financial appraisal.

Feedback on learning activities and self-assessment questions

Feedback on learning activity 11.1

There is no one right answer. An example might be as shown in table 11.2.

Table 11.2

Function involved	Current involvement	Ideal involvement
Procurement	Deals with sales and finance queries.	Coordinate contacts, and leads on communications strategy.
Customer	Deals direct with sales and production.	Deals with supplier via communication routes agreed with purchasing.
Quality	Deal with sales.	Deal with supplier's production and quality.
Senior management	Our MD knows their MD and plays golf occasionally.	Ideally only on a formal basis within the communications plan.
Receipts	Deal with delivery and despatch.	Deal with delivery and despatch.
Finance		Deal with finance queries.

Feedback on self-assessment question 11.1

Your model could look something like figure 11.2.

Figure 11.2: A communication model diagram

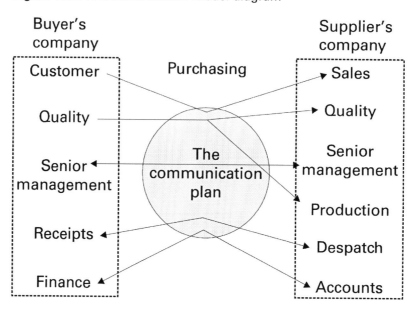

Feedback on learning activity 11.2

There is no specific feedback.

Feedback on self-assessment question 11.2

1 C
2 A
3 D
4 B
5 C

Feedback on learning activity 11.3

There is no one correct answer. An example would be as shown in table 11.5.

Table 11.5

Checklist	Comment
Description of contract	
This contract arrangement is for the supply of agency staff. Our organisation needs to use these staff quite regularly and at short notice.	
Relationships need to be established early	*We let this contract by electronic tender, and there was little attempt to establish relationships at the beginning. This caused problems at first.*

(continued on next page)

Table 11.5 *(continued)*

Relationships need to be actively managed	*This caused problems at first, as it was not clear who was really responsible for handling communications. It is now agreed that the contract manager leads on business issues and the lead customer on operational issues.*
Relationships are flexible and open	*Relationships are still guarded, but improving.*
Procedures are good	*Procedures are good, and agreed by both parties.*
Style (adversarial to partnership)	*We wish this to be adversarial at first, while the contract beds down, but our strategy is to move to a partnership style if the measurement system indicates good results.*
Level of resource commitment needed	*Has been significant; has reduced, but still takes too much time.*
Supplier's view of contract	*We have had some difficulty getting this view, as the supplier does not seem to think like this. We want to be a 'development' customer but at present we may be 'exploitable'.*

Feedback on self-assessment question 11.3

Your comments could include the following:

- Organisations required to use formal tendering can easily miss the communication opportunity to build up relationships by assessing suppliers thoroughly at the pre-award stage, and need to take positive action to correct this.
- Electronic tendering and communication can, in general, reduce administrative and printing costs, but does not help to build relationships.
- There was clearly little attempt to consider relationships and communications in the planning stages for this contract: hence the confusion with the lead user.
- There are clear indications in paragraphs 4 and 5 that planning and strategy discussions have taken place.
- 'Good procedures are in place' seems to conflict with other statements. Perhaps this refers to basic procedures for contract administration, payment etc. This might suggest an over-emphasis on this aspect at the planning stage.
- It is easy to underestimate the resources a project such as this can require, and contract managers must be very selective in applying measurement and monitoring systems where resources are insufficient.
- There is good awareness of the different views that suppliers may have.

Feedback on learning activity 11.4

There is no one correct answer. Your escalation path is likely to cover the following points:

- Resolve at operational level.
- Refer to relevant manager.

- Refer to senior management (or human resources if personality based).
- Refer to mediation or arbitration (internal or external).
- Refer to law.

Feedback on learning activity 11.5

- Company newsletter: not suitable for operational changes, but can be used post-event to highlight improvements
- Internal memo: limited effectiveness on its own; may not be read.
- Memo on noticeboard: may not be read, but useful if there is a known system of posting such details.
- Issue new procedure notice: good if necessary, and if procedures need updating. Effective if addressed to employees.
- Change IT-based procedural manual: necessary, but only as backup to another approach. Do operatives have regular IT access?
- Email to all operators: do operatives have regular IT access?
- Staff meetings: good, and a good place to confirm by memo or procedure note.
- Phone calls to operators: not likely to be effective.
- Management walkabout: helps to make a point, but needs follow-up action to sustain.
- Quality meetings: good if held, but staff meetings would do.

Feedback on self-assessment question 11.4

1 FALSE. they will be more important post-award.
2 FALSE. Disputes are best settled during the normal course of business.
3 TRUE. If not used regularly, communications may be missed.
4 FALSE. Recourse to law is a last resort, and is very expensive.
5 FALSE. Supplier award schemes are of little importance in an audit trail.
6 TRUE. Leaving communication planning until after an award is a poor way of working.
7 TRUE. The choice of media must be from those accessed by the recipient.
8 TRUE. Good performance measurement is not penalty based, so the manager should act for both sides.

11

Financial appraisal

Introduction

In many organisations there has in the past been rivalry or conflict between finance and procurement, and in many structures the purchasing and supply function has been part of the corporate finance function. The 'bean counters' are not seen as having a creative input to make to the purchasing process in general.

In this session we shall look in some detail at the role for the finance department in measuring supplier performance, and how they can make a very positive input.

'You know, we
accountants
are a much
misunderstood lot.'
Sir Kenneth Cork

Session learning objectives

After completing this session you should be able to:

12.1 Describe the role and input for the finance department in performance management.
12.2 Explain the benefit of undertaking corporate financial appraisal on appropriate suppliers.
12.3 Demonstrate the advantages of specialist third-party versus internal appraisal.
12.4 List specific financial assessment measurement tools, and understand some specific application examples.

12

Unit content coverage

This study session covers the following topics from the official CIPS unit content document:

Learning outcome

Use a range of accounting techniques to measure organisational efficiency.

Learning objective

2.6 Outline how a shared measurement approach will inform a process of continuous improvement, and employ appropriate financial and accounting tools to assess organisational efficiency including:
  • Various financial analyses
  • Use of appropriate ratios – activity ratio, liquidity ratio, working capital – to assess organisational efficiency
  • Identification of supplier fraud.

Prior knowledge

You should have a general understanding of the concept that finance and accounting staff can bring benefit to the measurement of supplier's performance.

You should have read from study sessions 7 to 11.

Resources

You will find a calculator useful.

It will be helpful to be, or to have been, involved in some aspects of financial appraisal of a supplier. If you have not, you may find it useful to discuss this topic with other students or colleagues, or with someone from your finance team.

Timing

You should set aside about 4.25 hours to read and complete this session, including learning activities, self-assessment questions, the suggested further reading (if any) and the revision question.

12.1 The role and input for the finance department

A comprehensive review of a supplier's financial data provides the purchasing manager with good information on where the supplier's organisation has been, and where it is going, in financial and business performance terms. In table 12.1 we can see various aspects of financial and business performance that are of concern in both pre- and post-award performance assessments.

Table 12.1 Role and inputs for finance department

Role	Description	Comment
Accounting measures, including ratio, income statement and balance sheet analysis	From balance sheets and income statements and other sources accountants can calculate: • return on capital employed • margin • asset turnover • liquidity, and many others. (We look at these measures later in this session.) A balance sheet analysis also provides a financial 'snapshot' of assets and liabilities.	Often they can be compared to those of other organisations in the same industry, providing useful performance benchmarks. Particularly useful pre and post award to check the financial strength and profitability of suppliers. Allow an on-going watch on the finances of key suppliers if checked regularly.

(continued on next page)

12

Table 12.1 *(continued)*

Role	Description	Comment
	These all provide a picture of the supplier's current financial condition.	
Audit and fraud prevention	We have already seen in study session 10 the contribution that can be made by audit including: • traditional financial procedures audit • process audit • value for money audit • audit trail.	A helpful range of services from the audit team which is typically a function of the finance department.
Cost control analysis	Has the supplier a history of attempting to reduce costs, and can they demonstrate this on a positive basis?	Particularly useful during pre award assessment to assess prices. It may be hard to obtain this type of data.
Credit rating checks	What is the supplier's credit history and, if poor, is this likely to affect the performance of the contract?	Useful at both pre and post award stages to help indicate the overall ability of the supplier to perform. Can provide an early view of future problems.
General financial support	An accountant can often provide useful support to all aspects of performance management especially when a team approach is involved. Typically they are good data analysts and provide a useful third party view on difficult decisions	Purchasing managers should use their financial support team skills whenever possible.
Review of annual report	Annual reports are produced by all publicly held companies at the end of the financial year. They hold data on many of the above aspects of financial performance	Especially useful at the pre award stage, and contain useful non financial information as well.
Third party financial report	Fee based services from third party suppliers such as Dun & Bradstreet. Their reports provide financial information about the supplier, including credit ratings, turnover, and so on.	A very useful and easily accessed service which finance staff can help interpret.

12

Learning activity 12.1

Consider supplier performance assessment and management in your own purchasing and supply organisation. Write a report (around 1.5 pages of A4) on the input (if any) from finance, accountancy or audit staff to this

(continued on next page)

Learning activity 12.1 *(continued)*

process at present, and how you feel this could be developed. You may wish to talk to a finance manager about this topic.

Feedback on page 206

Although a purchasing manager may be expected to understand these basic financial principles, he will usually call on colleagues for support as and when needed.

Annual reports and accounts should always be thoroughly reviewed. In addition to the core financial statements (profit and loss, cashflow and balance sheet), the explanatory notes should also be scrutinised. They may include a detailed breakdown of turnover by specific activity, changes in management staff, contingent liabilities, financial commitments and post balance sheet events. An analysis of turnover may identify or confirm a supplier's core business, and whether it is over-dependent on a particular customer.

Self-assessment question 12.1

Read this mini case study and provide answers, with comments, to the questions below.

Alan's appraisals

Alan is the procurement manager for a large local authority, reporting to the director of finance. He feels that, like many local authorities, they have paid insufficient attention to measuring the performance of their suppliers, and he would particularly like to improve their assessment of suppliers for a large service outsourcing contract on which he is about to start the planning.

He feels it would be especially useful to develop some financial and analytical skills, but is concerned that the staff in finance will not have the particular skill sets needed to appraise suppliers properly. He has, however, been impressed with the way the audit team have worked in the past, but feels this kind of traditional procedural audit has a very limited part to play in his plans.

In the past he has used D&B reports, and is familiar with annual reports that companies often present to the team, but he is unsure of the contribution they can make. He is a bit reluctant to raise this with the finance director (his boss) in case it exposes his ignorance.

1   Is Alan right that many local authorities are weak on supplier performance measurement?
2   Do service outsourcing contracts require more measurement than product-related contracts?
3   Why would he feel the finance staff may not have the skill sets needed?
4   Is he right to feel the audit role is limited?
5   Is he right to feel wary of revealing too much ignorance in front of his manager?

Feedback on page 207

12

12.2 The benefits of undertaking corporate financial appraisal

Today's business world is a complex place, both nationally and internationally. Although very few suppliers go into a contract knowingly promising things they cannot deliver, the purchasing and supply manager has a responsibility to his organisation to ensure:

- that before awarding a contract he is satisfied that the supplier has the financial resources and stability to perform acceptably for the period of the contract.
- that during the term of a contract he can check that the supplier's financial resources and stability are not affected by the supplier's own actions or other market situations.
- that in the event of the contract being heavily amended the supplier has the financial strength to cope.

Learning activity 12.2

Consider the suppliers with whom you deal regularly. Draw up a list of points that you need to consider when appraising a supplier's financial strength during the term of the contract. You may find it useful to discuss this activity with a member of the finance department.

Feedback on page 207

Corporate financial analysis (or appraisal) is an important tool for ensuring that the three criteria listed above are met, and although the purchasing manager should always retain overall responsibility, the finance department will often take a leading role in carrying out this appraisal.

Issues such as financial standing may have an impact up to the final award of contract, and ultimately even lead to cancellation. The credibility and stability of suppliers can change from month to month as their commitments vary, and, if possible, data and credit ratings from specialist online database providers (see table 12.1) should not be used as a substitute for detailed and ongoing examination of the audited accounts by the contracting team.

This examination should cover the prime bidder, subcontractors (if known), and, if applicable, the ultimate parent company/ies. (In a bid process the **prime bidder** leads the bid, and manages any other involved parties who are essentially subcontractors for the bid.) It should include an analysis of the latest available audited and interim accounts, and any other published information that may have a bearing on the company's financial position or ownership (eg credit facilities, debt rating, current takeover activity, restructuring, new capital investment). The analysis should draw attention to any significant items, including trading results and their trend, cash movements, and balance sheet strengths and weaknesses.

Undertaking such activity is time-consuming, and – as with all procurement tools – it should be applied only where the cost can be justified by the value or importance of the contract or purchase. Care should be taken

12

if doubts exist about a supplier's financial standing, particularly when a large-value, long-duration contract is being let. This can lead to interesting and rewarding discussions with the supplier, who will naturally try to put a positive spin on the published figures.

In the end the purchasing manager must be as confident of a supplier's financial ability to fulfil the contract as he is with other aspects of the supplier's performance.

Warning signals

Good, regular financial appraisal will help to indicate what may happen to a supplier in the future, and can often predict:

- falling profitability
- increasing debtor-days
- increasing debts and creditor-days
- increasing stocks, slower stock turnover
- deteriorating liquidity
- over-reliance on short-term debt
- high gearing
- late production of accounts
- qualified accounts
- changing auditor's and/or banker's name
- cash draining from the business
- major reductions in staffing.

Although poor performance in any of these areas may have a positive explanation, a buyer who has this information is well placed to ask probing questions at the next relevant meeting.

12

Self-assessment question 12.2

Give True or False responses to the following statements.

1 The responsibility for identifying a need for and carrying out financial appraisal usually lies with the finance team. TRUE/FALSE
2 Dun & Bradstreet type analysis can replace a more detailed and time-consuming appraisal. TRUE/FALSE
3 Because much information is public, it will not be difficult to get suppliers to reveal the real financial position. TRUE/FALSE
4 Financial measurements are good indicators of financial problems. TRUE/FALSE
5 Appraisal needs to go beyond the supplier, up as far as parent companies if possible. TRUE/FALSE

Feedback on page 207

12.3 Specialist third-party versus internally led financial appraisal

Although almost all organisations likely to undertake supplier performance measurement will have access to a finance department, there are often good reasons why it is appropriate to use external third-party support for a financial appraisal rather than to do it in-house.

Learning activity 12.3

Consider your organisation's procurement activity. Have you or your colleagues ever used external third parties to undertake financial appraisals or other performance-related activity?

If yes, please describe what it was, and your view of its overall effectiveness.

If no, why is this, and what scope would you see for doing so?

You may find it useful to discuss this activity with your manager or a member of the finance department.

Feedback on page 208

Most of the reasons for using third-party finance support in performance measurement are typical of the reasons why third-party contractors are used in any aspect of management. In a sense this is a typical 'make or buy' decision. Table 12.2 summarises the position. (In the table, the **Private Finance Initiative** refers to a politically driven process that tries to bring private sector skills and capital into the public sector. It is often said to be aimed at increasing efficiency, but critics of the scheme would argue over its long-term financial benefits.)

Table 12.2 Third-party versus internally based financial appraisal

Issue	Comment
Cost	Generally the use of third-party specialists is likely to prove expensive, particularly so in the case of banks or large accounting firms.
	Internal services will be cheaper, or not charged at all, depending on organisational policy.
	The costs of financial appraisal will have to be included in any value for money audit of the overall success of the performance measurement process.
Skills	In smaller companies, or some public sector functions, the internal teams may not have the necessary skills. In any organisation this will be true if financial appraisal has not been undertaken before, or is not undertaken on a regular basis
	On the other hand, if external contractors are used, the internal team will never acquire the skills, and this must be considered at the planning stage, especially if the skills will continue to be needed in the future.
	External firms sometimes change the staff provided from time to time, occasionally reducing the level of skills in the process!
Training	Following from the above, third-party support can be used to increase the competence of the internal resource. For example, initial appraisals

(continued on next page)

Table 12.2 *(continued)*

Issue	Comment
	could be undertaken by third parties supported by internal staff, who would gradually take over as the contract progressed.
Time	Such appraisal can be complex and time-consuming, especially on large contracts. Internal teams may need external support to be able to provide the desired level of support.
Political or procedural	There may be internal or governmental political or procedural constraints that lead to the choice of external third parties. Very often this would be for the provision of all financial services on a contract rather than just for the performance measurement aspects
Size	The size or complexity of the contract or purchase may mean that external third-party support is the only practical way of providing the resources.
Innovation and new methods	For example, the Private Finance Initiative (PFI) schemes in the public sector have introduced some unfamiliar concepts. Such arrangements tend to be intricate, particularly for large projects, and sometimes involve the formation of a separate company, a special-purpose vehicle, as the entity to deliver the required service.
	Usually the contracting authority will need specialist financial expertise to vet the PFI financing structure proposed by the bidders, and to undertake the necessary financial, sensitivity and risk analyses.
	It is advisable, at the start of the proposal process, to appoint financial advisers who have experience in the quantitative evaluation of complex contract pricing and funding structures.
Impartiality	Third parties may be used if the in-house operation is felt to be unable to be impartial in its evaluation. For example, if a major service is being outsourced or moved overseas the financial team might be biased in favour of the internal 'supplier'.
Conflict of interest	The reverse of the above happens when the contracting manager needs to ensure that there is no conflict of interest between the provider of advice to the buying organisation and the provider of advice or funding to the supplier.
	In this case an in-house operation may have the advantage of total independence.
Geography or location	Internal finance teams can appraise overseas or distant suppliers, but using a third party in the supplier's location will help that ensure local knowledge is applied and will minimise travel and logistical issues.

Clearly there is no right or wrong answer to the question of whether financial appraisal should be undertaken in-house of placed with a third party.

However, it can reasonably be assumed that third-party providers will be more expensive, and it should also be noted that not all third-party contractors will be capable of providing the required quality of advice. The problem is knowing which contractor can, and this type of sourcing may require a performance management system of its own.

Self-assessment question 12.3

Answer the following multiple-choice questions:

1   Generally speaking a third-party contractor will be:
    A more competent
    B more expensive
    C more acceptable to the supplier
    D more focused on results.
2   A conflict of interest can happen because:
    A the in-house finance team favours the buyer's organisation
    B an external third party is working for another buyer in the same market
    C the in-house finance team favours the supplier
    D an external third party is working both for the buyer and for the supplier.
3   Innovative purchasing causes problems because:
    A an in-house team may not have the skills
    B a third-party team may not have the skills
    C the type of analysis needed is new
    D there are no procedures to cover it.
4   Are the following statements true or false?
    I Third-party contractors cannot train internal finance staff.
    II Internal finance staff cannot deal with overseas suppliers.
    A I and II
    B II
    C I
    D Neither

Feedback on page 208

12

12.4 Financial appraisal measurement tools

There are many useful financial tools, but ratio analysis is probably the single most important technique of financial analysis. However, a ratio is unlikely to provide any useful information about a company in isolation; it must be used as a means of comparison. This can be done by comparing the trend of a ratio for a particular company over time or with the corresponding figure for other companies, particularly those in the same sector.

Ratios can be considered in two groups when appraising a supplier's ability to perform:

Performance ratios. These give an indication of how well the business is being run.

Financial status ratios. These indicate the financial position of the company; of them, liquidity ratios measure the ability of the company to meet its short-term liabilities.

Note also that not all organisations use exactly the same methodology for financial calculations (though the principles are the same). Check with your finance team if you have any doubts.

Performance ratios

Figure 12.1 shows three of the most important measures. Each of the following example calculations uses the following figures: sales of £300m, an operating profit of £60m, and capital employed of £80m.

Figure 12.1: Performance ratios

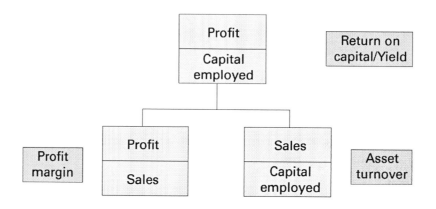

Return on capital employed

Return on capital employed (ROCE) is expressed as a percentage (figure 12.2). Capital employed is best defined as fixed assets plus stocks and trade debtors less trade creditors, ie the net operating assets in the business. This enables the ratio to measure the operating performance of the management.

Figure 12.2: Return on capital employed (ROCE)

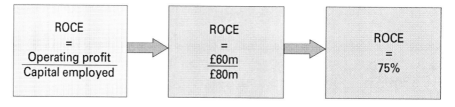

Profit margin on sales

Profit margin on sales (margin) is expressed as a percentage (figure 12.3). This gives the profit that is earned as a proportion of sales. Thus, if the margin is 10%, 10 pence of each £1 of sales represents profit. The margin will vary from sector to sector. A manufacturing company might have a margin of 10%, whereas a food retailer's margin would be more like 5–8%. Service sector companies' margins may be higher.

The margin can be improved either by putting up selling prices or by reducing costs.

Figure 12.3: Profit margin on sales

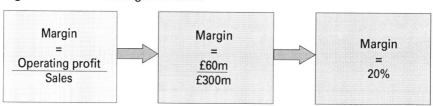

Asset turnover

This ratio shows the level of sales that a company can generate from a given level of capital employed (figure 12.4). Capital-intensive industries (eg heavy engineering) will tend to have low figures for asset turnover. The asset turnover can be improved either by generating a higher level of sales from a given asset base or by disposing of assets that are not productive.

Figure 12.4: Asset turnover

Financial status ratios

Figure 12.5 shows two of the most important measures. Each of the following example calculations uses the following figures: current assets £8m, stock £4m and current liabilities at £4m.

Figure 12.5: Financial status ratios

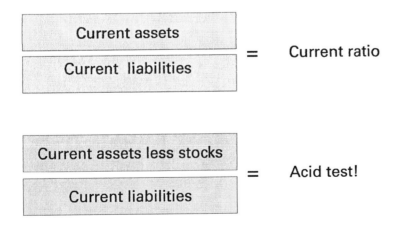

12

Current ratio

This ratio (figure 12.6) indicates the extent to which short-term assets are adequate to settle short-term liabilities. However, a current ratio of less than 1.0 does not necessarily mean that a company has liquidity problems, nor does a current ratio of more than 1.0 mean that a company does not.

This is because liquidity is essentially concerned with future cashflows, whereas the current ratio considers the position at a given moment in time.

Figure 12.6: Current ratio

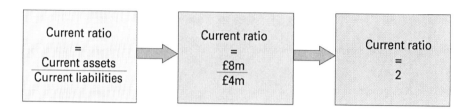

However, despite this limitation, the current ratio can still be a useful indicator, particularly when there is a sharp deterioration in the liquidity position.

It should be noted that whereas too low a current ratio may be worrying on the grounds of liquidity, too high a current ratio may be worrying on the grounds of profitability. Funds invested in working capital could be earning a return if invested elsewhere.

Acid test (or quick) ratio

The idea behind this ratio (figure 12.7) is similar to the current ratio. However, in this case the stock figure is excluded from the funds available to meet current liabilities, on the grounds that stock may take several months to turn into cash.

Figure 12.7: Acid test (or quick) ratio

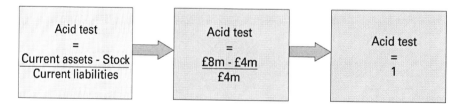

It is important to remember that these ratios represent the picture only at a moment in time. They need to be explored in more detail to find out what is behind them, and finance department staff should be able to help with this. It will also be helpful to record them over time, because a trend is often more informative than a snapshot.

Learning activity 12.4

Study the sample balance sheet and profit and loss statement in figure 12.8.

(continued on next page)

Learning activity 12.4 (continued)

Figure 12.8

Balance sheet ABC Ltd	Year 2002	Year 2003	Year 2004
Fixed assets			
Property	400	845	1,325
Plant and equipment	1,200	1,350	2,250
Current assets			
Stock	1,000	1,050	1,450
Debtors	1,400	1,300	1,850
Cash	50	250	0
Total	4,050	4,795	6,875
Current liabilities			
Creditors	1,100	1,400	1,600
Tax owing	270	250	230
Dividends owing	100	120	60
Profits distributed to shareholders in proportion to shares held in the business			
Long-term liabilities			
Long-term loans	400	500	1,100
Share capital (money invested by shareholders)	800	1,000	1,300
Reserves (balance on profit and loss a/c)	1,380	1,525	1,685
Total	4,050	4,795	6,875

Profit and loss statement	2002	2003	2004
Sales (turnover)	6,100	6,500	6,750
Cost of sales (cost of production)	5,400	5,850	6,025
Gross profit (turnover – cost of sales)	700	650	725
Selling, distribution and administration expenses	60	75	95
Operating profit (before interest and taxation)	640	575	630
Interest payable	45	68	76
Taxation payable	270	250	230
Profit after interest and taxation	325	257	324
Dividends	125	112	164
Reserves (retained profit for the year)	200	145	160

Calculate the following ratios:

1   return on capital employed (ROCE)
2   profit margin
3   asset turnover
4   current ratio
5   acid or quick ratio.

Feedback on page 208

Now go on to tackle the following self-assessment question.

Self-assessment question 12.4

Using the information from learning activity 12.4 above, answer the following questions.

1   The return on capital employed has gone down significantly. Why do you think this is?
2   The operating profit in 2004 is only slightly less than in 2002, but the margin is down by 1.2%. Why do you think this is?
3   Sales turnover has increased from 2002 to 2004, and so has stock. Studying these figures, what observation could you make?
4   Sum up your views of this business, and the immediate actions you could take.

Feedback on page 208

Revision question

Now try the revision question for this session on page 336.

Summary

In this session we have looked at the important role that financial appraisal plays within the overall supplier measurement framework, and we have considered the advantages and disadvantages of outsourcing this activity. We have then worked on some practical examples to show how financial appraisal can help us see problems arising for our suppliers.

In study session 13 we shall look at some other aspects of supplier performance measurement.

Suggested further reading

Students seeking more information on external financial inputs can check out Dun and Bradstreet report analysis in Lysons and Farrington (2006), chapter 11, page 376 or visit their website at http://www.dnb.com.

A wide range of other useful information on financial services can be obtained by searching for 'financial services' through your web browser.

Feedback on learning activities and self-assessment questions

Feedback on learning activity 12.1

There is no specific feedback. Your report should have picked up some of the points covered in the main text, and you should ensure you comment on the appropriateness of the level of input you identified.

Feedback on self-assessment question 12.1

1   Yes, this is generally true: much local government procurement (and other public procurement) has tended to be short- to medium-term and tender-driven. However, this weakness is increasingly being recognised.
2   Not necessarily; it is the overall balance of risk and benefit to the organisation that matters most. However, most large outsourced service contracts will generally benefit from good pre- and post-award supplier measurement, which is not always true for product-based contracts.
3   Local authority finance staff have many skills, but are likely to have spent less time on this type of activity than many private sector colleagues (see also question 1).
4   No. Audit does not need to be limited to procedural matters, and Alan may gain from open discussion with the audit team on possible roles and inputs.
5   No. In general terms an open admission of weakness accompanied by a proactive proposal for remedying this will not seem a show of weakness, given a normal management relationship. Also, it is better to acknowledge this now, rather than once planning is under way.

Feedback on learning activity 12.2

There is no specific answer, but you may have some of the following:

- Poor financial standing may lead to cancellation.
- Financial standing can change from month to month.
- Dunn & Bradstreet type analysis is not a substitute for detailed checks.
- Appraisal should cover the prime bidder, subcontractors and parent company/ies.
- Appraisal should always include the latest available audited information.
- Appraisal activity is time-consuming.
- Care should be taken if doubts exist about a supplier's financial standing.
- Financial ability is as important as any other aspect of performance.
- Early warning signals can be spotted.
- Poor performance may have a positive explanation.
- Appraisal keeps a buyer well informed and in charge.

Feedback on self-assessment question 12.2

1   FALSE. The purchasing manager should always retain overall responsibility.
2   FALSE. This type of analysis is useful for a 'quick picture', but cannot replace a more detailed appraisal.
3   FALSE. Suppliers are likely to be reluctant to confirm poor financial performance: hence the need for the team to have an accountant with a real skill in interpreting financial data.
4   FALSE. They are pointers to possible problems, and there may always be good explanations for the figures.
5   TRUE. This should happen unless there is insufficient time or risk involved.

12

Feedback on learning activity 12.3

There is no specific answer. Whether your response is yes or no, some of the issues that may have been considered could include:

- the cost of external support
- lack of internal skills or training
- lack of time
- political requirements
- size, scale or complexity of the transaction
- the wish to gain impartiality
- the need to avoid conflict of interest.

Feedback on self-assessment question 12.3

1 B
2 D
3 C
4 D

Feedback on learning activity 12.4

Based on the information in this study session, your answers should look like figure 12.9.

Figure 12.9: Answer to learning activity 12d

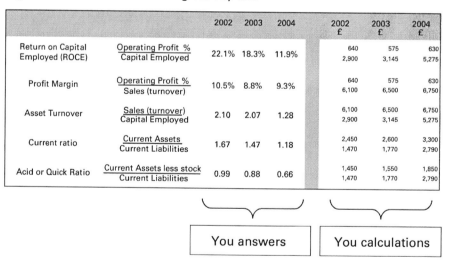

		2002	2003	2004	2002 £	2003 £	2004 £
Return on Capital Employed (ROCE)	Operating Profit % / Capital Employed	22.1%	18.3%	11.9%	640 / 2,900	575 / 3,145	630 / 5,275
Profit Margin	Operating Profit % / Sales (turnover)	10.5%	8.8%	9.3%	640 / 6,100	575 / 6,500	630 / 6,750
Asset Turnover	Sales (turnover) / Capital Employed	2.10	2.07	1.28	6,100 / 2,900	6,500 / 3,145	6,750 / 5,275
Current ratio	Current Assets / Current Liabilities	1.67	1.47	1.18	2,450 / 1,470	2,600 / 1,770	3,300 / 2,790
Acid or Quick Ratio	Current Assets less stock / Current Liabilities	0.99	0.88	0.66	1,450 / 1,470	1,550 / 1,770	1,850 / 2,790

You answers   You calculations

Feedback on self-assessment question 12.4

1 Essentially the operating profit in 2004 is the same as 2002 (£630 to £640), but the capital employed to achieve it has nearly doubled (£5,275 from £2,900). We can see that much of this is plant and equipment (which might be good for the future, but is not helping short term). You need to find out why when you meet this supplier.

2 The margin is down because sales are up, by around 10.1% (at £6,750), but the profit on these sales is slightly lower (£630) than in 2002: hence the margin is falling. You could ask how the supplier feels about this when you meet.

12

3   Sales turnover is up by 10.1%, but stock is up by 45% (at £1,450). This seems a large increase, and you will want to ask why this is when you meet the supplier.

4   On the face of it, you have cause for concern, because the company has clearly acquired significant extra assets in property equipment and stocks but these are not yet helping it, and margins are falling although sales are growing. In fact the trend on each ratio is downwards.

5   The problem for you is that if sales grow and margins fall the company could eventually go out of business. You need to:
   •   Discuss the position in depth with the company.
   •   Watch the position carefully.
   •   Prepare a contingency plan if this is a key supplier.

12

Study session 13
Other performance measures

Introduction

So far we have concentrated on the main activities of supplier measurement, and the important role for financial appraisal. If you really want to do a better job then you will need to consider the wider picture. In this session we shall look at some other aspects of performance management, the benefits of joint performance measurement, and benchmarking.

If you do things well, do them better – be daring, be first, be different, be just!
Anita Roddick – Body Shop International

Session learning objectives

After completing this session you should be able to:

13.1 Describe the internal and external commercial relationships found in most organisations.
13.2 Propose other areas for measurement activity.
13.3 Describe the potential for joint performance measurement initiatives.
13.4 Explain supplier surveys and benchmarking.

Unit content coverage

This study session covers the following topics from the official CIPS unit content document:

Learning outcome

Categorise types of performance measures that are available to supply chain managers.

Learning objective

2.8 Discuss possible measures relating to a supplier's R&D development, cultural adaptation or such similar qualitative performance
• Compare conformance to international/recognised industry standards or benchmarks.

Prior knowledge

You should have read study sessions 7 to 11.

13

Resources

It will be helpful to be, or to have been involved in, some aspects of benchmarking and other performance measurement activities.

Timing

You should set aside about 4.25 hours to read and complete this session, including learning activities, self-assessment questions, the suggested further reading (if any) and the revision question.

13.1 Internal and external commercial relationships

In study session 7 we looked at relationships, and at the development of partnerships between buying and supplying organisations. Before anything resembling a partnership can exist, good relationships must be developed both inside the buying organisation and between the buying organisation and the supplier.

Learning activity 13.1

In terms of your own purchasing department, can you identify any examples of relationships in which the supplier and the end user are closer than (from a procurement point of view) you might wish?

Write a short report (1 side of A4) explaining the problem, stating why it is affecting relationships and how this might be resolved.

Feedback on page 223

Often, at least at start-up, these good relationships do not exist. In fact it is surprising how often relationships, especially internal relationships, are a problem. Figure 13.1 shows how this might look in many organisations.

Figure 13.1: Typical commercial relationships

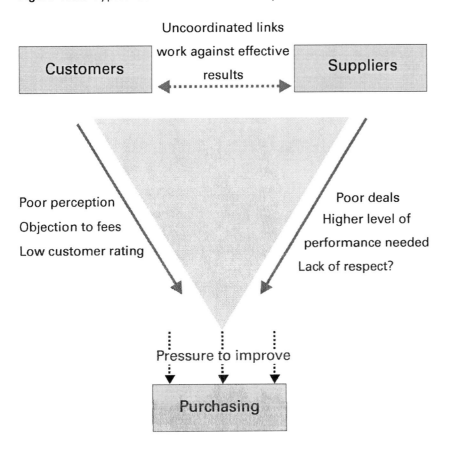

In this model the customers and the suppliers are in regular contact, which may include commercial issues, and there is little control exercised. Suppliers offer poor deals because purchasing has little effectiveness, and customers also have a low opinion of the service offered to them. The pressure is on purchasing and not on the supplier, and this is a problem in many organisations.

An example of this can be found in the NHS, where traditionally medical suppliers keep very close to medical staff, making it difficult for buyers to negotiate good deals.

Figure 13.2 shows how the relationships need to work if the buying organisation is to get the best from the relationship.

Figure 13.2: Relationships for effective buying

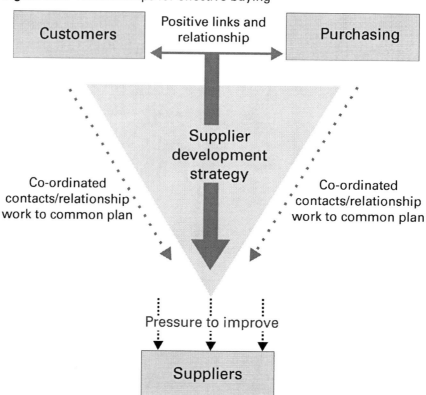

The customers and the purchasing team have managed to form a positive relationship, and develop a coordinated approach to dealing with the supplier. There is a development strategy for managing the relationship with the supplier, and the pressure is on the supplier to perform.

It will not always be easy to achieve this, but this type of relationship is essential if effective performance measurement is to work.

Note also that, although a relationship will often be focused on the purchasing team and the end user, other departments will be involved from time to time, and need to be integrated into the relationship management strategy:

- Senior management: contact through occasional meetings, trade associations, exhibitions and functions.
- Research and development: contact if joint development is taking place.
- Finance: contact through invoicing and payment plus financial appraisal.
- Health and safety: contact through any specific problems that may arise.
- Marketing: contact through any joint product or service development.
- Production: contact through any production problems or development sessions.

Self-assessment question 13.1

Answer the following multiple-choice questions:

1   In many organisations the closest relationships exist between:

(continued on next page)

13

Self-assessment question 13.1 *(continued)*

A purchasing and the supplier

B purchasing and the end user

C the supplier and the end user

D the supplier and the payments section.

2   In regard to contact with a supplier, purchasing will try to:

I keep contact to the minimum.

II develop a coordinated approach to dealing with the supplier.

Which of the above statements is true?

A I and II

B II

C I

D Neither

3   Generally speaking, the senior management role in relationship-building will be:

A solving problems

B promotion and development

C mediation or arbitration

D taking meetings.

4   Suppliers often like to deal direct with customers because:

A purchasing has set the deal up that way

B it saves time for sales staff

C customers' technical knowledge is better

D purchasing is not involved.

Feedback on page 223

13.2 Other areas of measurement activity

There are several aspects of a supplier's business that can be evaluated, especially if the contract to be awarded is large, complex or high risk for the buyer.

13

Learning activity 13.2

Draw up a checklist of the main aspects of a supplier's business that you feel you might need to measure at some stage in a comprehensive contract award and management process. Give a brief description of each header.

Feedback on page 223

Much of the focus in this section so far has been on the measurement of the basic services or products provided, and on the financial strength and stability of the supplier. However, the following are also important aspects of the supplier's business that are worth measuring on higher-risk projects.

The supplier's organisation and management

- General information: Who are they and what do you know about the company and its managers? The annual report can be helpful here, as can Dun & Bradstreet. How long has the management been in post?

Supplier account management techniques (see study session 14) can be useful here.

- History: What do you know about the company and its trading record with you and other customers? Is it known for any bad practice or unethical activities, or do other customers or suppliers constantly rate it badly?
- Future plans: Where are they going as a business, and how does this fit in with your expectations and business plans?
- What level of investment has been made in plant and equipment and is it in good condition?
- The level of training and academic background of individuals. Are they signed up to schemes such as 'Investors in People' (see study session 15)?
- Many companies these days contract out services and sub-assemblies. Is the product or service you require supplied by a subcontractor, and if so do you need to know more about how this process works and might affect your contract?
- Where does the company stand on public issues such as environmental policies, support to the community, health and safety, and so on?

The supplier's employees

- Skills and training provided: Many jobs now need higher-level skills and the supplier may well be able to show training plans and targets. Look also for evidence such as 'Investors in People' or the existence of a training needs analysis. (See study session 18.)
- Trade unions: Are employees represented by a union, or do they address their concerns directly to management? What is the public state of management and employee relationships, and is there a history of strikes?
- Employee turnover: What is the turnover rate among management and employees? High turnovers may indicate skill shortages or bad industrial relationships.
- Is there evidence of good morale? Look for evidence of pride and support for the company and try to talk to some employees. What is the state of 'housekeeping' on the site?

The purchasing and supply team may be supported by management, human resources and production staff when measuring some of these activities.

It is also important to note that some aspects, such as employee welfare and ethics, can require a different emphasis if dealing with overseas or multinational suppliers, or if your own organisation requires certain standards to be met, eg achieving certain environmental standards, or avoiding 'sweatshop' labour.

Self-assessment question 13.2

Give True or False responses to the following statements.

1   The use of subcontractors by a supplier is not the concern of the buyer.
    TRUE/FALSE

(continued on next page)

Self-assessment question 13.2 *(continued)*

2 High levels of management stability, and length of employment with the organisation, indicate a supplier who will do the job well. TRUE/FALSE

3 In the UK, strikes are now not so much of a problem as turnover and skills shortages. TRUE/FALSE

4 There can be a significant difference in the behaviour of multinational companies in different countries. TRUE/FALSE

5 A small team from purchasing and supply will be able to appraise all these factors as well as is necessary. TRUE/FALSE

Feedback on page 224

13.3 Joint performance measurement initiatives

We have seen from study session 7 that there is scope for joint benefit from performance measurement when the supplier considers that the buyer's organisation is important to its future plans. This can lead to the development of joint performance measurement.

Learning activity 13.3

Describe some 'win–win' opportunities for the buyer and the seller that can arise from the effective use of performance measurement indicators. Have you any examples of these occurring in practice?

You may wish to discuss this with your line manager.

Feedback on page 224

13

Table 13.1 Benefits of joint performance measurement

Buyer and supplier

Improved solutions to operational difficulties:

- delivery schedules
- lead times
- invoicing and payments
- expediting
- basic customer service
- better operational communications

Buyer	**Supplier**
Elimination of 'waste' at the interface between the buyer and supplier	Market advantage, and reduced selling effort

(continued on next page)

Table 13.1 *(continued)*

Improved quality with positive supplier input	Improved technological capability and product development
Unnecessary cost can be 'designed' out of products	Can be more innovative in what it offers
Improved security of supply	Improved and secured payment arrangements
An increase in purchasing contribution to the profitability of the organisation on a continuous basis	Improved financial stability and security
Cycle time reduction in product development	Opportunities to improve and refocus management capability
Ability to concentrate on supplier management, not sourcing and award	Ability to plan resources over the longer period

Joint performance initiatives are expensive to both parties because of the commitment and resources that are necessary to make them work, and continuous improvement should be seen as the basis of the relationship. This is not possible without a review process for assessing performance.

Until recently, such processes have been restricted to the assessment of the supplier's performance but there is an increasing move to '360 degree' assessment in which the two parties assess each other. In this way obstructions that were caused by either party to the performance of the relationship can be identified and mutually resolved.

Generally, a shared measurement approach is a type of partnership, and is based on:

- shared mutual objectives and compatible benefits for both parties
- agreed problem-solving methods
- shared risks according to who can best manage them
- an active search for continuous measurable improvements
- a way of managing the relationship proactively.

Joint performance measurement impinges on design, manufacturing, logistics and other functions as well as on the commercial aspects traditionally of interest to the buyer. However, cross-functional teams are usually needed to inject specialist expertise into the process, and at the start of the relationship both the buyer and supplier organisations will form teams. As the relationship develops it is possible that the two teams may merge, creating 'cross-functional, cross-organisational' teams, as shown in figure 13.3.

13

Figure 13.3: Cross-functional, cross-organisational teams

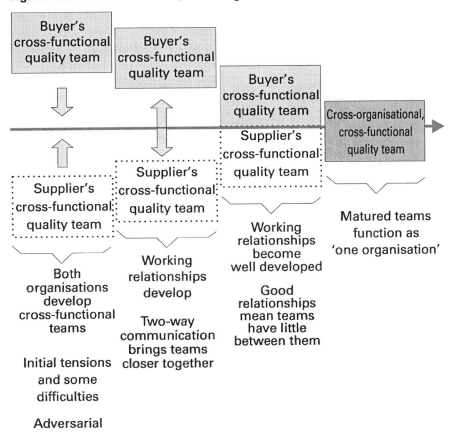

These teams have the task of analysing performance data, identifying the causes and effect of problems, and implementing solutions.

For example, the performance measurement data may show that the supplier is not meeting delivery targets. The cross-functional team examines the data, and finds that the late delivery is the effect of poor planning and scheduling by a buyer (the root cause of the problem). In traditional supplier measurement the 'blame' would lie inside the buyer's organisation. However, with cross-organisational cooperation one potential solution may be for the supplier to cross-transfer one of his production schedulers on either a temporary or permanent basis to help 'coach' the buying organisation until the problem is removed.

Self-assessment question 13.3

Read the following mini case study.

Flora's Flowers

Flora's nurseries supply flowers to a large florist chain, whose lead buyer has proposed the creation of a joint performance measurement action team, as part of a new five-year deal. The buyers already operate a vendor rating system, which has been running for some years, and internally Flora's have set up a cross-functional team that has effectively dealt with some of the problems weeded out by this system, working quite closely with the buyer.

(continued on next page)

13

Self-assessment question 13.3 *(continued)*

Flora's sales director John and his team have come to recognise that being measured has sharpened up their business in several ways, and John feels they have gained from the process (he thinks that the buyers probably suspect this is his view). He also feels there will be significant benefits from the joint approach, especially in reduced sales effort, financial stability and long-term planning.

His new MD Shirley is less sure, however, and thinks the joint team will struggle to stay equal with the buyers, who will use this as an opportunity to simply pressure Flora's for better service and prices.

Based on what you have read in this session please provide at least four single-paragraph comments on the above scenario.

Feedback on page 224

13.4 Benchmarking and supplier surveys

Benchmarking

Although measurement of our supplier's performance is always useful, we have already said that the data then needs to be put in a context before we can start to make effective judgements. At the most basic level we test the result against the standard or target we require, and the result will indicate whether or not we have compliance. This is a good start, but it leaves two important questions unresolved:

- What is happening to the measured performance? Is it improving, or getting worse over time?
- How good is our standard? Are we aiming too high or too low?

The process by which we try to establish the answers to these questions is called 'benchmarking'.

Learning activity 13.4

Study your organisation in its entirety. Can you identify three areas of activity in which benchmarking regularly occurs? What are they, why are they chosen, and how effective is the process, in your view?

For this activity, only one of the above should be procurement related.

You may wish to discuss this with your line manager.

Feedback on page 225

A benchmark is a measurement which can be used as a point of reference when comparing an aspect of business or personal performance. Typically the comparison is either with competitors or the 'best in class' (or relevant field of business) and the results highlight opportunities for improvement by showing where the purchaser is and where he or she could be in the future.

Virtually all aspects of an organisation's performance can be benchmarked, such as financial management, manpower statistics, operational performance, use of technology and so on. The technique is equally useful in the public and the private sector, though in the public sector it is sometimes used as a 'blunt' tool for such issues as council tax levels or hospital bed occupancy.

In this session we are concerned only with supplier performance management, and we would look to benchmark aspects of the supplier's performance, which might typically include:

- price and especially cost breakdown
- quality and quality control processes
- day to day performance and service delivery
- administration and overheads
- supply chain management
- employee performance standards.

As many of these are aspects of the supplier's business that we wish to assess as part of our performance management, it will be obvious that the ability to compare the results with the performance of other suppliers is essential if good decisions are to be made.

It is also important to note that the key issue with benchmarking is not obtaining the information, but understanding why the different performances are occurring.

For example, you have established that (on a like-for-like basis) a major competitor awards a contract at an average period of 12 weeks from notification of requirement to contract award. Your average is 16 weeks. However, this data is of little use. What you must find out is how this is achieved, and it is the investigation that will identify actions you may be able to take.

There are, however, some problems with benchmarking that you should be aware of, and table 13.2 provides a summary.

Table 13.2 Problems with benchmarking

Problem	Description
One snapshot compared with another	Unless the benchmarking is done well, comparisons are just snapshots and are less useful: your company may be doing badly and they may be doing well at the time of the exercise.
Resource heavy	Benchmarking is time-consuming if done properly, and should not be started without adequate resources. This includes the obtaining and processing of the information.
Be careful when benchmarking prices	There are many factors, such as volume and marketing, that can distort price differences unrealistically.
'Apples for apples'	Comparisons are undertaken for products or services that are not to the same specification: eg our printer paper is 100gsm, theirs is 80gsm.
Choose the benchmark with care	'Best in class' may not be the best benchmark to aim for: • The differences may be too fundamental. • The pursuit may be too expensive. • The process may be too demoralising.

(continued on next page)

13

Table 13.2 *(continued)*

Problem	Description
Getting the information	It may be necessary to benchmark to organisations with whom data can be shared, or about whom data is easily acquired.

Supplier surveys

We have talked above about joint performance measurement initiatives and the benefits they offer to both parties. One benefit that some companies offer to their suppliers is the opportunity to participate in occasional supplier surveys.

There is no particular form for these and the content will depend on what is to be achieved. Typically the issues covered relate to the ease of doing business with the company, how the buyers are seen to be performing, and whether payment processes are working effectively.

The buying organisation must however be prepared to accept criticism and suggestion for change. If it is not then the survey will have no effect, and future surveys will not be supported by the suppliers.

Surveys can be made anonymous, to avoid any suggestion of trying to please the customer, and they can also be undertaken through a third party if total impartiality is required. They can take many forms, ranging from telephone polls to formal visits and interviews, with questionnaires being a common approach.

Many organisations have been initially surprised by the negative feedback received from suppliers: some do not really care. However, it is worth bearing in mind that an organisation needs to be a world-class customer in order to obtain world-class suppliers.

13

Self-assessment question 13.4

Write a paragraph (3–5 lines) of critical comment on each of the following statements:

1 Benchmarking is not really relevant in my business.
2 Now the data tells us what can be achieved, we are halfway there.
3 We are pleased, because our supplier's performance has improved steadily from when we took the benchmark.
4 You have to be very careful to compare the right things to get meaningful benchmark data, especially on complex issues.
5 The problem with supplier surveys is that they always say what they think we want to hear.

Feedback on page 225

Revision question

Now try the revision question for this session on page 337.

Summary

In this session we have looked in detail at the quality of relationships, some other important areas for measurement of supplier performance, the scope for joint performance measurement, and the details of benchmarking.

Each of these can be helpful in taking the quality of our purchasing performance measurement to another level, and in study session 14 we shall have a brief look at the more sophisticated concepts of supplier development and supplier account management.

Feedback on learning activities and self-assessment questions

Feedback on learning activity 13.1

There is no one right answer. Depending on the organisation, such problems develop because:

- Procurement doesn't have a good reputation.
- Customer and supplier share technical knowledge.
- Procurement are 'just following the rules'.
- Suppliers are trying to 'divide and conquer'.

Depending on the organisation, solutions include:

- improving buyers' skills
- improving technical knowledge among buyers
- promoting procurement as an added value process
- pushing the rules and procedures
- managing and understanding relationships better.

Feedback on self-assessment question 13.1

1 C
2 B
3 B
4 D

Feedback on learning activity 13.2

Your list might include:

- Ability to perform: suppliers who appear to be good candidates on paper may actually have old facilities in disrepair, outdated technology, or an overall inability to meet a purchaser's needs.
- Financial status: a comprehensive review of the supplier's financial data provides the purchasing manager with good information on where the organisation has been, and where it is going.
- Cost systems: measurement systems designed to track an organisation's costs.

- Quality assurance, quality control, and related systems: close examination is critical, because purchasing is responsible for ensuring the quality of supplies and services.
- Organisation and management: close examination of top management commitment and involvement, stability, training and certification.
- Workforce: close examination of labour relations, morale skills and unionisation.
- Housekeeping: housekeeping is an indicator of discipline and pride in the workplace.
- Process/material flow: efficient process and material flow are required to keep a supplier competitive.

Feedback on self-assessment question 13.2

- FALSE. The buyer needs to ensure that audits of subcontractors are made by the supplier to ensure that standards are met.
- FALSE. Management stability and length of employment are factors to be looked at in the supplier's management structure, but do not in themselves offer a guarantee of performance.
- TRUE. High turnover and skills shortages are major problems for some companies, and need careful appraisal by buyers.
- TRUE. Consistent standards are not always applied by multinational companies, and are often driven by in-country legislation as much as by ethical concerns.
- FALSE. Done properly, such appraisal will need support from across other functions.

Feedback on learning activity 13.3

Table 13.1 shows some of the most common benefits, but your list may well contain others.

Don't forget to provide examples if possible.

Feedback on self-assessment question 13.3

Your comments could include the following:

- The buyer's scheme appears to be working well, and the sales team can see progress and don't appear to feel threatened. This could be a good basis for going ahead, provided there is no obvious change of attitude coming from the buyers.
- The setting up of the internal team has also worked well, and the fact that it already has positive links with the buyers argues for a joint set-up.
- The benefits that John can see are all possible advantages of a joint approach, which is in effect a partnership style of doing business.
- The MD's view is probably affected by being new in post. There is a natural suspicion inherent in buyer–seller relationships, which is often overcome only by involvement. Shirley needs to be prepared to discuss the issue with the team, and to look at the results to date.
- Where Shirley does have a point is in terms of the ownership of the joint team, and it would be reasonable to discuss the protocols around

13

this team, such as how it works, where it meets, and who is in the chair before finally agreeing.

Feedback on learning activity 13.4

There is no specific feedback. Your non-procurement examples should be significant to the organisation. Your procurement example is likely to include one of the following:

- quality
- operational performance
- value
- costs
- service
- processes
- labour and training
- technological innovation.

Feedback on self-assessment question 13.4

Your comment could look like this:

1 I think you're wrong. Benchmarking is widely used in many industries and across most sectors of business and management activity. As it basically consists of comparing your performance with a known better performer, it is unlikely that it is not relevant to any business. Even a known good performer will wish to check they are not slipping backwards!

2 Getting your data right is an important first step, but it is really only a beginning. The main task is to critically analyse why the results are different and what actions can be taken. If there is a halfway point it might be after the action plan is developed but before implementation starts!

3 You are right to be pleased, because this is clearly a step in the right direction. However, the problem is that benchmarking should provide both start-point position and a target position so you know how far you have come *and* how far you have to go.

4 You are right. It is essential to ensure that like-for-like comparisons are made. Even on simple exercises such as price comparisons slight variations in specification can distort the results. On complex issues such as buyer productivity many factors need to be carefully checked before results can be used.

5 This can happen if the buying organisation has not planned the survey properly. It is unlikely that this will happen where purchasing really own the project and genuinely wish to improve.

13

13

Supplier development and supplier account management

Introduction

In study sessions 7 to 13 we have discussed the benefits of supplier performance measurement, and have demonstrated that, properly managed, it can be a very powerful tool for purchasing and supply management. We have also seen how it can help facilitate partnerships, or at least move relationships towards more of a 'partnership' style. However, not all relationships suit this style, and not all organisations wish to have partnership-type relationships.

To boldly go where no buyer has gone before.
adapted from *Star Trek*

Session learning objectives

After completing this session you should be able to:

14.1 Develop and control suppliers in a more positive way.
14.2 Demonstrate the value of being able to identify key suppliers.
14.3 Define supplier development.
14.4 Define and understand supplier account management.

Unit content coverage

This study session covers the following topics from the official CIPS unit content document:

Learning outcome

- Categorise types of performance measures that are available to supply chain managers.
- Discuss the benefits of implementing a well structured approach to measuring organisational, functional and individual performance.

Learning objectives

2.5 Discuss the importance of close and frequent buyer–supplier communication and of its importance within supply contracts.
   - Demand–supply chain relationships
   - Inter-organisational partnering and long-term commitment
2.7 Discuss the use of performance measurement as a tool for supplier relationship development.
   - Measurement as a motivating factor for both parties
   - Mutual opportunities to create understanding to improve performance
   - Positive approach to relationship-building and continuous improvement
   - Identification of weaknesses and problems

14

Prior knowledge

You should have read and have a good comprehension of the preceding study sessions and general management principles.

Resources

It will be helpful to be, or to have been involved in, some aspects of supplier development, and in more positive ways of managing suppliers. You may wish to talk to other colleagues on the issues in this study session.

Timing

You should set aside about 5.25 hours to read and complete this session, including learning activities, self-assessment questions, the suggested further reading (if any) and the revision question.

14.1 Developing and controlling suppliers in a more positive way

'To partner, or not to partner; that is the question.'

Learning activity 14.1

Complete a Pareto analysis of your suppliers by spend value and identify the top five. In each case consider the nature of your relationship with the supplier, and the main customer, using table 14.1.

Rate the supplier relationship from 1 = well managed to 10 = badly managed.

Rate the customer relationship from 1 = well managed to 10 = badly managed.

Table 14.1

Supplier	Value of business	Supplier relationship type	Customer relationship quality
1			
2			
3			
4			
5			
Total			

What is your judgement on the result?

Feedback on page 238

While it is generally the case that there will be benefits from measuring the performance of suppliers, it does not follow that a partnership or cooperative approach will necessarily be the desired relationship in all cases. There are a number of reasons for this:

- Either the buying or the selling organisation may prefer a more adversarial style as part of its organisational culture.

14

- Either the individual buyer or the seller may favour a different approach. This is not uncommon, and many buyers and sellers see themselves in a 'game', where they are on opposite sides.
- Relationship styles (as with many aspects of business management) go through phases when they are in or out of fashion.
- Organisational policies work against true long-term partnerships. For example, public sector tendering requirements are often seen like this as contracts are renewed to timescales, and good performance is no guarantee of repeat business. (This does not mean that a partnership *style* cannot be achieved.)
- Geographical and market issues may influence the way the relationship develops.
- The size of the organisations may work against a partnership approach. For example, a large company may need to source a critical part from a small or medium-sized enterprise (SME), or vice versa.
- The nature of the relationship may be a problem. There may be some 'rogue' buyers or sellers who just cannot work together, even in a supportive environment.

Each organisation will develop its own approach, which may be summed up as shown in figure 14.1.

Figure 14.1: Relationship styles

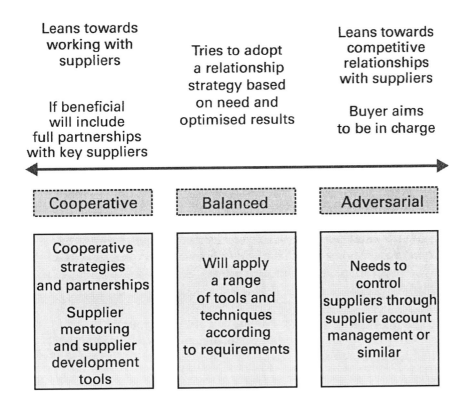

No matter what the chosen style of relationship, most buying organisations will wish to handle supplier relationships in a more positive way, and depending on the approach chosen there are other tools that can be used, including supplier mentoring, supplier development and supplier account management. These will be discussed later in this session. (The term **supplier relationships** refers to the range of relationships with suppliers, but with the implication of a more structured and organised approach.)

Whichever style or approach is chosen, good performance measurement needs to be part of the process, and the tools referred to are intended to complement not replace good performance measurement techniques.

Sometimes formal supplier measurement, appraisal or rating systems cannot be implemented. Buyers must recognise that it is still essential to have a method of monitoring progress and establishing targets and timescales. For each supplier there should be an agreed series of milestones, and progress against these milestones can then be reviewed on a regular basis and, if necessary, revised targets agreed. In this way, both parties have the reward of progress over time.

To provide an added incentive for the supplier, award schemes may be used or extra business may be offered. However, care must be taken to ensure that this is done in an open and transparent way.

Self-assessment question 14.1

Based on your analysis in learning activity 14.1 above, prepare a draft report (300–400 words) to explain why you wish to manage your top five suppliers more closely.

Feedback on page 239

14.2 The need to identify key suppliers

We have seen that cooperation is not necessarily the best approach in every situation, and that in some buying situations a more adversarial relationship might be more appropriate. Also, from a practical point of view purchasing resources are usually scarce and need to be allocated to where they can have the most benefit, and developing partnerships takes time. In this more balanced approach, how can the buyer decide what type of relationship to aim for with each supplier and, in particular, how can the key suppliers be identified?

In many organisations simple techniques will often identify the key, strategic or important suppliers, and no further sophistication may be needed. These may include:

- value of spend
- problems in a relationship (continued poor service)
- commodity issues (eg the price of a raw material such as copper)
- buyers' professional and business knowledge
- political or organisational sensitivity (eg potential environmental hazards)
- clear business exposure to risk from supply failure.

In other organisations buyers may wish to augment such knowledge with a more systematic approach, and in study session 9 we looked briefly at this concept using a 'four box' matrix (P. Kraljic). It will now be helpful to revisit this idea in more depth, because it provides a very useful model for breaking down the supplier base. Figure 14.2 shows the traditional model.

Figure 14.2: Traditional four-box matrix

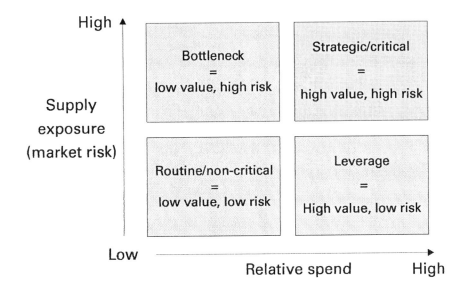

In purchasing, the term **product portfolio** denotes the range of goods or services purchased by the buyer; by implication it leans towards a commodity base rather than a customer base approach. The concept of the four-box matrix has been in circulation for around 30 years. You use it to classify your product portfolio within the four boxes, according to a balance of spend and risk:

- Critical/strategic items: high cost and therefore profit impact and supply risk to your business if supply fails. Any suppliers supplying these products must be highly competent, and purchasing resources can be concentrated here.
- Bottleneck items: little cost and profit impact, but failure could be disruptive. For example, cheap parts for a conveyor system could stop production. This high criticality or risk justifies some investment of time in supplier measurement and proactive management.
- Leverage items: you spend a lot on these but there is little supply risk, and so as a buyer you have the upper hand. Performance data is less important because supplier substitution is easier, and you can be much more adversarial if you choose.
- Routine/non-critical items: buy as you like, with little need for effort. Often these items can be delegated to users to acquire.

14

Learning activity 14.2

Take the top five suppliers identified in learning activity 14.1 above. Using the four box matrix (figure 14.2), categorise each of the five suppliers,

(continued on next page)

231

Learning activity 14.2 *(continued)*

and comment on the result, bearing in mind the report you wrote in self-assessment question 14.1 above.

Feedback on page 239

When using this model you are starting with the intrinsic qualities of the products you buy, not the suppliers you buy them from. The model acts as a basis for further consideration of the supply base available to you, and it is quite possible that a supplier may fall into two boxes. For example, the supplier could be supplying a critical production component and a routine spare. The buyer then makes a further choice:

- Determine the supplier as 'critical', dealing with all products supplied by the company.
- Continue with the product as 'critical', concentrating only on this item from this supplier.

As with all models of this kind you can design variations to suit your specific requirements: it is the principle of classifying the products (and hence the suppliers) in a consistent and structured way that is particularly useful.

Self-assessment question 14.2

Give True or False responses to the following statements.

1 In Kraljic's model critical/strategic items are those that have little supply risk but which are critical to keeping your business going. TRUE/FALSE
2 In many purchasing organisations shortage of resources means difficult decisions need to be taken when considering relationship development. TRUE/FALSE
3 You don't need complex models to know which are the key suppliers. TRUE/FALSE
4 Kraljic's model is based on product analysis. TRUE/FALSE
5 This type of model works only if you apply it exactly as written. TRUE/FALSE

Feedback on page 239

14.3 About supplier development

Imagine that you are dealing with a supplier and your performance measurement system indicates that the supplier is not performing well. If your general style for handling suppliers is adversarial, and if the market allows, you may move towards termination of the supplier.

If, on the other hand, your style is more cooperative (or if there are few suppliers), you may decide that it would be worth putting effort into helping the supplier to improve. More rarely it may be the case that you have a limited number of suppliers in a certain market and would like to encourage some new suppliers.

This is often known as supplier development or sometimes supplier mentoring.

Learning activity 14.3

Consider your suppliers and identify five suppliers who are not performing well. Using the template below, indicate whether you feel that your company could help these suppliers to perform better, and what support would be needed.

Supplier	Problem	How we could help
1		
2		
3		
4		
5		

Feedback on page 239

Supplier development means the provision of help to a supplier. There are no limits on what this might be, but it typically includes:

- Advice – on any issue that might help the relationship, such as quality or customer service.
- Finance – to help with capital purchases or even on occasions in time of hardship.
- Technology – large companies may provide access to their technology to help smaller or less competent suppliers.
- Personnel – key personnel may be loaned to the supplier for assistance, for example loaning engineers to give technical assistance with a manufacturing problem.
- Procurement – large buyers may help add 'muscle' to smaller companies' purchasing power.
- Supply chain benefits – allowing the supplier to access your supply chain for a particular purpose.

This is generally to enable the supplier to offer a product or service that better meets the buyer's needs, or to interface with the buying organisation in a mutually appropriate way. Suppliers are often selected for development as a result of supplier assessment or vendor rating. The use of supplier development is determined by supplier strategy, and will generally be targeted at those suppliers categorised as being of strategic importance. Where several suppliers are strategically important to an organisation, supplier development programmes may be used.

14

Supplier development is a practical series of steps, based on developing more effective relationships, designed to get the best out of a supplier. You should note that:

- Supplier development is normally undertaken with existing suppliers who can be (and agree to being) improved. This agreement is important, and is a key characteristic of supplier development schemes.
- Supplier development depends on good communication. Suppliers will tend to view any client initiatives as just another means of exploitation – driving down the buyer's costs at the expense of the seller's profits. The key starting point, therefore, is to have a clear set of objectives, which are agreed internally. This should then form the basis of explaining and selling the concept to the supplier. The supplier needs to participate as a 'willing partner'.
- Supplier development is a good way in which larger companies can bring on SMEs that they feel have future potential, and this can help create competition and stimulate innovation.
- Before the programme starts, the supplier's performance must be measured against the agreed criteria in order to 'benchmark' the scope for development. This also allows the monitoring and measurement of improvement over time.
- Supplier development teams will generally be multifunctional, so that they can look at all aspects of any particular process or initiative. The aim is to identify areas where improvements can be made on a joint basis.
- Supplier development is not impossible in the public sector, but is often limited to advice or personnel rather than financial support, except on rare occasions.
- Even in a supplier development programme it is essential that the development should be bespoke to each supplier, and targeted at their particular needs.
- Supplier development in this context should not be confused with diversity and other such programmes, which aim to help small and ethnically owned businesses, by ensuring a more level playing field for business, and which may have grant support attached.

14

Self-assessment question 14.3

Write a paragraph (3–5 lines) of critical comment on each of the following statements.

1   We have a supplier development programme that supplies loan equipment and technical training to all suppliers on the programme.
2   I don't believe in helping suppliers – we have enough problems already!
3   Most of our problems with suppliers seem to be with administrative issues such as specifications, orders and invoicing problems. Supplier development won't help here.
4   I have a feeling that a team approach would be useful here!
5   Supplier X is a real problem and I think needs developing!

Feedback on page 240

14.4 About supplier account management

You will have seen that supplier development works in a cooperative type of business relationship. Supplier account management, on the other hand, recognises and prospers in a more adversarial type of relationship.

Many procurement departments are at a disadvantage relative to suppliers' sales departments in terms of the amount of resource available, and the level of training received. As a result the supplier often 'manages' the relationship better, and often has undue influence on the user (see internal and external commercial relationships in study session 13).

Supplier account management is a sophisticated technique that aims to reverse this relationship, placing the buyer much more firmly in charge of the relationship. As with all such techniques it should be applied only where the time and effort required are likely to have a positive result, and is likely to be applied only to carefully selected suppliers.

A complicating factor is that some suppliers provide a range of products through various buyers to different end users. How this is to be handled will require some internal discussion, perhaps with one buyer taking the lead and a number of users being in the team.

As with supplier development, before the programme starts the supplier's performance must be measured against the agreed criteria in order to 'benchmark' the scope for development and allow the monitoring and measurement of improvement over time. However, unlike supplier development, cooperation is not essential, and indeed there may be some supplier resistance.

For the rest of this session we shall discuss a simple model of account management that most organisations could apply. Simplistically there are three stages:

1 Fully understand the supplier, your own business requirements of the supplier and the current state of business and relationships. This may sound simple but can be quite difficult to achieve, especially in large, complex businesses.
2 Develop a strategy for dealing with the supplier and building the internal relationships to implement this strategy. This will usually require a team approach, but can be very difficult to achieve, especially where internal relationships are poor. The internal relationship-building is needed to answer the question 'What do we want from this supplier and how do we get there?'
3 Design an action plan and implement the strategy, measuring progress over time, and having regular reviews within the internal team to take the necessary corrective action.

Once the strategy is working well the buying side may, if they wish, try to build the supplier into the arrangement, thus moving away from the adversarial approach to some extent.

Supplier account management requires significant time and resources to carry through well, though this will reduce as the principles become part of

14

your organisation's standard way of working. It will often take a long time to get a result, and patience and some continuity of personnel will be useful.

Supplier account management requires data, and table 14.4 shows some minimum requirements. You can see that many of the techniques and tools mentioned in these study sessions form part of this schedule.

Table 14.4 Supplier account management

The current relationship

Activity	Description
Supplier background	• Basic supplier information: name, contacts, etc • Annual reports and other documents • Details on supplier's management (study session 13) • Overview of products/services supplied • Supplier's other major customers • Recent major news items of note • Main customer units served
Financial and commercial status	Current financial performance indicators *with your analysis* (study session 12) Current and forecast value of business transacted Value of your business to the supplier
Contract information	• Details of current contracts with supplier, including number, dates, type and products/services covered • Any special contractual commitments • Details of any non-contract supply (leakage, out of scope, etc) • Details of actual spend against contracts • Trend data relating to spend
Performance information (study session 10)	• The supplier's current performance • Benchmark information • Price/cost information • Have you any information on customer satisfaction in regard to this supplier? • If you have customer satisfaction data, what is the trend?
Account analysis	• SWOT and PESTLE on the supplier and the relationship (study sessions 9 and 11) • Supplier classification (this study session) • Reverse positioning – how the supplier sees the business (study session 7) • Details of supplier's account/sales management style

The future relationship

Activity	Description
Future relationship objectives	• What benefits are sought • Target relationships internal and external • New performance targets including specific price/cost targets • Any changes required to the supply chain.

14

(continued on next page)

Table 14.4 *(continued)*

	• Supplier conditioning – our special ways of working we need the supplier to comply with • SWOT analysis of the attractiveness to supplier of your business *after* you have implemented your proposed changes • Details of roles and responsibilities within the 'virtual team' managing the relationship with the supplier
Management points	Administrative details of all scheduled meetings, reviews, etc Communication plan that details of all scheduled communications, reports, contact points, news flows Escalation plan for disputes (study session 11)
Action plan	1 2 3 4 5 6 7 8 9 10

Management executive summary

Analysis summary, conclusions and recommendations with regard to supplier management approach based on above information

Learning activity 14.4

Note: This activity utilises table 14.4. It will take some time to complete.

Take a supplier with whom you would like to prepare a draft account plan and on whom you feel you already have a fair amount of knowledge. Study the draft checklist in table 14.4 and amend it to cover anything you feel is missing.

Work through the checklist, acquiring the data you require, and taking a view on each header. You can do this individually, but may find working with a colleague useful. You may wish to open a file for this information.

Go as far as completing the action plan.

Feedback on page 240

Now go on to tackle the following self-assessment question.

Self-assessment question 14.4

Using the work you did in learning activity 14.4 above write the management executive summary and recommendations for the chosen supplier (300–400 words).

Feedback on page 240

Revision question

Now try the revision question for this session on page 337.

Summary

In this session we have looked mainly at how data used to measure purchasing performance can also be used in more unusual forms of supplier management, and in building up an extensive picture of a supplier to allow for supplier account management techniques to be developed.

This ends our work on measuring the performance of the supplier. We shall now begin to consider measuring the performance of another key player – you, the buyer!

Suggested further reading

Details of Pareto analysis (also known as ABC analysis or the 80:20 rule) can be found in Lysons and Farrington (2006), chapter 10, page 319.

Details of Kraljic's 'four box' matrix can be found in Lysons and Farrington (2006), chapter 2, page 64.

Feedback on learning activities and self-assessment questions

Feedback on learning activity 14.1

Your chart could look like the example in table 14.2.

Table 14.2

Supplier	Value of business	Supplier relationship type	Customer relationship quality
1	£3m	7	6
2	£2.7m	4	2
3	£2.1m	5	5
4	£1.6m	10	5
5	£1.2m	8	7
Total	£10.6m	34/50	25/50

For our top five suppliers I judge that we are generally operating with badly managed relationships, and that of supplier 4 is particularly poor. Our customer relationships are slightly better managed than those with our suppliers. I feel that for our organisation some repositioning of supplier relationships towards better managed would be beneficial.

Feedback on self-assessment question 14.1

There is no specific answer. Your report may include issues such as

- better relationships with customers
- better service, quality and prices
- earlier supplier involvement
- less interference by supplier's sales force
- placing the buyer in charge.

Feedback on learning activity 14.2

Your response may look like this example (as these are your top five by value, they will be either critical/strategic or leverage items):

- Supplier 1: Critical
- Supplier 2: Leverage
- Supplier 3: Leverage
- Supplier 4: Critical
- Supplier 5: Leverage.

Having done this analysis I feel we should not worry about suppliers 2, 3 and 5 but concentrate on suppliers 1 and 4, both of which scored as badly managed on both supplier and customer relationships.

Feedback on self-assessment question 14.2

1 FALSE. This describes 'bottleneck' items.
2 TRUE. We must concentrate resources to get maximum benefits.
3 TRUE. Many buyers will know this easily. However, in some organisations portfolios are large and harder to manage. Also, new buyers may find this technique useful.
4 TRUE. This model starts by looking at the product and then considers the supplier.
5 FALSE. You can modify the model to suit; the main thing is to apply it consistently.

Feedback on learning activity 14.3

Your chart could look like the examples in table 14.3.

Table 14.3

Supplier	Problem	How we could help
Supplier example 1	Performs well, but never understands our need for on-time deliveries.	Provide training on how we work – exchange personnel for short periods.
Supplier example 2	Is a very willing performer, but struggles to hit quality because of outdated equipment it cannot afford to replace.	Consider financing equipment, or purchasing and loaning/hiring.

(continued on next page)

Table 14.3 *(continued)*

Supplier	Problem	How we could help
		Loan surplus plant from own operations
3	Etc	Etc
4	Etc	Etc
5	Etc	Etc

Feedback on self-assessment question 14.3

Your responses could be as follows:

1   Be careful, as your programme may be too prescriptive. Each supplier may have different needs, and the programme needs to respond with what is needed, not just determine a requirement for loan equipment and technical training.
2   Fair enough – but helping the supplier could be the easiest way of solving *your* problem, because supplier development is not done for the supplier's benefit but because it helps the supplier to offer a product or service that better meets the buyer's needs.
3   You may not appreciate it, but much supplier development is about helping to get administrative systems working better. This often includes exchange of personnel and 'training' schemes to improve contacts.
4   You are absolutely right. A cross-functional team approach (see study session 13) is most likely to be the way forward, unless the supplier's problems can clearly be related to one aspect of business performance.
5   Simply being a 'problem' is not a development issue; there has to be an identified underlying problem. Also, the supplier has to agree to be 'developed', and this may not happen if relationships are not right.

Feedback on learning activity 14.4

You should end up with a file of information on the supplier, and a series of judgements such as the SWOT analyses.

- Are any gaps in the data critical pieces of information you really should know about the supplier?
- Compare your future objectives with the current position. Are you being realistic?
- Look at your action plan – is it achievable?

Remember: this is only an exercise, but the information can be very useful in a real situation.

Feedback on self-assessment question 14.4

Your summary should explain how you propose to improve the management of this supplier. Your report could include:

- background and overview
- summary of current position

- outline of desired changes
- proposed actions to achieve this.

14

Why measure buyers' performance?

Introduction

This may seem a trite question, but if we do not perform, why are we here at all? We therefore need to **manage and measure the performance** of the purchasing and supply department. The importance that is attached to this will often reflect the profile that purchasing has within the organisation.

Performance management of purchasing and supply staff is *not* just about staff appraisal, although this may be a part of it. Performance management looks at all aspects of the purchasing and supply function.

Performance management should:

- include any measurement processes
- be continuous rather than scheduled
- focus on the business objectives and the 'bottom-line' performance
- be owned by everyone, rather than an end in itself
- not be driven by process or paperwork
- include inputs from **stakeholders** other than the manager and employee – all those people or bodies with an interest or 'stake' in the issue of buyer or supplier performance
- be something that employees want to be part of.

> 'In business, words are words; explanations are explanations, promises are promises, but only performance is reality.'
> **Harold S Geneen**

Session learning objectives

After completing this session you should be able to:

15.1 Describe the benefits to the buyer of good performance management.
15.2 Summarise the aims of measuring buyer performance for the organisation.
15.3 Distinguish between periodic, ongoing and annual measurement options.
15.4 Explain the links to reward and advancement.
15.5 Summarise problems with poorly managed measurement schemes.
15.6 Explain the wider national view and structured approaches such as Investors in People.

Unit content coverage

This study session covers the following topics from the official CIPS unit content document:

Learning outcome

- Discuss the benefits of implementing a well-structured approach to measuring organisational, functional and individual performance.

15

Learning objective

3.1 Discuss the benefits of a well-managed and structured approach to measuring an individual's performance including:
  - Investors in people guidelines and structure
  - Performance against target assessments
  - Planning for improvements>
3.4 Discuss and demonstrate how an individual's knowledge, expertise and skills can be developed to the benefit of both that individual and the organisation.
  - Individual benefits: level of responsibility, job satisfaction, career progression, skills development
  - Organisational benefits: better-trained workforce
  - Improved productivity and profitability
  - Competitive advantages>

Prior knowledge

No specific knowledge is required for this session. However, if you are already subject to a personal measurement system you may find some aspects of this session easier.

Resources

No specific resources are required. However, there is much general research information available on the internet, which you can use to support the recommended textbooks and learning materials.

Timing

You should set aside about 5.5 hours to read and complete this session, including learning activities, self-assessment questions, the suggested further reading (if any) and the revision question.

15.1 Performance management and the buyer

Organisations should be continuously helping to develop their employees' skills and knowledge. Clearly, this benefits both the individual employees and the organisation as a whole, but it requires a structured and well-managed approach that ensures that individuals:

- Have the skills and knowledge that they need to do the job, and to develop their full potential.
- Can improve their contribution to the organisation.
- Can participate more fully in the organisation, and understand the overall aims and business strategies better.
- Are motivated, and that their morale is high.

15

Feedback on page 254

Learning activity 15.1

Reflect on any personal experience of performance measurement that you have had. How effective do you feel it has been? What benefits has it provided for you and for your organisation?

Let's look at these four areas in more detail.

Improved skills and knowledge

A prime objective of the performance management process is to help employees improve their performance, particularly by developing useful skills and gaining relevant and up-to-date knowledge. This can be a continuous process, if say a manager interacts regularly with the employee, acting as a coach and mentor; or it may come from employee requests, or as output from a formal **appraisal** system. Appraisal is a systematic approach to checking aspects of performance, usually used for suppliers and employees. The term is often interchangeable with 'evaluation'.

A **training needs analysis** (TNA) can be of benefit here by providing a better view of the employee's learning needs. This is a systematic analysis undertaken to establish the training needs of staff in relation to the needs of the organisation. (See study session 18.)

The skills and knowledge acquired will benefit the employee in all future employments, but they must bring benefit to the organisation as well.

Making a better contribution

Well-skilled and developed employees can make a better contribution to the activities of the organisation activity, and they should therefore find their work more involving and enjoyable. Remember also that the employer is investing time and money in performance management, and will require a return on this investment. This may be measured in various ways (see below).

Having a better view of overall aims and business strategy

In many organisations employees complain that 'they never tell us what is going on', and that communication is poor. A good performance management system requires regular dialogue between staff and managers. It normally includes objectives and targets, which should be derived ('cascaded') from company business plans and objectives. We describe this cascade process more fully in study session 16.

Improved motivation and morale

Low morale among buyers is likely to lead to poor day-to-day performance, lack of interest in the job, and higher staff turnover. This in turn will mean that procurement targets are not achieved, expertise is lost, and recruitment costs increase.

There are many reasons for poor morale in an organisation, but a regular, well-managed performance and appraisal system should provide a positive improvement in morale.

Of course, some buyers might take a narrower view, and consider the main benefit of performance measurement to be merely the rewards that may be linked to it. This is understandable, but buyers who see this as the only benefit have failed to understand the wider aims and objectives of such measurement.

Self-assessment question 15.1

Give True or False responses to the following statements on the benefits of performance management for the buyer:

1   Bonus payments or rewards may be considered as a wider benefit of performance management for buyers. TRUE/FALSE
2   Internal communications should be directly improved as a result of a well-managed employee measurement system. TRUE/FALSE
3   Almost any training and development that an employee wants will help to benefit the organisation. TRUE/FALSE
4   The employing organisation will be looking for a measurable return on its investment in measuring and appraising employees. TRUE/FALSE
5   Individual departments should set their own targets and objectives derived from departmental plans. TRUE/FALSE

Feedback on page 254

15.2 Performance management and the organisation

An organisation will invest time and resources in a good performance management and measurement system. It will have various aims in introducing such a system.

Learning activity 15.2

Reflect on your organisation's aims for buyer performance management. You may need input from your line manager or HR department. What does the organisation see as the benefits?

Feedback on page 254

Improving employee performance

A performance management and appraisal system is designed to increase employees' performance in the long term. It does this by measuring performance against objectives and targets, and by providing the skills and training that employees need to support any areas of weakness.

For buyers this should eventually result in better prices, deals or contracts for the organisation, improved quality and service, and a bottom-line improvement. This is often difficult to measure directly, and improvements in the perception and profile of the purchasing and supply function within the organisation will be equally important.

Better communication and feedback

Most organisations recognise that there can be benefits from improving communication, especially around the business-planning process. Also, good 'honest' appraisals can provide valuable feedback to management on how the organisation is felt to be performing.

With good processes for setting objectives, regular appraisals and good feedback, an organisation can receive excellent input from staff on improvements to the systems and processes with which they are involved. This input can be taken into account when corporate and departmental plans are reviewed.

Gaining information

The system produces information about the employee, the manager, and the organisation. This can help in developing the employee, the team, and the recruitment process.

For example, appraisal might reveal a weakness in negotiation skills. This would lead to successful training across the team, spin off into other parts of the business, and become a key part of the job profile for future recruitment.

Procedural or legal requirements

An effective performance management system must be professionally sound, and should enable managers to ensure the organisation complies with all relevant legislation and organisational policies.

For example, a good appraisal system might help identify issues such as harassment or prejudice, so that appropriate action can be taken.

A structured approach ensures that personnel-related decisions (such as promotion or termination) can be supported if they are subsequently subject to legal challenge.

15

Self-assessment question 15.2

From the above material, arrange a list of benefits in the best order for your organisation, and explain why you have chosen this order.

Feedback on page 254

15.3 Periodic, ongoing and annual measurement

In any performance management system, the frequency of measurement and review is important.

A good process requires effective communication between employee and manager all year round, and it will suffer if this is not the case. The employee and the manager must both feel comfortable with the system. If they have little regular contact, the process will be less effective.

The manager's key appraisal tasks are to observe and identify performance that has occurred, and communicate those observations to the employee. The manager should also look for feedback and make suggestions for improvement.

The employee's key appraisal tasks are to accept assessments that are fair, and defend himself or herself against assessments that are not. He or she should also provide sensible feedback, and consider the suggestions made. There can be a degree of negotiation in such reviews, especially if financial rewards are involved.

Learning activity 15.3

Consider any appraisal or measurement systems that apply to your own job. What frequency is used? Is this effective? If not, what frequency would be best?

Feedback on page 254

Typically, we find three different frequencies:

- Ongoing. In an ongoing process there is regular contact on performance and appraisal matters throughout the year. Often this contact is informal. There may be milestone meetings as well, especially if quantitative data has to be produced and considered. This approach may be particularly useful in fast-moving businesses, or in smaller organisations where contact is easy to arrange.
- Periodic. This usually involves a series of scheduled appraisal interviews, typically either quarterly or half-yearly, for which both manager and employee prepare. This is helpful if external sources need to prepare data or statistics as it provides a series of target dates. Quarterly meetings are better if manager/employee contact is less frequent.
- Annual. Managers who view the process as only a once-a-year activity lose significant opportunities for performance improvement. Annual interviews, even with a manager with whom the employee has regular contact, can be uncomfortable and hard to handle. Also, it is harder to change objectives and apply corrective actions if you only meet once every 12 months.

Self-assessment question 15.3

List the advantages and disadvantages of each of the approaches described above.

Feedback on page 255

15.4 The links with reward and advancement

In many organisations, performance and appraisal information helps to determine career paths for individuals and identify talent. Often it is also linked to salary or bonus payments.

Learning activity 15.4

Reflect on your organisation's policy or process in relation to linking appraisal to reward and advancement. Does it bring benefit to the business, and increase employee motivation? If not, why not? (Your HR department or line manager may be able to help you.)

Feedback on page 255

Developing talent

Appraisal can allow employees (especially those comfortable in such situations) to 'advertise' themselves within the organisation. They can be monitored, given special training or extra objectives, or even **fast tracked** according to organisational policy. (Fast tracking is scheduling a supplier or employee for advancement or development faster than the norm.)

Their performance in a more demanding role can also be monitored closely, and in a formal system the results can be seen by managers elsewhere in the organisation (if this is allowed by confidentiality rules).

Care should be taken to ensure that the talent is genuine; the ability to perform well in an appraisal is not the only test for a good buyer.

Improved motivation

When good rewards follow from a fair and respected system there should be increased morale, greater effort, and more ideas and innovation.

Financial reward

Financial rewards significantly sharpen employees' perception of the measurement and appraisal process. There are different types of reward. They can be:

- Manager's discretion. The manager has full authority to reward as he or she sees fit. This is a powerful role for the manager, and it can easily be abused unless there is some type of rigorous checking system.
- Next increment. Performance to a certain level automatically moves the person to a new salary point.
- Organised bonus schemes (performance-related pay or similar). These are schemes devised by the organisation and based around the performance measurement process. There are usually have limits on the

15

249

size of the payments, and there may be opt-out clauses for staff who do not wish to participate, especially in the public sector.

The danger is that employees may see financial rewards as the key reason for a performance appraisal. Managers should ensure that this aspect does not predominate, or the other benefits of performance measurement will be lost.

Self-assessment question 15.4

Give True or False responses to the following statements:

1 Although many staff might disagree, reward or promotion are not the key reasons for performance appraisal. TRUE/FALSE
2 The performance appraisal process provides good opportunities for employees to be identified for promotion or development. TRUE/FALSE
3 Next increment reward schemes are no longer common because organisations do not wish to pay financial rewards. TRUE/FALSE
4 The power that a manager has in a system where rewards are at the manager's discretion is not a problem. TRUE/FALSE
5 Appraisal interviews give all staff an equal opportunity to present themselves for consideration for reward or advancement. TRUE/FALSE

Feedback on page 255

15.5 Problems with poorly managed measurement schemes

Measurement and appraisal requires the interaction of several different individuals and systems to work effectively. As you might expect, there are plenty of opportunities for problems to occur.

Learning activity 15.5

Reflect on performance management in your organisation. Can you see any problems with the way it is managed? How do these affect the credibility of the system?

Feedback on page 256

Some of the most common difficulties are as follows:

- 'We have an appraisal system because we feel ought to.' To work effectively, measurement and appraisal must be owned by the management and given real priority within the organisation. Without this they fall into disrepute. For example, if a manager is called to a meeting when he has an appraisal organised, the appraisal must be given priority.

- There is too much pressure and slippage. Managers and employees have full diaries, and it is easy for four meetings a year to slip. If an appraisal has to be cancelled, it should be immediately be rescheduled. Failure to hold meetings is always a sign that the system isn't being taken seriously.
- There are changing targets and priorities. Fast-moving organisations often need to change targets and objectives. This must be allowed for, but it can make results hard to judge. It is important not to arrive at a yearly interview to discuss performance and targets against objectives that are no longer high priority.
- There is a lack of confidentiality. Information is often quickly available to all; staff often tell each other how they 'got on'. Management must assume that information will leak out; fairness and equality are essential.
- 'You're not listening.' Managers don't listen to feedback from review sessions. This is self-defeating, and employees gradually lose confidence in the system and provide less input as time goes on.
- There is a lack of good information. This can be a problem for both management and employees, and if the appraisal process requires data that is unavailable there may be disagreement over what has actually been achieved.
- There is a failure to review and update. The measurement and appraisal process has been operational for a long time, but has not itself been 'reappraised'. Employees easily spot this, and the process becomes discredited.
- There is a lack of training and practice. Often, training takes place when a scheme is introduced, but is not then continued to cover new staff and managers. Personal measurement can be difficult, and many people are uncomfortable in such situations. Training can help. So too can regular participation and attendance, which acts as practice, and significantly improves contributions.

Self-assessment question 15.5

Mini case study with questions: Jack's dilemma

Jack works for the purchasing department in a large local authority. The authority has operated a performance measurement system for several years, linked to some well-understood and fair performance targets. Good performance is recorded on an employee's record and used in interviews for promotions, but staff sometimes share these comments, which they often find interesting. The measurement system has always been quite strong on qualitative data, but the authority shows little sign of improving the level of quantitative input.

The authority wishes to introduce a financial reward for achieving savings targets. Jack has no problem with the principle of this, but he does have some concerns, because of what he sees as weaknesses in the current system.

1   From the information given, what might be Jack's main area for concern given the need to link rewards to savings made?
2   From the information given, what could be his second concern now that financial rewards are involved?

(continued on next page)

15

Self-assessment question 15.5 *(continued)*

3   In this scenario, does it seem sensible for the authority to consider this
     type of target?
4   What might be done to ensure that the scheme continues to work well?

Feedback on page 256

15.6 The wider view, and Investors in People

Increasing the measurement of performance in the workplace is seen
as part of the wider educational and development framework for the
country at large; it is not just an organisational tool for improving in-house
performance. It is argued that a well-measured and developed workforce
will ultimately benefit everyone, and should be supported both by both
individual organisations and by a national initiative.

In the UK, the basic components of a structured approach are set out in
the national standard **Investors in People**, a national scheme that aims to
provide a 'kitemark' of excellence in training.

Learning activity 15.6

Disappointment for Jill

Jill has just started working in a company that proudly displays an Investors
in People plaque in the reception area. This was one of the things that drew
her to this company, but she has found that her colleagues and managers are
not concerned with training and development, and that few plans have been
drawn up for training.

Identify some key issues that you would expect Jill to see in a company that
has achieved this standard. (You may wish talk to your line manager or HR
department, or look on the internet for companies with IIP policies.)

Feedback on page 256

The Investors in People standard is a benchmark of excellence in training,
based loosely on the total quality management model. It comprises the
following elements:

- Commitment from senior management to develop all employees to
  achieve business objectives. Organisations need written flexible plans
  that set out business objectives, how employees will help the business
  meet its objectives, and how their personal and development needs will
  be assessed and met.
- Regular senior management review of the training and development
  needs of all employees.
- Action to train and develop individuals, not only when they are
  recruited bur throughout their employment;

15

- Set out in the organisation's business plan a mechanism for continuous evaluation of the effectiveness of the investment in training, to assess and improve its future effect.

These are good management practices and disciplines in their own right, irrespective of whether the organisation goes on to achieve formal recognition in the form of the IIP standard or a similar standard of quality.

Self-assessment question 15.6

Write a short memorandum on the importance (or otherwise) of a national framework of performance management for the nation, the organisation and the individual.

Feedback on page 256

Summary

We have looked at the reasons why we should consider measuring buyers' performance, and we can now identify the following key issues:

- Measuring performance is part of the wider process of managing performance.
- Benefits should accrue both to the employee and to the employer.
- There can be differences in the frequencies with which measurement is undertaken, and these can have significant implications for effectiveness.
- Reward and advancement are common outcomes of performance measurement, but they need careful management to be effective
- Performance management can also be said to have a wider benefit to the economy as a whole, by steadily increasing the skills and competence of the workforce.

Suggested further reading

For study sessions 15 to 19 students will find that chapter 8 of Neely et al (2002) provides a useful view of performance measurement from the perspective of employees as stakeholders. Students should also look at Lysons and Farrington (2006), chapter 17 for brief information on employee-related issues especially:

17.2 Management by objectives

17.8 Miscellaneous approaches to measuring purchasing performance

17.11 Ethical codes and training.

For this session in particular students can find useful information on the Investors in People initiative at their website http://www.investorsinpeople.co.uk.

15

Feedback on learning activities and self-assessment questions

Feedback on learning activity 15.1

You should reflect any experiences you have had to date, asking yourself:

- What did you gain?
- What was learned or improved?
- Did you feel more or less motivated after the involvement?
- What did the organisation gain?
- Were there any benefits or failures in communication or participation?

Feedback on self-assessment question 15.1

1 FALSE. Rewards are a narrow way of considering the benefits of performance measurement.
2 TRUE. This is one of the key benefits of a well-managed scheme.
3 FALSE. The skills and knowledge must bring benefit to the organisation as well as to the employee.
4 TRUE. Ultimately, the organisation has to improve performance for all stakeholders, not just employees.
5 FALSE. Objectives and targets should be derived from company business plans and objectives.

Feedback on learning activity 15.2

You should be able to identify why your organisation operates a buyers' performance measurement system, and what its *main* reason is for doing so. The reasons might include:

- improved employee and business performance
- better communication and feedback
- better information
- compliance with procedural or legal requirements
- more employee benefits
- benefits specific to your organisation.

Feedback on self-assessment question 15.2

There is no one right answer. Your list should include most of the above points, plus others that you feel are relevant. In general, you should include improved business performance towards the top of your list.

Feedback on learning activity 15.3

You should examine the approach used for any appraisal or measurement that you are involved in. Does it:

- Happen all the time?
- Happen to a schedule?
- Happen only once a year?

15

Do you feel this is the best frequency? Explain why, or, if not, why a different frequency would be better.

Feedback on self-assessment question 15.3

Your answer might include some or all of the following:

Ongoing

- Advantages: regular contact, less formality, better relationships, fast and adaptable.
- Disadvantages: time input, lack of milestones, difficult in some organisations.

Periodic

Advantages: allows coordinated inputs, more structured; formality may mean it is taken more seriously.

Disadvantages: generally more difficult to manage; relationships are more difficult.

Annual

- Advantages: less time input.
- Disadvantages: formal, lack of relationship, hard to change or develop objectives.

Feedback on learning activity 15.4

You should be able to look at your own organisation and identify whether there is a direct link between measurement of buyers' performance and the rewards they receive. You could have identified:

Pros

- identifying talented staff
- positive motivation and rewards
- bottom-line performance improvements
- innovation and effort.

Cons

- focused too much on rewards
- perceived unfairness
- power of managers.

Feedback on self-assessment question 15.4

1   TRUE. This aspect can become too dominant. If it does, the other benefits of performance appraisal will suffer.
2   TRUE. Performance and appraisal information will help the organisation to determine career paths for individuals and spot and develop talented staff.

15

3   FALSE. Many organisations are happy to give financial rewards but dislike next increment systems.
4   FALSE. Rigorous checks are necessary to prevent abuse and favouritism.
5   FALSE. Staff may perform well in general, but feel uncomfortable in this particular situation.

Feedback on learning activity 15.5

By now you should have thought about your own organisation's measurement process in some detail. Problems could include any or all of the following:

- The scheme exists, but it has low priority in the business.
- There is pressure and slippage in the process.
- The scheme doesn't allow for change.
- There is a lack of confidentiality.
- Management ignores feedback.
- There is a lack of good information.
- There is a lack of training or practice.

Feedback on self-assessment question 15.5

1   Jack's main concern should be the lack of measurable data. To measure savings targets effectively, very clear numbers will be needed.
2   Jack's second concern could be the current lack of confidentiality, though this does not come from the organisation.
3   Probably not. A savings target is perfectly reasonable, but setting targets without ensuring the data is available for measurement is likely to lead to faults with the measurement scheme.
4   First, the authority needs to put effective data collection systems in place. The issue of confidentiality can perhaps be covered more easily by discussion with the staff involved. In any case, a major change such as this would be a good opportunity to review the way the scheme works.

Feedback on learning activity 15.6

Your list of issues might include the following:

- commitment from senior management
- written flexible plans for personal and development needs
- regular review of training and development needs of all employees
- action to train and develop individuals
- a mechanism for continuous evaluation.

Feedback on self-assessment question 15.6

Your memorandum should cover several of the points covered in this section of the study session, including:

- commitment from senior management
- written flexible plans
- regular senior management reviews

15

- action to train and develop individuals
- action throughout an individual's employment
- mechanisms for continuous evaluation of training effectiveness
- accepted standard of standardisation
- goes beyond one organisation.

15

15

Cascading targets and objectives

Introduction

'The odds of hitting
your target go up
dramatically when
you aim at it.'
Mal Pancoast

It may seem an obvious statement, but the activities any group of staff need
to be 'aimed' via a series of targets and objectives. This is the concept of
management by (or through) objectives (MBO). In this study session we
shall look at how this concept works, and at how objectives cascade down
from the business-planning process. We shall consider some of the issues
and problems of objective-setting.

Session learning objectives

After completing this session you should be able to:

16.1 Define the concept and benefits of managing through objectives.
16.2 Summarise the way in which targets and objectives cascade down from
the business-planning process.
16.3 Design positive objectives that conform to the SMART approach to
objective-setting.
16.4 Demonstrate the possibilities of different timescales for objectives.
16.5 Analyse some of the problems that can arise during objective-setting.
16.6 Demonstrate the benefits of feedback, audit and review of the
objective-setting process.

Unit content coverage

This study session covers the following topics from the official CIPS unit
content document:

Learning outcome

- Determine how measuring performance in supply chain activities fits
into the overall management process of an organisation.

Learning objective

3.3 Review how individual components of a purchasing job link to the
overall objectives of the organisation.
- Contribution of individuals to an organisation's profitability
- Management of basic workload
- Development of purchasing infrastructure

16

Prior knowledge

You should have read study session 15. Some familiarity with corporate or departmental planning processes would be useful, as would participation in an objective-setting process.

Resources

No specific resources are required. However, there is much general research information available on the internet, which can be used to support the recommended textbooks and learning materials. You may find discussion with your manager or HR department to be useful.

Timing

You should set aside about 5.75 hours to read and complete this session, including learning activities, self-assessment questions, the suggested further reading (if any) and the revision question.

16.1 Managing by objectives

Managing by objectives (MBO) requires that the aims and objectives for the business are cascaded down through the organisation, providing direction for departmental planning, staff and management targets, and eventually personal objectives.

MBO can be misused, and this can lead to an overemphasis on results, competition between staff, and workers being pushed to accept inappropriate targets. A balance needs to be struck between:

- a proactive set of objectives that provide employees with a clear indication of what the organisation expects and why and
- an over-demanding set of rigid objectives that override every other consideration.

16

Learning activity 16.1

Reflect on the term 'managing through objectives'. What do you think this means, and what would be the benefits for the employee and the organisation?

Feedback on page 271

If properly implemented, management through the use of objectives should:

- lead to focused, business-driven objectives at all levels in the business
- encourage individuals to become involved in setting and reviewing their own objectives

- help identify skill shortages and bespoke training opportunities for the participants.

The basic steps to establishing an individual employee's objectives are as follows:

1   Management should ensure that all employees clearly understand the corporate business direction and departmental objectives. (This may require some special briefing or communication.)
2   Manager and employee need to review the employee's job description and responsibilities, preferably by discussion and agreement. The objectives should not conflict with this, or the job description may need to be amended.
3   Jointly match the targets for the business and department with ideas from the employee. Usually this results in objectives for a defined period, for example one year ahead.
4   Discuss and agree the objectives. The employee should take ownership of them as far as is practical within the cascade process. Whenever possible the manager's role should be that of questioner and developer, rather than director.
5   Agree the evaluation criteria that will be used in evaluating progress towards achievement of the objectives. Typical examples might include project due dates, profit contributions, savings targets, quality targets, or contract coverage.
6   Agree the timetable for joint review of performance and comparison with the plan.
7   Agree the required outputs, because feedback from the subsequent review sessions may provide business challenges for the manager and highlight training and development needs for the employee.

Self-assessment question 16.1

Fill in the blanks in the following text:

If we have a good process for management through objectives, then employees will have more _____ and _____ objectives, which typically results in more _____ job performance and allows _____ training and development for each individual. Care should be taken that there is a high degree of employee _____ in the process, or else _____ may suffer.

_____ from the process is essential if management is to _____ the scheme over time.

Feedback on page 271

16

16.2 Targets and objectives, and the business-planning process

Many larger organisations will have a high-level corporate business-planning process. This should include a procurement plan, or at least a reference to procurement's role within the business. Smaller businesses may lack a formal structure for doing this, but they are often better at more informal communication of organisational strategies and plans.

The basic question is always 'What is the function and direction for procurement?'

Learning activity 16.2

Look at your department's objectives. Can you track them back up the organisation and into the planning process?

Feedback on page 271

High-level planning should cascade down through the business. This is summarised in figure 16.1: the thick black track highlights the individual employee's objective-setting process.

Figure 16.1: High-level planning should cascade down through the business

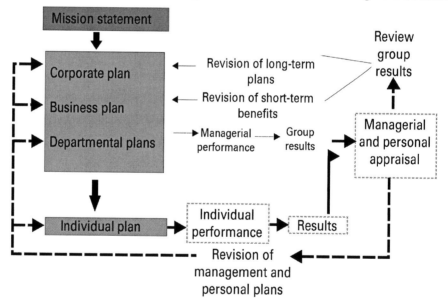

The various parts of this cascade are described below.

Mission (statement)

This is a broad statement of why the organisation exists, and what it hopes to achieve. This is often aspirational. For example, a car manufacturer's mission might be:

'To lead the market in the development of low-cost, environmentally safe transport'

From this we might assume that the company will emphasise low-cost, environmentally friendly manufacturing, and safety.

The mission statement gives focus and direction to the organisation. We should see the key issues of cost, safety and the environment echoed throughout the objective-setting process. These aspirations are turned into positive actions for the company in the corporate plan and the business plan.

Corporate plan

This is long-term and strategic, looking ahead perhaps 3–10 years. It focuses on the larger issues: for example, a decision to cease manufacturing in high-cost countries.

Business plan

This is medium-term, covering perhaps the next 1–3 years. It contains more detail on particular projects within the corporate plan: for example, the planned transfer of an engine-manufacturing facility from the UK to China.

Departmental plan

This is short-term, covering typically 12 months. It includes the department's contribution to the business and corporate plans. It provides the manager's objectives, and therefore influences those of his or her staff: for example, re-sourcing components in the project to move the UK engine-manufacturing facility.

Employee plan

This is usually short term, covering typically 12 months, and is derived from the departmental plan. Its content influenced by the job description and responsibilities: for example to re-source components X, Y and Z in line with the project to move the UK engine-manufacturing facility.

Outputs from departmental and individual plans are reviewed and fed back into the planning process; organisational demands can result in changes to individual targets.

This is an ideal model, but if individual employees cannot track their objectives back through the organisation they would have a reasonable case for asking 'Why am I doing this?'

Self-assessment question 16.2

Write a short essay analysing how this process of cascading objectives works in your organisation. (Maximum one side of A4)

Feedback on page 271

16

16.3 Designing positive and SMART objectives

As we have now seen, individual objectives should be derived from the main business-planning process, with of course the inclusion of some internal departmental and personal objectives.

How many objectives should there be? This is often a problem. There is no one correct answer to the question, but consider the following points when setting objectives:

- If there are too many objectives, this can be both unrealistic and demotivating.
- If there are too few, this is not sufficiently challenging.

Objectives are not tasks, but they do *contain* tasks. They should be broader than tasks, and should allow the employee some creativity.

The optimum is probably between eight and ten well-developed objectives.

An objective will typically have four elements. A simple example for a purchase order controller is shown in table 16.1.

Table 16.1 Elements of an objective

Objectives	Example
The key task (May be in several employees' objectives)	Improve the payment of invoices
The objective (A description of the objective for *this employee*)	To ensure that invoices received are checked for accuracy and paid in a timely manner
The performance measures (*How the performance or improvement will be measured*)	Average time (days) from receipt of invoice to payment date
	Monthly total of settlement discounts claimed (£s)
	% of inaccurate invoices received
The timescale (by when) (The objective milestones and review timetable)	By December 200? – review every month

It is not easy to write good objectives. To ensure good 'quality' objectives it is sound practice to follow the principles embodied in the acronym **SMART**:

- Specific: The objective should be clear and unambiguous. It should refer to a specific area of activity, and be clearly expressed.
- Measurable: It should be possible to measure the outcome. If not, employees or managers will not know whether it has been achieved. **Quantitative** measures (measurements that are based on figures and data) are popular, but they are sometimes difficult to obtain. For example: 'To undertake a survey of customer perceptions of the purchasing service'. The only measurable here might be whether or not the survey has been undertaken.
- Achievable: It is clearly undesirable to set objectives that are unachievable by the employee or unrealistic in their scope. For example, it might be unrealistic or not achievable to set the employee the objective 'To improve the perception of the purchasing service'.
- Realistic: As 'Achievable'.
- Timed: Objectives should have a timetable for achievement and review. Some objectives may need special reviews outside the normal object review process. For example, if our invoicing objective is a high priority,

it may need a special monthly review outside the regular quarterly review.

Learning activity 16.3

Compare any two real examples of objectives used in your organisation with the model described above. How do the real-life examples stand up?

Feedback on page 271

When we choose a measurement, we need to decide whether to make it **zero based** or continuous. Zero basing starts each period from zero: it effectively forgets previous performance, and looks afresh at what is achievable. Continuous improvement builds on data all the time, but this can be a problem, because improvement in a given area usually gets harder to achieve over time.

Self-assessment question 16.3

Read the following:

Mr X is a contract manager looking after a range of very good, well-priced hotel service contracts in an NHS hospital. He has 14 objectives this year, of which two are detailed below. He has a wide authority to take actions.

Comment on whether each of the two examples shown below meets the SMART criteria for objective-setting.

Do you have any other comments?

Table 16.2

Objective 1: To achieve savings of around 10% across all your contracts during the financial year subject to progress review at two-monthly intervals.	
	Comment
Specific	
Measurable	
Achievable	
Realistic	
Timed	

Table 16.3

Objective 2: To improve the service provided to the catering department in response to complaints received on quality and payment of invoices by the end of July	
	Comment
Specific	
Measurable	
Achievable	
Realistic	
Timed	

Feedback on page 271

16

16.4 Timescales for objectives

Learning activity 16.4

Reflect on how different objectives need different timescales to achieve. Use the table below to write a brief outline of the relevance of timescales to aspects of your job, your work environment (team or colleagues) or your department.

Table 16.6

Area of activity	Main timescales	Relevance
My job		
My immediate environment		
My department		

Feedback on page 272

Objectives have different timescales, which fit broadly into the level they occupy within the cascade process we described above. In general we can see five broad levels of timescale as we move down through this process. These time periods are just suggestions; the actual periods will vary from one organisation to another.

Very long-term (10 years plus)

The mission statement and the higher-level strategic aims and objectives fit here. They should be carefully chosen, because constant change at this level will cause more problems than it solves.

Long-term (3 to 10 years?)

The corporate plan fits here. Corporate plans are not rigid; they change over time as the organisation moves forward. They also have to reflect changes outside the organisation, such as developments in technology and new legislation. However, as for the mission statement, rapid changes at this level can have negative effects.

Medium-term (1 to 3 years?)

The business plan fits here. Some flexibility is desirable at this level, because of the shorter timescale and the need to incorporate issues such as design and marketing, which move on faster cycles. Here the organisation can respond to business pressures (or government policy in the case of public services).

Short-term (up to 1 year?)

The departmental and individual plans fit here. There is more scope for change and adaptability here, as activity is largely tactical, and fast moving.

Day-to-day

These are department and individual actions and plans, which vary and develop to suit immediate organisational needs. These are always fast moving, but can still have a major impact on business success. Too much day-to-day focus can easily distract management from the need for longer-term objectives.

Self-assessment question 16.4

Give True or False responses to the following statements on timescales for objectives:

1 Different timescales apply at different levels in the organisation because the nature of the objectives set is different. TRUE/FALSE
2 Operational buying staff have lots of long-term objectives. TRUE/FALSE
3 If possible, buyers should be set some longer-term objectives. TRUE/FALSE
4 It is the day-to-day activity that really drives a business forward. TRUE/FALSE
5 Dedicated planning teams and process can sometimes become 'divorced' from the rest of the business activity. TRUE/FALSE

Feedback on page 272

16.5 Problems with objective-setting

Learning activity 16.5

Sometimes objective-setting does not work well. Compare the list of reasons in table 16.7 with any real examples you have experienced or come across in your career.

Table 16.7

Reason	My experience
Failure to write SMART objectives	
Inadequate information for measuring success	
Constantly changing plans	
Failure to hold review sessions	
The organisation likes to dictate the objectives	
Lack of qualitative objectives (too much emphasis on numbers)	
Objectives are too easy	

Feedback on page 272

16

Clearly, there are many things that can go wrong with the objective-setting process. Some of the more common ones are listed below:

- *Changing plans and focus:* Probably the greatest cause of problems with objective-setting. The cascade process works badly, so objective-setting drifts from core business aims. Sometimes objectives are changed by instruction from further up the organisation. This causes frustration for both management and employees.
- *Failure to review adequately:* This leads to an assumption that the objectives do not matter. It is unreasonable to set regular reviews and then to fail to do this but still demand results at a yearly review. Failure to review also means that changes cannot be properly incorporated into the objective-setting process.
- *Failure to be SMART:.* This is a failure of both manager and employee. The objectives do not meet the SMART criteria, perhaps because of poor construction or lack of development time and thought
- *Inadequate information:* It is often difficult to obtain the information needed to measure the objectives. This means the objectives fail to be properly measured, or there is disagreement over the values used.
- *Too much organisational control:* Employees discover that there is less 'give' in the system when it comes to selecting objectives than they were led to believe. If they disagree with an objective, the manager forces it through. Participative goal-setting becomes top-down objective-setting, and the entire process loses credibility.
- *Lack of qualitative objectives* (those based more on perception and opinion, rather than on figures and data). Evaluation criteria need to be SMART. However, sometimes effective performance management requires the evaluation of behaviours and subjective issues, which are often avoided because they are harder to evaluate.
- *Setting easy objectives:* Performance theory suggests that best results are achieved when challenging objectives are set. However, employees who receive linked rewards may prefer easier objectives to ensure a good financial reward. Also, some managers may set easier objectives to avoid difficult issues with employees, or to give a false impression of departmental success.

Self-assessment question 16.5

Write a short report (around one sheet of A4) critically analysing a couple of sample objectives from your organisation, bearing in mind your responses to learning activity 16.5 above. You may include other problems in the analysis if you feel they are important

Feedback on page 273

16.6 Feedback, audit and review of the objective-setting process

Regular review will help to validate the objective-setting process and ensure that both manager and employee treat it seriously. It will also provide advance notice any difficulties or problems that the employee is experiencing, and allow the manager or the employee to change the objective in the light of real world developments.

Learning activity 16.6

Identify the key points in regard to review and feedback on objectives from the following short scenario.

Oliver is a new buyer (9 months in post). He has inherited an objective to improve the lead time on some pumps kept in stock for ready-use spares. He was previously a stationery buyer. These pumps are critical items and during his investigations he discovers that the long lead time is caused partly by major problems with the single supplier used. During his first review in month 8 the topic is discussed, but he doesn't mention the cause, as he feels this will look as though he is trying to avoid coming up with good ideas and is just blaming the supplier.

Three months later (month 12) the supplier fails, and there is a temporary supply crisis with lost production for his company. His manager calls for a review in the next month, at which this will be discussed.

Feedback on page 273

Feedback should be a two-way process: the employee needs to know how the manager sees his or her performance, and the manager needs to know whether the employee is experiencing difficulties or problems.

Provided the atmosphere is right, there should be useful feedback during appraisal review sessions, and the manager should ensure that whenever possible this includes some positive elements as well as any negative ones.

Feedback should generally be:

- Precise: Both manager and employee should avoid speaking in general terms, as what they say could be interpreted in different ways. This will make it more difficult to achieve any correction or change.
- Timely: As soon as possible after the poor (or outstanding) performance or behaviour has taken place, or when there is a major issue around one of the objectives.
- Impersonal: Criticism of personal traits should be avoided unless essential: it can cause emotional reactions that are both undesirable and obscure the main issue
- Given often: Understanding of performance is enhanced when there is frequent review, and when feedback is received early enough to identify problems in achieving goals.

As well as the day-to-day feedback from appraisal meetings it is also necessary for the organisation to review and perhaps audit the operation of the entire measurement and appraisal process. This will help ensure that:

- The organisational and employee benefits are being obtained.

- No major problems are occurring.
- The scheme is up to date and relevant.
- The necessary outcomes are being dealt with effectively.

Organisations with the Investors in People award are under a requirement for senior management to undertake such checks and audits.

Self-assessment question 16.6

Arrange the following measurement process steps in a suggested correct sequence:

1   Appraisal meetings take place.
2   Senior management review and audit progress and outcomes.
3   Manager and employee agree/confirm job roles and responsibilities.
4   Manager and employee discuss/propose individual objectives.
5   Manager ensures employee understanding of corporate business direction and departmental objectives.
6   Manager and employee agree evaluation criteria and appraisal meeting outputs.
7   Manager and employee agree appraisal timetable and process.
8   Manager evaluates feedback from appraisal/measurement process.
9   Manager and employee agree and sign off objectives.

Feedback on page 273

Revision question

Now try the revision question for this session on page 337.

Summary

In this study session we have seen:

- How objective-setting should be part of an overall cascade of planning and performance measurement, beginning at the top of the organisation. Without this the objective-setting process will lack real focus.
- How to write well-structured objectives using the SMART criteria, and some of the problems that can arise when objective-setting does not happen properly.
- How failure to feed back and review can negatively affect the objective-setting process.
- Although sometimes managing through objectives may lack flexibility, or convey a 'command and control' image, it can be very useful when properly applied with these limitations in mind.
-

16

Feedback on learning activities and self-assessment questions

Feedback on learning activity 16.1

Benefits could include:

- a good information 'cascade'
- realistic and acceptable objectives
- involvement of employees
- feedback to management
- agreed measurement criteria.

Feedback on self-assessment question 16.1

You should have found words close to or equivalent to the following:

focused – business-driven – effective – bespoke – involvement – morale – feedback – improve

Feedback on learning activity 16.2

You should demonstrate that there is some link between your department's aims and objectives and those of the organisation. Preferably this should include reference to organisational documents such as annual reports, business plans and mission statements.

Your own objectives should also clearly 'fit' within this process.

Feedback on self-assessment question 16.2

Your essay should track the cascade process described above, as applied in your own organisation. You may decided that not all the stages described are applicable: if so, it would be equally interesting to know why they do not apply in your organisation.

Feedback on learning activity 16.3

You should have identified two example objectives from your organisation and have provided a short analysis of their effectiveness or otherwise, measured both against the main content of an objective and against the SMART criteria.

Feedback on self-assessment question 16.3

Table 16.4

Objective 1: To achieve savings of around 10% across all your contracts during the financial year subject to progress review at two- monthly intervals.	
	Comment
Specific	OK, but could perhaps define what type of saving
Measurable	Easy to measure provided data is available. Yes provided the data is available
Achievable	Yes – he owns the contracts and has a wide spread of authority

(continued on next page)

Table 16.4 *(continued)*

Objective 1: To achieve savings of around 10% across all your contracts during the financial year subject to progress review at two- monthly intervals.	
	Comment
Realistic	Perhaps not - the contracts are already very well priced
Timed	Good – clearly states regularity of review

Table 16.5

Objective 2 – To improve the service provided to the catering department in response to complaints received on quality and payment of invoices by the end of July	
	Comment
Specific	Reasonable in pointing at the broad objective
Measurable	Harder to measure, perhaps using reduced complaints. Poor overall
Achievable	Not clear. The contracts are his responsibility, but some of the issues, eg invoicing, may not be
Realistic	Not as written, though he could obviously make a contribution
Timed	Very precise

Other comments could include the following:

Two-monthly review conveys priority on savings.

14 objectives may be an overload.

Objectives may need more detail; they look rushed.

Feedback on learning activity 16.4

Your outlines should identify different timescales (or explain why they are all the same), and pick out which aspects of your job, environment and department have different timescales and why.

Feedback on self-assessment question 16.4

1   TRUE. It is the job of the objectives set at senior level to give direction to the business over longer timescales.
2   FALSE. Operational buyers generally work on day-to-day through to medium-term timescales.
3   TRUE. Although most objectives will be short-term, it may benefit the individual to have, say, one objective that runs over a longer period of time.
4   FALSE. Successful companies get the day-to-day right, but they are driven by good medium-term and long-term planning.
5   TRUE. Dedicated teams can be very effective, but sometimes they can make the planning an end in itself.

Feedback on learning activity 16.5

You should be able to identify at least two or three examples from your own experience.

Feedback on self-assessment question 16.5

You should evaluate by using the above list of problems and identifying new ones if relevant.

Feedback on learning activity 16.6

Key points should include the following:

- Did the buyer have the chance to feed back?
- Was the 8-month delay acceptable?
- Should the buyer have asked for a review?
- Should a critical item have been reviewed more often?
- Feedback was not given to the manager, who could have taken action.
- Is the final review too late?

Feedback on self-assessment question 16.6

The response should be broadly in the following order:

5 – 3 – 4 – 6 – 9 – 7 – 1 – 8 – 2

16

16

Appraisal and evaluation techniques

Introduction

Does this sound familiar? This session focuses on the appraisal process and interview – still very common in many organisations – which can be a stressful experience for many employees (and some managers).

It's that time of year again, and your organisation has gone into performance measurement frenzy. There's panic to complete the appraisal process and sign off this year's objectives, and a hectic round of appraisal interviews for all concerned.

Session learning objectives

After completing this session you should be able to:

17.1 Describe informal and formal appraisal and evaluation techniques.
17.2 Evaluate the benefits of a quantitative or qualitative approach.
17.3 Explain the main components and issues in an interview-based appraisal process.
17.4 Summarise the self-assessment approach to appraisal.
17.5 Propose the involvement of others in the appraisal process.
17.6 Define the issues that can arise if the appraisal process fails to work effectively.

Unit content coverage

This study session covers the following topics from the official CIPS unit content document:

Learning outcome

- Categorise types of performance measures that are available to supply chain mamagers

Learning objective

3.2 Outline the appraisal and evaluation techniques that can be employed within such an approach.
  - Periodic reviews
  - Informal and formal appraisals

Prior knowledge

You should have read study sessions 15 and 16. Some personal experience will be beneficial, especially experience of appraisal interviews.

Resources

No specific resources are required, but you may find it useful to discuss this issue with other students or colleagues.

Timing

You should set aside about 5.75 hours to read and complete this session, including learning activities, self-assessment questions, the suggested further reading (if any) and the revision question.

17.1 Formal and informal appraisal and evaluation techniques

In many organisations, appraisal includes an interview, typically between the line manager and the employee. These interviews take different forms but in broad terms we can identify two extremes of formality in interview structure (see figure 17.1).

Figure 17.1: Two extremes of formality in interview structure

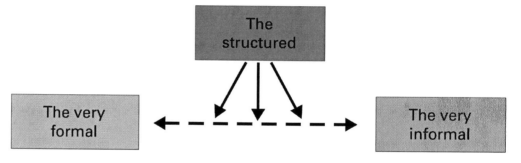

Learning activity 17.1

Look at your organisation, and make brief notes on the degree of formality in the appraisal or measurement process for buying staff. What strengths and weaknesses result from this choice?

Feedback on page 286

Formal

Formal interviews are often included in organisation-wide appraisal schemes, which typically have fairly tight rules and requirements, precise written objectives, set interview requirements and standards for measurement of achievement. Such schemes often include a requirement to keep records for administration purposes.

There may also be guidelines on the interview structure, and the minimum interview timetable is often dictated by the rules. For example, there may be a requirement for at least four interviews per year.

17

In the formal interview the buyer and his or her manager are more likely to attempt to use scoring mechanisms as part of the evaluation process, and this can be likened to the vendor rating used for suppliers. Good preparation is needed for this type of interview to work effectively.

Informal

This appraisal process will be far less structured and disciplined, and is often based on regular day-to-day discussion or shorter, more relaxed meetings. Undertaken well, this can still be very demanding, and is well suited to organisations where employees are able to demonstrate their progress without significant preparation. Equally, however, informal systems can simply hand control to the manager to praise and reward as he or she sees fit.

The paperwork content is likely to be minimal, or absent all together.

Structured

This represents a balance of the above two approaches, with a minimum of control and formality but designed to avoid the ad hoc nature of the informal system.

Self-assessment question 17.1

Fill in the blanks in the following text:

Mr Johnson is manager of a small printing company with two buyers. He favours a formal system of measuring their performance with precise _____ objectives, set _____ requirements and standards for _____ of achievement. He has also taken steps to produce _____ on interview _____ and technique.

He is aware that this can make the interviews quite _____, and therefore he tries to ensure that the atmosphere is as _____ as possible when he meets with the buyers.

Feedback on page 286

17.2 Quantitative and qualitative measurement approaches

As when we are evaluating supplier performance, the measures used to evaluate buyers' achievement of their targets and objectives may fall into two categories – quantitative and qualitative.

We need to understand the difference between these, and how this can affect the appraisal process.

Learning activity 17.2

Look at your objectives or those of a colleague, and make brief notes that assess the balance between quantitative and qualitative objectives.

Does your organisation tend to favour one or the other, or is the balance about right?

Feedback on page 286

Table 17.1 shows some of the main characteristics of each approach.

Table 17.1 Quantitative and qualitative measures

Quantitative measures	Qualitative measures
Based around numbers and values	Based around quality or service issues
Objective and measurable	Subjective and less easy to measure
Easily turned into targets	Difficult to turn into targets
More task orientated	Designed to measure satisfaction and service rather than efficiency at tasks
Common where purchasing is seen as a process driven or clerical activity	More likely where purchasing is seen as a key contributor
Focus on efficiency and improvement (in numbers)	Focus on perception, effectiveness and contribution
Examples	Examples
1 To increase the number of orders processed from an average of 4 to 5 per hour	1 To strive for significant improvement in relationships with key internal customers
2 To increase business margin from 21% to 25% over 12 months through better procurement	2 To improve product quality over a range of goods

Most purchasing teams will be exposed to a mix of these measures, and indeed this is often desirable. If the appraisal process is very demanding, or is linked to rewards, employees may well prefer quantitative measures if they feel measurement will be easier or more accurate.

Self-assessment question 17.2

Give True or False responses to the following statements on timescales for objectives:

1   Quantitative measures are concerned with numbers and data; qualitative measures are concerned with facts and opinions. TRUE/FALSE
2   Qualitative measures are usually easier to turn into targets. TRUE/FALSE
3   Failure to obtain good data is more likely to cause problems in quantitative measurements. TRUE/FALSE
4   Task-related functions tend to be measured using qualitative measures. TRUE/FALSE

(continued on next page)

17

5   Quantitative measures may be preferred by employees when bonus payments are involved. TRUE/FALSE

Feedback on page 286

17.3 Interview-based appraisal

The interview is by far the most popular way of undertaking formal appraisal. This interview is an important part of the process, but it is one that both parties – employee and manager – can find difficult. Although the term 'interview' is most frequently used, the general aim should be to have a relaxed atmosphere, and a supportive approach from the manager.

Of course, managers undertake many sorts of interview, and it is important that the right style be used in appraisals in order to get the best results. Some of the different styles that could be used are listed below:

- Interrogative/forceful
    - Used in a disciplinary session, or when interviewing a difficult supplier.
    - The interviewer is an interrogator, and has total control, which may have to be exercised in a forceful way.
    - Very inappropriate as a style for appraisals.
- Planned/directive
    - Used in job interviews, and with suppliers and customers.
    - The interviewer has an agenda, but tries to guide the process positively, rather than exerting control directly – to steer the direction the interview takes, but not try to control the whole process.
    - Might be suitable in a very formal appraisal session. Not ideal.
- Loose/relaxed
    - Typical style for appraisals, counselling and personal issues.
    - The interviewer tries to create a sympathetic 'partnership' relationship with the employee, to reduce the possibility of friction or tension, and help ensure the individual feels able to contribute. There is a minimum of direct control, but a result is needed, and the employee must have a large input.
    - The style to aim for in appraisals.

17

Learning activity 17.3

Reflect on what you have now read about interview style. Prepare a short comparison between the theory and any practical examples or situations in which you have taken part.

Feedback on page 286

We can break an appraisal interview down into three main stages:

Before the interview

- Plan and prepare for the interview. Failure to do this is a common cause of difficulty in appraisals.
- Identify new objectives, remembering the links to the business planning process. You may have to do some 'negotiation' in the interview.
- Review existing objectives and form your view of progress. You may need to ask for data to be available.
- Review last year's interview notes, especially if you do not know the other person well.
- Book rooms and appointments.

The interview

- Must be in private, with as few interruptions and distractions as possible.
- The atmosphere should be informal, but performance improvement and problem solving should be the main item for discussion.
- Managers must give employees adequate time to speak, allowing them to describe their performance throughout the year.
- Data should be tabled and agreed.
- A set of objectives with performance targets should be produced, or drafted for completion at a later session.
- Changes and amendments to the objectives can be discussed and agreed.
- Notes should be kept as required.

After the interview

- Notes should be written up and agreed. Both parties will keep their own notes.
- Unagreed points can be confirmed.
- Actions can be set in place.

The outcomes from the interview should include:

- A clear view of the employee's performance over the period concerned.
- A recommendation for reward or for counselling/development.
- A review of the objectives and the job, with changes to both objectives and job descriptions as required.
- Feedback from both parties on the wider view of the business.
- Identification of skill and knowledge gaps that may need training or development.

This last point is important: one of the great benefits of a sound appraisal system is the input it provides to the development of training. (See study session 18.)

Self-assessment question 17.3

Fill in the blanks in the following text:

The HR department at Company X is very concerned about some aspects of the appraisal interview process. At least one manager has adopted the

(continued on next page)

17

Self-assessment question 17.3 *(continued)*

wrong _____ in interviews, being rather _____, which employees feel is inappropriate for these interviews.

Several other managers are failing to undertake the necessary pre-interview _____, and some have not held interviews in _____ owing to a failure to_____ _____.

_____ are not being taken, and the necessary _____ from both parties is often missing.

Feedback on page 287

17.4 Self-assessment

Self-assessment is the process by which an individual assesses his or her performance either as part of, or instead of, a wider evaluation process. Typically self-assessment will involve a form or questionnaire in order to ensure consistency for all participants. Usually the outcome will be evaluated by the line manager or an appointed group.

Self-assessment builds on the employee's undoubted knowledge of his or her own personal strengths and weaknesses and as such should create a more open and honest appraisal. However in practice employees usually find it difficult to be objective and often either under or over estimate their performance.

Learning activity 17.4

Reflect on whether you think self-assessment could work in your department or organisation, and prepare a short management report on your views. (If it is already in use, report on how successful you feel it is.)

Feedback on page 287

There are several points to considered in regard to self-assessment:

- It can feed a bigger process, where the self-assessment becomes part of the preparation work that the employee should be undertaking anyway.
- It can be rigid in application. If the self-assessment uses a rating or measuring system it can create a very mechanistic or 'tick box' approach to performance measurement.
- It can be useful for training and professional development. Self-assessment is particularly useful in helping to identify skill gaps and training and professional development opportunities.
- Filling in forms, especially if they are complex, is usually unpopular.
- It is hard to avoid personal bias, and if rewards are linked to the appraisal process then staff may have a vested interest in overstating their success.

17

When self-assessment replaces an interview this may remove a difficult stage from the process. However, it can also remove an opportunity for feedback and relationship-building as well.

The content of a self-appraisal form will vary, but typically it will be a mix of verbal responses, numbers and dates. It is also common for such forms to include simple rating of the '1 equals low, 6 equals high' type. There may be sections for each level of management who will sign the form.

Typical content of the form might include:

- the key objectives
- the progress made on each objective
- appropriate numbers for measuring progress
- perceived skill shortages or training needs
- personal initiatives outside the main objective process
- a signing-off section for all participants
- a rating section for the manager.

Self-assessment question 17.4

Fill in the blanks in the following text:

It is always difficult to assess the value of self-assessment in performance measurement. When it is _____ of a wider scheme it forms part of the employees' _____, and it is also extremely useful for assessing _____ gaps and _____ needs.

On the other hand it often means completing a _____, which can be unpopular, and _____ _____ can often make the results less satisfactory.

Simple forms often include a numerical _____ system, and different levels of _____ may need to sign off the forms. The whole process can create a '_____ _____' mentality towards performance management

Feedback on page 287

17.5 Involving others in the appraisal process

Most appraisal takes place down the line management structure. There is nothing wrong with this, but the wider performance management concept discussed in study session 15 envisages other inputs to this process. In particular, it envisages input from those who can be considered as 'stakeholders' of the purchasing department.

(Stakeholders can be defined as groups with similar characteristics who have a 'stake' in a particular issue, function or organisation. For example, passenger groups can be considered as a stakeholder for a transport company.)

Learning activity 17.5

Write a management report on how other stakeholders could be (or already are) involved in performance measurement of buyers in your organisation. You may wish to discuss this with your manager.

Feedback on page 287

Some potential stakeholders for purchasing and supply staff are listed below:

- Team and/or peer input
    - Used for many years in education and the military.
    - Peers often have unique first-hand knowledge, which supervisors do not.
    - Must be handled carefully, as it can cause stress, bad relationships and undesirable competition.
- Internal customer input
    - Particularly useful when assessing staff or functions that provide a service, for example expeditors or stores staff.
    - The manager may obtain useful performance appraisal data, such as whether the internal customers' needs are being met promptly, courteously, and accurately.
- Suppliers
    - If the organisation is keen to improve relationships with suppliers, their input can provide a very different focus to the appraisal.
    - Many buyers have been surprised by what suppliers say about them and their organisation.
    - However, suppliers may tend to say 'nice things' to avoid upsetting their customers.
- Other stakeholders
    - Could include senior managers, board members, end customers, trade unions etc
    - The principle is that the stakeholder should be involved because their input provides a useful and different contribution to the appraisal process for purchasing staff.
- Junior staff
    - Unsurprisingly not especially common, but can be applicable in organisations that place a premium on good employee relationships, or where very close teamwork is common.
    - Would need very careful design and management to work effectively.

17

Self-assessment question 17.5

Give True or False responses to the following statements on stakeholders:

1   Stakeholders are generally people with shares in an organisation.
TRUE/FALSE

(continued on next page)

2   Stakeholders have always been involved in the performance
     measurement of buyers. TRUE/FALSE
3   Involving junior staff as stakeholders is best suited to organisations with
     strong trade unions. TRUE/FALSE
4   Internal customers can provide a valuable insight into buyers'
     performance. TRUE/FALSE
5   Suppliers' input may tend to be distorted for fear of avoiding upsetting
     a buyer. TRUE/FALSE

Feedback on page 287

17.6 Problems with the appraisal process

If the appraisal process is not undertaken properly, there are two major
consequences:

- The employee fails to be motivated, and begins to lose confidence in the
  whole process, perhaps seeing it as a management 'game'.
- The organisation fails to gain the benefits it seeks, which include
  employee participation and empowerment. Ultimately it also begins to
  see a fall-off in performance and a failure to achieve targets.

Learning activity 17.6

Arrange the following list of statements in order of priority in terms of
the problems you feel they cause in an appraisal process. Show the biggest
problem first.

Give a brief explanation of your reasoning for the order you have chosen.

The problems of poor appraisal can include the following:

1   The rewards in our systems are not worth the effort we put in.
2   We often lack the data we need for measuring performance.
3   Our interview techniques are poor, and need improving.
4   There is favouritism and unfairness in our appraisal process.
5   A failure of the 'cascade' of communication means we sometimes do not
     know how our objectives relate to the business objectives.
6   Failure to prepare is a major problem in our appraisal process.

Feedback on page 287

The problems of poor appraisal can include the following:

- Failure to prepare. The interview dates are adhered to, but very little
  preparation is undertaken. Significant harm is done if only one party
  has devoted a lot of time to preparation.
- Favouritism and unfairness. The good manager will make every attempt
  to avoid this, but appraisal is an emotive time, and managers must be
  prepared for such feelings even where they are not justified. It may be
  helpful to document the process.

17

- Poor interview techniques. Many managers do not like this type of interview, and consequently are not good at it.
- The process becomes mechanistic. The danger in regulated systems is that, over time, a comfortable process can develop, but there is little real achievement.
- Failure of the 'cascade' of communication. The best systems have a good relationship between appraisal and organisational targets, but this is frequently a weak link in many systems.
- Failure to follow up. Often interviews can reveal skill shortages and weakness, for example a need for some negotiation training, but there is no follow-up, and the training is not provided.
- Lack of data. Systems fail to provide the data necessary to allow the achievement of targets to be measured.
- Inappropriate rewards. Where appraisal is used as part of the reward system, managers must ensure that employees can receive large enough pay increases. Well-structured and managed appraisal processes that lead to very small rewards may be perceived as not worthwhile.
- Trading success. Employees frequently try to trade off success in some objectives against failure in others. Although this is understandable, objectives are set against business needs, and cannot be substituted in this manner except when formalised as part of the review process.

Self-assessment question 17.6

Analyse the following short case study, and identify possible problems and any plus points.

Sam is attending his end of financial year appraisal interview on Tuesday 30 April, after having returned from two weeks' sick leave.

This interview has been postponed twice, (once in March, because the manager had to cancel at the last minute, and two weeks before, when Sam went off sick), and there is now some pressure to have the meeting.

Through no fault of his own, Sam has had a lot of sickness this year, and he is worried, as he has not achieved all his targets, and his manager doesn't always appear sympathetic. However, Sam has some very good data on all aspects of his performance, and he believes that he has exceeded a couple of targets. He feels that this may help him against those targets that he has not done so well in.

Feedback on page 288

17

Revision question

Now try the revision question for this session on page 338.

Summary

In this session we have considered various surrounding the appraisal and evaluation process, especially appraisal interviews, which are still a core component of many performance measurement schemes for buyers. We have also considered:

- self-assessment
- the inclusion of other stakeholders in the process
- the problems that can occur during appraisal.

Suggested further reading

Students may enjoy Goodworth (1989) which, though quite old, makes a number of good points in a humorous way.

Feedback on learning activities and self-assessment questions

Feedback on learning activity 17.1

Your notes should show:

- Whether your organisation leans to the formal or the informal.
- The strengths and weaknesses of this approach.
- Some examples to illustrate the process.

Feedback on self-assessment question 17.1

You should be able to identify the following words from the text:

written – interview – measurement – guidelines – structure – difficult – relaxed

Feedback on learning activity 17.2

Your notes should show some objectives, with your comments on whether they are quantitative or qualitative measures. You should also indicate how you see the balance, and why.

Feedback on self-assessment question 17.2

1 TRUE
2 FALSE. They work more on subjective judgements, and are therefore harder to turn into targets.
3 TRUE. Quantitative data is more dependent on numbers.
4 FALSE. Tasks are often more suited to quantitative measures.
5 TRUE. There should be less scope for disagreement with quantitative measures.

Feedback on learning activity 17.3

Your comparisons should bring out some of the issues around:

- The different interview styles, and whether they were wrongly applied.

- The structure of the process, and whether it was broadly followed.
- Whether there were good outcomes from the process.

Feedback on self-assessment question 17.3

You should have the following words:

style – interrogative – planning – private – book rooms – notes – feedback

Feedback on learning activity 17.4

You should provide a view as to why you feel self-assessment will or will not work in your organisation or department. This could include the following points:

- as part of a wider process
- rigidity or formality in application
- use in training and professional development
- problems of personal bias
- lack of interview – a good or bad thing.

Feedback on self-assessment question 17.4

You should have identified the following

part – preparation – skill – training – form – personal bias – rating – management – tick-box

Feedback on learning activity 17.5

There is no set response. You should identify some groups who could be involved, and show the contribution they could (or do) make.

Feedback on self-assessment question 17.5

1   FALSE. Stakeholders can generally be defined as groups with similar characteristics who have a 'stake' in a particular issue, function or organisation.
2   FALSE. Involving stakeholders is a relatively new idea in most organisations.
3   FALSE. It is best suited to organisations that place a premium on good employee relationships.
4   TRUE. Customers' perceptions are tremendously important but often overlooked.
5   TRUE. Supplier input is valuable, but care must be taken to check its validity

Feedback on learning activity 17.6

There is no one right answer, but a good order would be: 4 – 6 – 2 – 5 – 3 – 1.

17

Number (4) is first, because any perceived favouritism and unfairness will cause the whole scheme to be badly viewed by staff (and by some managers). Following this is number (6), because failure to prepare is always likely to be a major problem. Lack of data (2) causes many problems, as does (5), failure of the objective 'cascade' process. Poor interviewing (3) is relatively easy to improve with practice and training, and inadequate rewards (1) are rarely a 'showstopper' in practice.

Feedback on self-assessment question 17.6

Your responses could include the following:

- Cancellation by the manager at this stage in the year should have been avoided. Had the March session gone ahead, there would be far less pressure.
- Sam has had little chance to prepare for the Tuesday interview, which might have been better later in the week. (Of course, he should have prepared for the earlier sessions.)
- Lack of sympathy in a manager may be common, because sickness and absence cause operational problems. However, this does not mean that the manager is likely to be unfair in his treatment of Sam.
- Sam has done well to get good data. This will always be helpful in this type of interview, whether it reveals a good or a bad result.
- Exceeding expectations on a couple of objectives is good, but not if it is at the expense of the other objectives. Sam is being optimistic to hope for a trade here, as the organisation is not getting the results it requires.

17

Study session 18
Training and staff development

Introduction

Thirty years ago people worked for the company; now they work for themselves. Organisations need to recognise that different employees are motivated in different ways: some by their career aspirations, some by reward, and many others who just want to do a good job and contribute usefully to the organisation.

By continuously helping to develop their employees' skills and assisting them in achieving their aspirations, managers are also enabling the organisation to achieve its business objectives.

Session learning objectives

After completing this session you should be able to:

18.1 Describe the stages and benefits of developing a training needs analysis (TNA).
18.2 Distinguish between job profiles and job descriptions, and how they influence a TNA.
18.3 Argue the benefits of focused rather than non-focused approaches to training and staff development.
18.4 Summarise the different types of training available.
18.5 Explain the concept of continuous professional development.
18.6 Evaluate the success of training for the individual and for the business.

Unit content coverage

This study session covers the following topics from the official CIPS unit content document:

Learning outcome

- Determine how measuring performance in supply chain activities fits into the overall management process of an organization.
- Discuss the benefits of implementing a well structured approach to measuring organisational, functional and individual performance.

Learning objective

3.5 Identify and appraise the training needs of individuals, using appropriate analytical approaches, including:
- Job profiles
- Key objectives

18

289

- Performance measures
- Appraisals

Prior knowledge

You should have read study sessions 15, 16 and 17. Some previous experience of participating in organised training courses will also be of benefit.

Resources

No specific resources are required, but you may find it useful to discuss this issue with other students or colleagues, and with your training department or responsible manager.

Timing

You should set aside about 6 hours to read and complete this session, including learning activities, self-assessment questions, the suggested further reading (if any) and the revision question.

18.1 Developing a training needs analysis

In many organisations training is a 'scattergun' process. When an organisation makes a positive attempt to structure training, based on what is needed to help the employees achieve the organisation's business goals, the result is a training needs analysis (TNA). The TNA process concentrates on matching the skills of the individual with the needs of the organisation. The result shows strengths, which can then be utilised, and weaknesses, which can be dealt with through training and development programmes.

Learning activity 18.1

Reflect on the approach that your organisation takes to analysing staff training and development needs, and prepare a short critical outline of the good and bad points. You may find it useful to talk to colleagues and your training department.

Feedback on page 302

18

Often an organisation's training needs are identified through the activities shown in figure 18.1. Of these, the data from the appraisal interview is the key, because it allows for a two-way comparison between what the organisation requires from the employee and whether the employee understands his or her roles and responsibilities.

Figure 18.1: Identifying training requirements

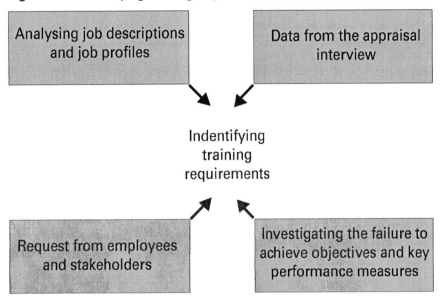

The information obtained can be analysed, and particular areas of weakness can be identified and remedied. This is specialist work, and it may require input from the human resources or training departments.

When the 'normal' processes shown in figure 18.1 are not working well, information on training needs will be poor. There may also be a need to establish a longer-term training plan, or to set a **benchmark**, perhaps after a restructuring or before a major change in direction. (A benchmark is a target that is established – benchmarked – and against which performance can be compared. It is often used in comparisons between organisations.)

In this case a special training needs analysis may be required, and this can be undertaken in various ways. Two common methods are by self-assessment and by interview, as follows:

- Self-assessment
    - Using a questionnaire to establish how employees see their own skill base and training needs, and to identify strengths and weaknesses.
    - Relatively easy to organise, but results can be subject to personal bias, and can easily form a 'wish list'.
- Interview based (internally or externally led)
    - Employees attend an interview similar to an appraisal interview, to discuss their strengths and weaknesses.
    - This is led by a manager or delegated member of staff. In order to encourage open discussion it is usually best if this is not the line manager.
    - Employee and interviewer discuss and agree the areas of strengths and weaknesses. Difficulties with this approach are the possible lack of open discussion, and the amount of management time required.
    - External interviewers, perhaps from a training or consultancy firm, can be used. This is more expensive, but can be faster, and it helps to ensure the open debate that is necessary.

18

In general, the steps in arranging a TNA are as follows:

1 Agree the method to be used (and recruit external interviewers if you need to).
2 Agree the group(s) of staff involved.
3 Agree and prioritise the areas of performance and the skills and competences that the organisation requires (that is, the desired benchmark).
4 Undertake the interviews or self-assessment.
5 Compare the results with the benchmark requirements, and identify any major problem areas (the skills gaps).
6 Devise and implement suitable training to remedy these skill gaps.
7 Review and feed back as appropriate.

A TNA can be a complex process, but if it is well managed, it can provide good results and a training and development programme that is capable of driving a business for several years.

Self-assessment question 18.1

Draft a management-type report on how training needs are (or could be) assessed within your organisation, with a shortlist or timetable of actions required.

Feedback on page 302

18.2 Job profiles, job descriptions and their influence on a TNA

A **job profile** defines the skills and abilities necessary for the successful performance of a job. A **job description** defines – both for the organisation and for the employees – all the essential functions of the job.

Job profiles and job descriptions can make a major contribution both to the appraisal process and to a training needs analysis. They do this by defining what the job is, what the expected outcomes are, and the key skills, knowledge and attributes that it is believed are necessary to do the job well.

Job descriptions and job profiles are both used extensively in recruiting staff, as well as in appraisal and performance management.

Learning activity 18.2

Compare your job description with the list of contents in table 18.1. Note any significant points of difference and any useful additions, and state whether you feel these have a positive or negative effect on your job. (If you

(continued on next page)

Learning activity 18.2 *(continued)*

do not have a job description, ask a colleague or friend to work with you – it
does not need to be purchasing-related)

Table 18.1

Model	Included in my job description? Y/N	Comment
Job title		
Job outline and position in the organisation		
List of essential activities (prioritised if appropriate)		
Specific output measures (if appropriate)		
Reporting relationships		
Other working relationships		
Size of budget or impact of job		
Tools and technology to be used		
List specific behaviours that might be required		
Conditions of service, and pay issues		

Feedback on page 302

Job profile (sometimes called job specification)

This defines the skills and abilities that are needed to perform the job
successfully. The following are typically included in a job profile:

- The knowledge, skills and abilities required to perform the task,
  together with some indication of the degree of ability required. These
  are often known as the key competences, and they are very important
  when developing a TNA.
- Any educational requirements, usually stated as 'a minimum of…'
  or 'must be studying for…'. This is useful if the TNA is to cover
  educational requirements and qualifications.
- The level of experience required, often including the markets and
  industries, and perhaps with stipulated time periods in each area of
  experience. May also refer to skills gained and tasks accomplished
  during these employments. Useful in the TNA because it can help
  highlight experience gaps.
- Any professional certificates or training required, often including
  evidence of continuous professional development. This is useful if the
  TNA is to include professional development requirements.

The job profile therefore provides a very useful checklist when preparing
a TNA, as well as being used in short-listing and selection activities. Job
profiles need to be updated over time – as do job descriptions.

Job description

This defines – both for the organisation and the employee – all the essential
functions of a job, and also what makes it different from other jobs.

18

Job descriptions have sometimes had a bad press, accompanied by images of employees waving a piece of paper and stating, 'It's not in my job description.'

In reality this is more an issue of morale and industrial relations. However, managers must appreciate that, having gone into some detail to explain the content of a job description to an employee, it is necessary to take equal care when explaining the need for changes and developments.

Table 18.2 shows the contents of a typical job description.

Table 18.2 Job descriptions

Content	Contribution to TNA
Job title	A broad indication of the nature of the job
Job outline and position in the organisation	Helps outline the broad skills required and wider reporting relationships
List of essential activities (prioritised if appropriate)	Helps determine the core skills that will be needed
Specific output measures (if appropriate)	Helps determine some specific skills that will be needed
Reporting relationships	Contributes to communication skills needs
Other working relationships	Contributes to communication skills needs
Size of budget or impact of job	Indicates a need for financial skills
Tools and technology to be used	Indicates a need for technical skills
List specific behaviours that might be required	Picks up more specialist skills that may be needed
Conditions of service and pay issues	N/A

Job descriptions are extensively used in recruitment, but often they are not updated in line with organisational developments. As a result, it is not uncommon for different employees doing the same job to have different job descriptions.

Self-assessment question 18.2

Fill in the blanks in the following text:

In most businesses both job _____ and job _____ can provide good inputs for the development of a _____ _____ _____. They are also very useful documents in the _____ process: the job _____ is especially useful to the interviewers and the job _____ to the interviewee. In the past, job _____ have sometimes been misused, and it is essential that both documents are _____ regularly to keep pace with changes in the organisation.

Feedback on page 303

18.3 Focused versus non-focused training and development

We have seen that, if an organisation has the necessary activities in place, training needs flow out of a well-managed process, which is itself directly linked to the organisation's needs and objectives. We may consider this to be a process in which the organisation – from the senior management down – has focused on training, and on the need to make it work for the organisation.

Learning activity 18.3

Consider the above statement, and then prepare a short report on whether you feel the process of determining training requirements in your organisation can be considered as 'focused'. You may wish to talk with your manager or training department.

Feedback on page 303

Focused training

The advantages of adopting a focused approach to training are as follows:

- Employees are trained only in skills or competences that relate directly to their jobs or their role in the organisation. For example, they may be trained in word-processing because it is a skill they need in their job, *not* because it is part of the IT training package.
- Employees are trained only in areas in which they have a skills or knowledge gap. This allowing training to be targeted at individuals, and not at a group or department.
- Training can be targeted to address real weaknesses, rather than being generic in nature, because all those taking part have similar knowledge gaps. For example, in the public sector negotiation training needs to concentrate on internal negotiation rather than supplier negotiation.
- The results from the analysis are very helpful in course development, which ensures that trainers deliver less generic training.
- Training budgets can be utilised better. Without this type of approach many people receive training that provides little benefit – a clear waste of money and time.
- Identifying staff or departments with skills gaps will also identify those with particular strengths in any given area of activity. This means that internal resources can often be used to supplement or replace external training.

Unfocused training

In many organisations training is unfocused, and as a result is less effective than it should be. When training *does* take place, it may arises from various sources:

- As a result of an employee's request: 'I have seen this supplier-sourcing seminar advertised, and would like to attend.'
- As a result of a manager's initiative: 'I have seen this excellent course on supplier sourcing, and think we should send some people on it.'
- As a result of senior management policy: 'We always send all our people on supplier-sourcing courses, and they really benefit from it.'

18

- As a result of a training company sales push: 'We are organising training sessions on supplier sourcing, and think your staff would benefit.'

Sometimes training is rushed to ensure that a budget is spent, and as there is no internal guidance the first available courses are chosen. Whatever the source of the initiative, this type of unfocused training is less likely to achieve the results or to be as cost-effective for the organisation.

It is also debatable whether it is better than no training at all!

Self-assessment question 18.3

Give True or False responses to the following statements on training:

1 Sometimes training is rushed through to spend a budget. TRUE/FALSE
2 Providing training as a result of an employee's request is not a good way of choosing training. TRUE/FALSE
3 Senior management play no part in establishing focused training needs. TRUE/FALSE
4 Focused training allows skilled employees to become involved in training others. TRUE/FALSE
5 External trainers can develop good courses without TNA outputs. TRUE/FALSE

Feedback on page 303

18.4 The different types of training available

Once the training need has been identified, there are several different ways in which training can be provided, and a number of different sources of the training.

Job-based training

This is training that takes place in the job situation, generally using existing staff and resources. It may include:

- Orientation or induction of new employees. Good induction is recognised as a factor in developing employee morale in the first few days.
- Learning by doing ('sitting with Annie'). An employee picks up a job by trial and error or sits with another employee for a period. Still common, though not especially effective and can easily allow the passing on of bad practices.
- **Buddying**. Employees are allocated a 'buddy' with whom they can work and learn, usually at a similar level to themselves. This can be effective, especially in the early days, but some skill is needed to select the right people to place together.
- **Mentoring**. Development or training is provided by a more senior employee, or by an equal with greater skills in a particular area.

18

This can work very well where a gap analysis has shown both strengths and weaknesses in a team, and can also help build up good staff/management relationships
- Rotational. Employees move around the organisation learning different jobs and gaining a wider view of the business. This is used more in supervisor or management training, and may be best not undertaken until the employee has had some time to settle in and learn the business
- Involvement and practice. Many skills, such as negotiation, presentational skills and taking meetings, benefit from involvement and practice. Whenever possible management should arrange this for those employees who need it.

Specific skills-based

This is training aimed at learning how to do something specific, such as operate a new machine or computer program, or understand a new staff appraisal process. It may be an external course, or it may take place in the workplace. It is often delivered by external trainers, or by representatives of the supplier or installer involved.

Generic

This is training aimed at broadening generic skills used in the job, and which form a 'toolbox' for the employee that grows over time. In procurement, examples of such skills might include negotiation, cost price analysis or sourcing overseas. Generic training is often delivered by external trainers, and may be open access (available to all) or bespoke (tailored to one company or market). This type of training is often difficult to apply immediately in a job, and its real benefit is in developing a knowledge base that can be used when required.

Professional or academic

This is training based around the addition of formal educational requirements, such as GCSEs, A-levels, degrees or masters degrees. Typically it will be focused on a few individuals, and will be taken though a college or e-learning route. This category also includes professional exams such as those offered by CIPS, the principle procurement qualifications body in the UK.

Many organisations require employees of a certain grade and above to have a professional qualification.

Learning activity 18.4

Examine training and training courses that you have been on (or have been offered) and match them to the categories in this section.

Feedback on page 303

Now go on to tackle the following self-assessment question.

Self-assessment question 18.4

Give True or False responses to the following statements on the different types of training:

1 Nowadays experience is most important, and it is rare for organisations to expect buyers to have professional qualifications. TRUE/FALSE
2 The problem with generic training is that it is often hard to apply in the job. TRUE/FALSE
3 'Buddying' is the term for development or training provided by a more senior employee or an equal with greater skills. TRUE/FALSE
4 Externally sourced training is always better than internal training, but it is usually more expensive. TRUE/FALSE
5 Orientation of employees early on is a very useful training technique. TRUE/FALSE

Feedback on page 303

18.5 Continuous professional development

A manager who expects to use employees effectively over a long period must recognise that training and skill development is not a one-off exercise. Equally, employees, especially those wishing to progress their careers, must recognise the need to keep updating their skills, training and experience if they are to be attractive to an employer.

Indeed, for some professionals (doctors for example) this is compulsory, and is built into their contract of employment.

Also, under risk management requirements many organisations see **continuous professional development** (CPD) – the process of keeping skills, training knowledge and experience up to date – as a way of demonstrating that employees are competent in their jobs.

Learning activity 18.5

Reflect on what you have read, and comment on whether the concept of CPD could (or does) apply in your current position, and what benefits it could (or does) offer you and your employer. How would it work? You may wish to discuss this with your manager or HR department.

Feedback on page 303

The concept of CPD is based on formalising the need to constantly review and update knowledge and skills. This can personally driven, or it can be organisationally or professionally driven.

Personally driven CPD

The employee or the manager takes it upon themselves to ensure this happens, by actively reviewing and refreshing their skills, or those of their employees, from time to time.

Organisationally or professionally driven CPD

In this case employees are part of a formal process, usually run by the employer or a professional body. Often there is a requirement to record a specific amount of development per year, and training courses often carry contribution ratings to help the individuals achieve their CPD ranking.

Typically CPD can be achieved through a mix of the following:

- your own efforts, using any available resources and activities such as audio/DVD/video tapes, books/publications, computer-based training and internet research
- professional association meetings and involvement
- evening courses or 'distance learning'
- seminars and workshops sponsored by academic bodies, professional associations and suppliers
- management training courses
- formal training programmes and courses
- site visits
- job rotation both inside and outside your own department
- acquiring additional qualifications including professional certificates, formal education or advanced degrees.

Self-assessment question 18.5

Fill in the blanks in the following text:

Continuous professional development is based on the need to constantly _____ and update _____ and _____ For employees this helps to keep them _____ to an employer; for an organisation it ensures that _____ from poor employee skills is minimised.

Even when an employer does not require it, employees can develop _____ CPD for themselves to keep _____ _____ _____ with their training and experience. In some professions, however, CPD is a _____ requirement.

Feedback on page 304

18.6 Evaluating the success of training

An organisation that is prepared to make a high level of commitment to training must be equally clear on the need to review and evaluate the success (or otherwise) of the training provided.

Unfortunately, it is difficult to evaluate the success of training, because it is often hard to apply quantitative measurement to the process. Also, the

18

amount of time required can be significant and costly. For these reasons many organisations do not evaluate training properly, and because of this they lose confidence in training, sometimes even abandoning projects while they are still running.

The value of training becomes harder to measure as its complexity increases. For example, it will be relatively easy to place a value on training employees to work a new procurement software system, but less easy to assess the value of negotiation training.

Learning activity 18.6

Reflect on what you read, and comment on the degree to which evaluation of training takes place in your organisation. Do you feel money is being wasted in this area? You may wish to talk to your manager or training department.

Feedback on page 304

A good training evaluation should answer a couple of reasonable questions:

- Is there evidence of a link between the training and a performance improvement?
- What is the bottom-line value to the organisation of the training (has it saved us more than it cost?)

Evaluation is also important because it can help in the design and delivery of future courses by providing clear feedback into the training planning process on the quality of the training undertaken. This ensures that the content of training courses is also the subject of continuous improvement, and helps when designing requirements and briefing training suppliers.

We can evaluate training in various ways:

- By asking participants: verbal feedback, usually on an informal basis. This needs recording and analysing to be of real value.
- By questionnaire: commonly done at the end of the training session to get a quick reaction. Needs to be done quickly, and not left for weeks. Often 'knee jerk' reactions prevail, and the job is rushed so that the attendee can leave.
- By discussion with the trainers: In particular, when external or funded training is provided there should be a follow-up to review the results.
- By a review group: a complex process, justifiable only on large training projects. The review may be by questionnaire or by interviews, or by a combination of the two. The training providers could be present.
- Through the appraisal process: This has the benefit of providing distance, and allowing the attendee to put the knowledge into practice.

A widely used model for training evaluation was devised by Donald Kirkpatrick (1975). This is a complex model, which basically attempts to evaluate training across four levels: reactions, learning, behaviour and results (see figure 18.2).

Figure 18.2: Kirkpatrick's model of training evaluation

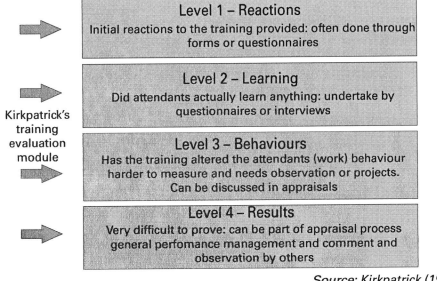

Source: Kirkpatrick (1975)

Obviously, training must deliver a return for the business, but there should be a benefit for the trainee as well. The benefits for the individual can be seen as:

- better, more enjoyable training
- responsibility and job satisfaction
- career opportunities and rewards
- skills and knowledge development.

Self-assessment question 18.6

Identify some potential issues and problems in the following statement, received confidentially from a purchasing manager:

'Our organisation has little time for the evaluation of training, which we feel is virtually impossible, except for easily measured skills such as using equipment or programs, or health and safety. We know external trainers sometimes ask for feedback, but we don't usually see this, and are not sure it would be helpful, as usually they simply want to show how well they have performed. Occasionally we do have complaints from delegates, and then we do not run the training again; however, we are always under pressure from HR to spend the training budget, so we often have to push a series of courses towards the end of the financial year.'

Feedback on page 304

18

Revision question

Now try the revision question for this session on page 338.

Summary

In this study session you have seen that training undertaken in an unfocused way is a waste of time and money, both for the organisation and for the employee. TNAs can provide this focus, and when they are combined with well-managed job profiles and job descriptions, and the encouragement of continuous professional development, there are great benefits to be gained for the organisation and the employee.

However, you have also seen that there is little point in doing all this without attempting to evaluate the success or otherwise of the training and development provided.

Suggested further reading

Students can find excellent references and checklists on training in Bailey (1997). A wide range of other useful information on training and staff development can be obtained by searching for 'training and staff development' through your web browser.

Students looking for more information on the subject of evaluation in general or on the Kirkpatrick training evaluation model should consider Kirkpatrick (1975) and Kirkpatrick and Kirkpatrick (2005).

Feedback on learning activities and self-assessment questions

Feedback on learning activity 18.1

You should show how training and development needs are assessed in your organisation, and whether or not this works well. Points to be brought out from this learning activity might include the following:

- Is there any type of formal or informal TNA process?
- If not, how is training developed in your organisation?
- What are the strengths and weaknesses?
- Any personal experience.

Feedback on self-assessment question 18.1

In learning activity 18.1 you identified how training is currently planned. This short report should turn this reflection into a management report that outlines some positive steps for improvement in your organisation.

Feedback on learning activity 18.2

Your responses should indicate which items are in your job description, with comments. You should also show useful additional items, and explain what you feel they add to the job description.

Feedback on self-assessment question 18.2

profiles – descriptions – training needs analysis – recruitment – profile – description – descriptions – updated –

Feedback on learning activity 18.3

Your response should bring out the nature of the training you (or your colleagues) have had to date, and whether you felt it fitted the definition of focused training or not.

Feedback on self-assessment question 18.3

1   TRUE. Many organisations cannot carry over training expenditure to a new financial year.
2   TRUE. Just because it is requested does not mean the employee or business will benefit.
3   FALSE. Senior management support is essential for the creation of a focused training environment.
4   TRUE. The process identifies such employees, who can then become involved.
5   FALSE. Without the TNA input the courses will be more generic and less useful to the organisation.

Feedback on learning activity 18.4

You should have provided a list of courses, showing which category you feel each one best fits into.

Feedback on self-assessment question 18.4

1   FALSE. Experience is important, but many organisations still require professional qualifications for the wider knowledge they can bring.
2   TRUE. Its real benefit is in developing a knowledge base that can be used when required.
3   FALSE. This is mentoring. In buddying, employees are allocated a 'buddy' with whom they can work and learn, usually at a similar level to themselves.
4   FALSE. Externally sourced training is usually more expensive than internal training, but it is not necessarily better.
5   TRUE. Good induction is recognised as a factor in developing employee morale in the first few days.

Feedback on learning activity 18.5

Your response should bring out whether you feel CPD could or does work for you, and the benefits to both parties. Under 'How would it work?' you may have picked up some of the points in the text:

- personal or business-driven
- a professional requirement
- many different sources and inputs.

18

Feedback on self-assessment question 18.5

review – knowledge – skills – attractive – risk – personal – up to date – compulsory

Feedback on learning activity 18.6

Your response should bring out whether you feel training is evaluated properly in your organisation, and whether or not value for money is being obtained. Some of the points in this section could appear, including:

- Why do you do the evaluation?
- How do you do it?
- Do you use a particular model or technique?

Feedback on self-assessment question 18.6

You should be able to identify the following inaccuracies:

- Evaluating training is not virtually impossible, but it does require some time and effort to do well, especially on more advanced material.
- There is no reason at all why the trainer's feedback cannot be shared with the organisation, and many external trainers will welcome the opportunity to do this.
- Of course trainers wish to see good results, but they are often genuinely anxious to identify any areas for improvement, especially if the training is likely to be repeated.
- Delegates' complaints should be investigated, and are a good source of feedback, but simply not doing the training again is not necessarily the right answer.
- End-of-year spending on training often places the training system under pressure and is likely to result in poor results. This is a bad reason for initiating training.

Information and individual performance management

Introduction

We saw in study sessions 15, 16, 17 and 18 the benefits to both the employee and the organisation of good performance management systems, positive appraisal processes, and a well-focused training and development programme. We can identify many things that are important if these systems are to work well, but one of the most important is the availability of good data.

The use of the wrong data, or data that is disputed by managers or employees, is highly likely to cause problems in a buyer performance measurement system, and can lead to the process (especially appraisal) falling into disrepute.

In this context 'data' means statements and views as well as figures, and it can therefore be both objective (based on facts) and subjective (based on opinion).

Session learning objectives

After completing this session you should be able to:

19.1 Describe the importance of data to the measurement process.
19.2 Explain the need for access to the corporate and departmental planning process, and effective systems design.
19.3 Summarise the types of data that may be used.
19.4 List the sources of data that may be used.

Unit content coverage

This study session covers the following topics from the official CIPS unit content document:

Learning outcome

• Interpret and apply statistical data used to measure performance.

Learning objective

3.6 Suggest and evaluate relevant statistical data and/or information as a basis for measuring an individual's performance including:

19

- Measuring performance against pre-set targets relating to cost reduction, profitability and productivity

Prior knowledge

You should have read study sessions 15, 16, 17 and 18, and also study session 6 (IT and data management). Knowledge of data acquisition issues and problems will also be useful

Resources

No specific resources are required, but you may find it useful to discuss this issue with your IT department or responsible manager.

Timing

You should set aside about 4 hours to read and complete this session, including learning activities, self-assessment questions, the suggested further reading (if any) and the revision question.

19.1 The importance of data in the measurement process

It may seem obvious that lack of suitable data will be a problem, and yet appraisal systems often fail because objectives are chosen that prove to be hard to measure. In addition we often find that insufficient thought has been put into ensuring that the necessary data will be available when required.

Of course objectives should not be chosen just to fit the information that *is* available. When an objective is necessary, and measurement information is not available, the employee and his or her manager need to carefully agree some terms of reference for assessing progress.

Learning activity 19.1

Reflect on any measurement data you are currently collecting that contributes to your appraisal or measurement process. Present a short report indicating whether the data is easily obtained, and whether you are happy with the quality of the data.

Feedback on page 316

Useful data needs to fit into the following categories:

Relevant

The data needs to be as closely relevant as possible to the issue or the objective that is being measured. There is little point in having information on a closely related subject just because the data needed for the main objective is not available.

For example, if we wish to reduce lead times on transactional purchasing we cannot measure this without data on all aspects of lead time (requisitioner to purchasing, inside purchasing, purchasing to supplier, and supplier to requisitioner). Without all the data, any individual pieces of data are less useful.

The same applies in more qualitative measurement. For example, when assessing presentation skills in business meetings it is not directly relevant that an individual plays a leading role in the organisation's amateur dramatic productions.

Properly targeted

An employee should be judged in relation to what is expected of them at their level or position. Avoid average measures wherever possible.

For example, it might be unfair to use a common measure of achieved savings for a group of buyers if they each have different commodities or groups of customers. In this case it would be unfair to have the same targets. Can the data be made to allow for these distinctions?

The same applies to a department. It would be unfair to set a department a savings target based on a given budget if the department cannot influence all of this budget.

Accurate

Is the data accurate, or from a trusted source? Very often, data is provided from corporate systems such as financial systems that were not set up to provide purchasing information, at least in a form suitable for accurate appraisal.

For example, we may have obtained a list of all suppliers from accounts and started a supplier rationalisation exercise, only to discover that the data does not include information for several key departments.

The need for accuracy is a particular problem when we are using subjective opinion, and in appraisals linked to rewards. Whenever possible, opinion-based data should be supported by multiple sources. For example, there is a big difference in emphasis between 'One of your customers says...' and 'Several of your customers have said...'.

19

Timely

Data should be as up to date as possible, and should be available at the requested time. This ensures that it reflects recent efforts and developments, but it can pose a strain on systems, and requires significant collection effort.

- Can the data sources keep up to date?
- Is the data available on request?
- Does the data require batch processing or special request?

Fair and impartial

All subjective data must be scrutinised to remove, as far as possible, any chance of unfairness or impartiality. This is both ethically desirable and essential for the good workings of the systems; it is also necessary by law.

Usable

Data collection on a large scale will be complex and can be expensive, especially if we are seeking personal opinions and views. Care should be taken that all data collected is used to avoid wasting time and effort. It is all too easy to have piles of data and printouts produced that are hardly used.

Self-assessment question 19.1

Give True or False responses to the following statements on the importance of data:

1   The more data you have available, the easier it will be to measure a result. TRUE/FALSE
2   If there is no data for measurement, you should not set the objective. TRUE/FALSE
3   It is best to set buyers individual targets, even if the department has an average overall target to achieve. TRUE/FALSE
4   Subjective opinions should always be sought from more than one source. TRUE/FALSE
5   Data from corporate systems is always directly usable in performance measurement. TRUE/FALSE

Feedback on page 316

19.2 Accessing corporate and departmental planning

We have seen that performance management systems should operate as part of the overall business-planning process. As with the organisational and supplier performance measures discussed in study sessions 1 to 14, much of the quantitative data needed for individual performance measurement *should* be available from corporate systems. However, we cannot assume that this means it *is* available, or that it is in the form we need. Much

19

thought and planning may be needed to access this information as and when necessary.

Learning activity 19.2

Prepare a list of any areas of your own activity where data flows seem inadequate to allow good measurement of your performance. Can you say why this data is poor? Do you feel the provision of data has been well thought through?

You may wish to discuss this with your IT department or line manager.

Feedback on page 316

We can see two main categories of information requirements: ongoing, and specfic or bespoke.

Ongoing requirements

This is data that an employee (or a department) needs to access over the long term in order to perform properly. It does not follow that all of this data will be used for performance measurement at any given time, but elements of it will be used when required. Much of this will be operational or day-to-day performance data.

In procurement, this type of data might include measurements relating to:

1 transactional activity, such as orders placed, invoices cleared or customers visited
2 budgetary conformance, such as staffing budgets, non-pay expenditures or training budgets
3 operational performance, such as savings targets, supplier appraisal or vendor rating system management
4 strategic contributions, such as margin improvements, supplier rationalisation programmes or international sourcing initiatives.

Often this type of data will come from corporate systems such as ERP (enterprise resource planning) systems, financial systems, HR systems and indeed dedicated procurement or logistics systems. However, such systems do not always provide the data needed, and frequently do not provide it in the desired format. The procurement department may need to set up local PC-based systems to extract and manipulate data to its own requirements, especially for use in performance measurement. However, where there is a consistent shortfall between the data required and the data available, purchasing management need to make every attempt to have the corporate systems enhanced.

It will also be necessary to establish regular information flows with other departments and perhaps customers and suppliers, and this will also take

19

time. These links cannot be established quickly, and need to be carefully designed, often with support from IT staff.

Much of this data is objective or quantitative, either transactional or process driven, and it is likely to be less easily available for categories 3 and 4 above, where we begin to have more bespoke data requirements (see below).

Specific or bespoke requirements

This is data that is needed so that a specific task or objective can be measured, and it could be required for any period from a few months to several years. So careful research is needed when writing and agreeing the objective, to ensure that adequate data is available to evaluate the performance achieved.

Examples of this sort of requirement might include information on:

- timescales and budgets for a specific purchasing project or capital scheme
- supplier or customer relationship initiatives
- special sourcing and market initiatives, for example overseas sourcing
- staffing or training and development initiatives
- quality of service surveys with suppliers or customers
- quality initiatives, value analysis or value engineering projects
- strategic initiatives.

Some of this data will be quantitative, but much of it will be qualitative, and therefore it will be dependent more on subjective opinion and less on figures. But, whether quantitative or qualitative, it is also less likely that the data will be easily available from existing systems.

Whether the requirement for information is ongoing or specific, the links to the business-planning process and the interaction with the organisation's business systems are critical, and need to be thought through during the process of cascading objectives. Equally, it is essential that the organisation has the skills and flexibility to create a new data flow when needed. In the case of more qualitative measures this may need some good **relationship management** as well as good systems design. Relationship management is the process of positively managing all the internal and external relationships with which the individual is involved. In procurement it is often linked to the internal customer and the supplier.

Self-assessment question 19.2

Give True or False responses to the following statements:

1 Qualitative data is often harder to get hold of and process accurately than quantitative data. TRUE/FALSE
2 Data for measuring strategic activity will be no harder to obtain than other data. TRUE/FALSE
3 The time to consider the data flow for an objective is during the business-planning process. TRUE/FALSE

(continued on next page)

19.3 Types of data used

The data and information used in performance management will vary according to the task or objective and the organisation. For a purchasing and supply organisation some typical measurement and target areas include those listed in table 19.1.

It is also important to recognise the nature of this information, which we can categorise as quantitative or qualitative, or a mix of both. This is important because, as we have seen earlier, there can be difficulties with the quality and availability of some information.

These lists are just typical examples, and you should be able to identify measures of your own that are not shown here.

Table 19.1 Measurement and target areas

Typical measurement	Category
Basic or transactional activity	
• Number of requisitions handled, orders placed etc	Quantitative
• Speed of turn round (purchasing lead time)	Quantitative
• Overall lead time (from request to receipt)	Quantitative
• Number of complaints	Mix
• Number of invoice queries	Quantitative
• Expediting activity	Quantitative
• Quality and effectiveness of service	Mix
• Internal and external customer satisfaction	Mix
Departmental or internal performance	
• Staffing costs and levels to budget or targeted reductions	Quantitative
• Non-pay cost to budget or targeted reductions	Quantitative
• Staff appraisal and development/training targets	Mix
• Activity ratios per employee	Quantitative
• Personnel and welfare issues	Qualitative
• Staff recruitment/retention targets	Mix
Operational performance	
• Savings or margin contribution	Quantitative
• Amount of delegated procurement activity	Quantitative
• Use of procurement cards	Mix
• Inventory reduction	Quantitative
• Quality or service improvements	Qualitative
• Environmental targets	Quantitative
• Impact on current business objectives	Mix
• Performance against corporate milestones	Mix
• Legislative and process compliance targets	Mix
• Project milestones	
Strategic performance	

(continued on next page)

Table 19.1 *(continued)*

Typical measurement	Category
• New sourcing strategies	Mix
• Product and materials development	Mix
• Supplier relationships and development	Mix
• Contribution to company performance	Mix
• Make or buy strategies	Mix
• Value analysis and value engineering	Mix
• Globalisation targets	Mix

Learning activity 19.3

Complete table 19.2 to analyse the type of data needed to measure the key tasks in your job description. Is it shown in the list of typical measures in table 19.1? Comment on the quality of data used to measure you.

Table 19.2

My key objectives	Shown in list? Y/N	Comment
1		
2		
3		
4		

Feedback on page 317

Now go on to tackle the following self-assessment question.

Self-assessment question 19.3

Answer these multiple-choice questions.

1   Quantitative data is more concerned with:
A opinions
B views
C facts
D reviews.

2   Which of these statements does *not* apply to qualitative data:
A It is harder to obtain.
B It is harder to judge as right or wrong.
C It is generated from IT systems.
D It comes from many sources.

3   Generally. measures used for assessing strategic level performance will not be:
A based on quantitative measurements
B based on others' judgements
C based on a wider view of business activity
D based on qualitative measurements.

(continued on next page)

Self-assessment question 19.3 (continued)

4 Many performance measurements will be based on:
A a mix of different inputs
B inputs from ERP systems
C inputs from human resources
D inputs from the employee.

5 Welfare targets for employees would generally be considered as:
A strategic measures
B departmental measures
C transactional measures
D operational measures.

Feedback on page 317

19.4 Sources of usable data

Clearly there will be a wide range of sources of data available, depending on the performance measure in use and the sophistication of the organisational systems. Those working in smaller organisations may have less access to corporate data systems (though this is not always a disadvantage), but note that volume of information is not the most important factor.

We should not assume that all data comes from IT systems. Although much data *is* available from IT systems, many organisations still have substantial paper records available, and much of the qualitative or subjective information will be written (or emailed) or verbal.

Learning activity 19.4

Investigate the sources of performance management data that your organisation uses, list then in table 19.3, and comment on how useful you feel each one is. Identify any other sources that you feel could be used, and state why.

You may wish to discuss this with you IT department or line manager.

Table 19.3

Data sources used	Comment
Other source	
Other source	
Other source	

Feedback on page 317

19

Sources of data for use in performance measurement might include organisational systems, personally managed systems, forms and pro formas, internal customers, suppliers, external organisations and research.

Organisational systems

These could include ERP, MRP and DRP systems, financial systems, HR systems, logistics systems and organisational procurement systems.

Departmental systems

In some organisations, systems are run only at departmental level. These can often be adapted more quickly than corporate systems, and may be more suitable for bespoke measurement data.

This is often the best level for gathering, storing and processing subjective data.

Personally managed systems

Most procurement staff will have access to a PC, and will have some sort of personal filing system of their own. This can often be used or modified to provide data for a performance management activity, though some validation of the data may be necessary from time to time. Personal systems are often kept as backups, or as duplicates when employees are not entirely happy with the main recording systems.

Forms and pro formas

Much long-term procurement can be monitored during delivery to ensure that performance of both the contractor and the procurement team is satisfactory. The completion of regular returns of this nature is common in service contract monitoring and vendor rating systems, and can provide a useful contribution to procurement performance measurement.

Input from internal customers

Many areas of performance can be measured with the help of input from internal customers who are the recipients of procurement services. This input will tend to be subjective, and will need to be used carefully to ensure accuracy. It can be especially usefully in the measurement of purchasing service quality and when measuring supplier performance. Customer surveys and questionnaires can be useful, but it is worth bearing in mind that improvements over time cannot be measured unless these are undertaken regularly, which can be time-consuming.

Data from suppliers

Supplier data is commonly used (especially where e-business links are in place), to monitor such measures as service levels, lead times and delivery performance. Many organisations also still rely on supplier information to find out what product ranges and volumes they are using.

This is basically transactional activity, and some organisations go further and look to measure aspects of buyers' performance by asking for suppliers' views. This can either be direct or via supplier surveys, and the results can be revealing, to say the least.

External organisations

Sources such as trade organisations, professional bodies, government agencies and statistical organisations can provide good sources of up-to-date and independent data that can be used in performance management. For example, buyers may wish to use the RPI index of inflation or the CIPS market price indices when calculating price savings or analysing cost breakdowns. Such organisations would not usually have a direct input into a buyer's measurement or appraisal, but the data they provide can be very useful.

Research

Data suitable for use in performance measurement can also be gained from newspapers, magazines and the media, library research, and of course the internet. However, this 'raw' data will often need validation before it can become acceptable evidence.

Self-assessment question 19.4

Draft a short report critically examining what you have found as detailed in learning activity 19.4 above, and making recommendations for widening the sources used for performance measurement data in your organisation.

Feedback on page 317

Revision question

Now try the revision question for this session on page 338.

Summary

We have looked in some detail at the availability and need for good data if our performance measurement systems are to be effective and if they are to retain credibility with both the organisation and the employees who are being measured. Clearly, there are many aspects of good performance management schemes, but good data is always essential, and the absence of this data has created weaknesses in many systems.

We have also looked at several activities that are commonly measured, and have suggested the degree to which data needs to be quantitative or qualitative or a mix of both.

Finally we have looked at potential sources of performance data.

19

Feedback on learning activities and self-assessment questions

Feedback on learning activity 19.1

Your report might include some comments on the following aspects of the data in question:

- Is it relevant?
- Is it properly targeted?
- Is it accurate?
- Is it timely?
- Is it fair and impartial?
- Is it in usable format?

Feedback on self-assessment question 19.1

1   FALSE. Too much data is as bad as too little, and is unlikely to be used.
2   FALSE. If the objective is a necessary organisational requirement, it must be set.
3   TRUE. Setting the departmental average for each buyer does not allow for differences in buyer portfolios, training and ability, or market conditions.
4   TRUE. This helps to remove bias and provide a more realistic view of performance.
5   FALSE. Corporate data needs editing, as does all data, to fit the specific measurement criteria required.

Feedback on learning activity 19.2

You should have prepared a list highlighting inadequate data flows in relation to your job and organisation, with comments on the inadequacy of the data where possible. Issues could include:

- shortage of day-to-day data
- poor paper or IT systems
- no longer-term information
- no qualitative information
- bad interdepartmental communication.

Feedback on self-assessment question 19.2

1   TRUE. Quantitative data is often available from existing systems.
2   FALSE. Data for strategic or bespoke projects will be harder to obtain, and may need special data collection methods.
3   TRUE. At this stage a new data flow can be developed if needed.
4   TRUE. Customers and suppliers may provide quantitative and qualitative data.
5   TRUE. Procurement may need to set up local PC-based systems to extract and manipulate data to its own requirements.

19

Feedback on learning activity 19.3

There is no specific answer. You should be able to identify with some of the points listed in the text or, if not, identify your own objectives. You should also analyse how satisfied you feel with the quality of the data.

Feedback on self-assessment question 19.3

Answers

1 C. Quantitative data is concerned more with facts.
2 C. Qualitative data generally does not come from IT systems, though such data may be used in making qualitative judgements.
3 A. Strategic-level performance will generally be based less on just facts and figures.
4 A. Many measures, especially those above transactional level. require a mix of inputs.
5 B. Welfare issues would be departmental targets or objectives.

Feedback on learning activity 19.4

You should have completed the table and provided details of other sources that you believe could be used. You may have identified some of the following broad categories:

- systems in your organisation
- systems in your department
- systems of your own (or a colleague)
- existing or new forms and pro formas
- input from internal customers
- input from selected suppliers
- inputs from external organisations or stakeholders
- research data.

Feedback on self-assessment question 19.4

You should provide feedback in report form on the data sources used, which should include a number of those mentioned above. Your criticism should be balanced to show good and bad points, with suggestions for improvement and for widening of the sources of data used.

19

Buyer and supplier performance links

Introduction

Many organisations are increasingly recognising that purchasing departments have to be able to prove they are adding value to the procurement process or the supply chain. It is certainly not always acceptable that judgements on good performance should be left within procurement, and it is becoming more important to take a wider view of procurement success.

Often the problem with measuring buyers' performance is that it satisfies the purchasing and supply management team, but it rarely addresses the views of everyone else who comes into contact with the purchasing service.

In study session 17 we looked briefly at the role that other stakeholders could play, and perhaps the only real way to measure any department's performance is to ask those who have dealings with it for their views. In this session we shall develop this idea further.

> Involving suppliers in our performance measurement is like sleeping with the enemy – we may find it interesting in the short term, but what will the long-term implications be?

Session learning objectives

After completing this session you should be able to:

20.1 Evaluate the weaknesses of existing approaches to performance measurement.
20.2 Argue that there is a need and benefit from relating performance to wider issues.
20.3 Define potential performance measurement links to suppliers.
20.4 Define possible performance measurement links to other stakeholders.

Unit content coverage

This study session covers the following topics from the official CIPS content document:

Learning outcome

Appraise measures that can be used to improve supplier performance.

Learning objective

3.7 Compare the relative performance measures of the buyer with those of his/her respective suppliers.
 • Key measures of supplier performance: competency, commitment, capacity, control

20

- Key measures of buyer performance: skill and knowledge, plus contribution to an organisation's goals and targets

Prior knowledge

You should have read sessions 15–19.

Resources

No specific resources are required, but you will find it useful to discuss this issue with fellow students, with other colleagues, and perhaps with line managers.

Timing

You should set aside about 4 hours to read and complete this session, including learning activities, self-assessment questions, the suggested further reading (if any) and the revision question.

20.1 The weaknesses of existing approaches to performance measurement

We have already seen that there can be difficulties in establishing a performance measurement system that works well, and that there are various processes and relationships that must work effectively over a long period of time for good schemes to make sustained progress. Inevitably, this fails to happen in many organisations. Indeed, even where the processes within performance and appraisal systems appear to be working well, the results may not provide the real benefits that the organisation deserves and requires.

Learning activity 20.1

Consider your organisation, and list any broad weaknesses of its approach to buyer performance measurement.

Feedback on page 329

Why may a performance measurement system not provide the benefits the organisation needs? There are several reasons for this.

The programme satisfies only the 'owners'

A measurement system has been developed that is believed to be working well at all levels within the purchasing department. Management and staff are broadly satisfied, and the results are good in terms of the numbers and the targets used. However, in reality the scheme has lost sight of the wider picture, and is measuring only what purchasing believe is important. It is 'inward-looking'. This can be the case if the measurement system no longer links to the wider business goals, or is not really being monitored from senior management level.

There is too much information

We have talked about the difficulties that may arise if data is not available to support measurement and appraisal. However, the rapid growth of data management systems in the last 15 years has often resulted in a situation where there is too much data or too many 'numbers', and this can effectively swamp appraisal systems. Indeed, the latest thinking in IT terms is that a decision management system should now sit above an ERP system in order to sift data and present only the absolutely key information. The same thinking needs to be applied to personal performance measurement. In particular, an overemphasis on measurables can reduce the qualitative content of the measurement process.

Setting unachievable targets

On occasions the targets and objectives set in even the best-managed systems are incapable of being achieved. This is not uncommon in the public sector, where political pressure can set targets for which the structure or resources of an organisation are inadequate or incapable. Closely linked to this is the issue of unrealistic timescales.

As an example, over the last 20 years the UK government has regularly changed the structure and ownership of the central purchasing function in the National Health Service, largely in order to improve procurement practice and achieve savings. At the same time it has also encouraged a great deal of procurement freedom and autonomy at hospital and clinic level. The two strategies may well be incompatible with the hoped-for savings gains, and lead to the setting of unachievable targets.

When this sort of thing happens consistently, performance measurement schemes begin to fail, or seek easier targets.

Unsuited to this department

Not all organisations and departments lend themselves to the kind of measurement systems that we have discussed in the study sessions so far. This is especially the case if the nature of their work does not fundamentally lend itself to measurement, or is almost entirely subjective. In purchasing this might be the case with strategic policy units or 'think tanks', IT or data analysts, commodity advisers, or quality control teams.

Nobody wants to drop it

Sometimes faults within the performance measurement system have caused it to become a mechanistic process, driven only by the fact that the organisation will not face up to (or is unaware of) the need to review the arrangements. This is often the case in public sector schemes, and in organisations without good two-way communication. It is also a problem when the system is 'championed' by a director or senior manager.

Blame cultures

Good performance and appraisal process require open, two-way communication and regular, managed feedback up the organisation. They also need performance management to take place in a 'no blame' environment, where those involved do not fear making mistakes or occasional failures. If this is not the case communication becomes limited, and the measurement system becomes unwieldy and penal.

However, although the above factors are important, many of those involved in performance measurement are now arguing that failure to adequately take into account the views and wishes of stakeholders is the greatest weakness of all.

Self-assessment question 20.1

Fill in the blanks in the following text:

The HR department of Big Factory plc believes it has identified weaknesses in the purchasing performance measurement system. It has become _____ as the process has taken over, and seems to have lost sight of the _____ _____. There are several processes and _____ that must work _____, and this sometimes fails to happen, and some targets are _____, causing employees concern. However, the biggest problem is that some _____ feel the department fails to take their views into account.

If purchasing was less _____ _____ it could consider involving its _____ or _____ in the process, with positive results.

Feedback on page 329

20.2 The wider involvement of stakeholders

The argument used for the positive inclusion of stakeholders is that, in today's global economy, the perceived performance of many organisations is about more than just the balance sheet.

For example, at a corporate level several oil companies have experienced bad publicity around environmental issues, and car manufacturers are occasionally shown to be disregarding safety issues. When this happens the stakeholders are the general public (and investors), and their confidence in these organisations can be significantly undermined by such problems.

Figure 20.1 shows some of the common stakeholder groups for any department.

Figure 20.1: Common stakeholder groups

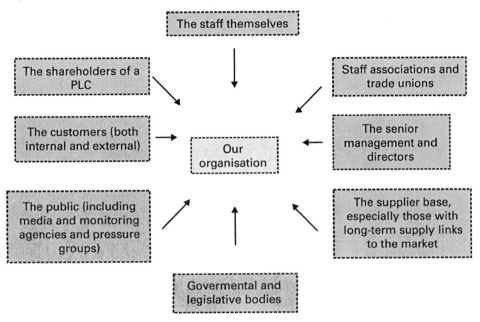

In addition, the involvement of stakeholders helps to ensure that performance management does not become too 'cosy' as discussed above.

Learning activity 20.2

Reflect on what you have read and write a short analysis of the scope for involving other stakeholders in the measurement of purchasing performance in your organisation. You may wish to discuss this with your line manager.

Feedback on page 329

In purchasing departments there are generally three major stakeholders to be considered: the corporate management team, the internal customers, and the suppliers.

The corporate management team

The corporate management team will have two main concerns:

- In a narrow sense, they will wish to see purchasing perform well to the performance targets set through the type of cascade process we have considered already.
- In the wider sense, the corporate team will have views on how these targets are achieved. and on the wider implications for the business.

For example, the buyers in a food manufacturing business will be expected to maintain or improve quality while improving margins and reducing costs. However, if in the process of doing this they fall out with farmers, who then start lobbying Parliament and the media, this may be seen as a

20

failure at corporate level. The procurement objective is met, but the business consequences can be unforeseen.

The internal customers

As we have seen elsewhere in this course, there is often tension between the traditional role of the purchasing function and the wishes of the end users or customers, who see purchasing as a mechanistic organisation that interferes with their getting the products and services they want. This can in part be resolved by better communication and stronger links between the functions, and involvement in the purchasing performance measurement process can be a very useful contribution to this process.

If the purchasing function is not perceived to be providing its customers with the service they require, then arguably it is failing to satisfy a major stakeholder.

For example, a hospital wishes to buy Brand A physiotherapy equipment because it sees it offering improved facilities, but purchasing buys Brand B, which is more cost-effective and compatible with existing equipment. The procurement objective is met, but the customers perceive purchasing to be ignoring their views as users and experts.

If we are an internal customer (and stakeholder) we shall expect two levels of performance from our purchasing colleagues. At one level we expect them to provide us with the operational service we require, and this can be summed up in ensuring that the 'five rights' apply: 'the right products, of the right quality, at the right prices, at the right timing and delivery, and in the right quantities'.

However, we also expect a reasonable level of service and professionalism, and increasingly we expect what might be considered as added value services: services that place purchasing high on the list of departments helping to drive the business forward. These include strategic contributions such as sourcing strategies, supplier and product development, and cost reduction programmes. They might also include softer contributions such as expanding product knowledge, training and development of non-purchasing staff, and developing better customer relations.

The suppliers

It has often been argued that a purchasing department is only as good as its suppliers. This view has been around for many years, but is especially true from the perspective of other stakeholders in the organisation who use the suppliers that purchasing has chosen.

Of course, there is often a problem even in well-structured organisations, because the demands of stakeholders conflict. This is quite normal, and in this situation purchasing and supply management will have to prioritise its stakeholder input – not always an easy thing to do.

In the next section we shall discuss this link between buyers and suppliers in more depth.

20.3 Performance measurement links to suppliers

A supplier is a stakeholder for the period for which it holds a contract to supply a particular organisation with a given product or service. That is to say, it has an interest in how the organisation performs, not least because it wishes to do business under the contract.

However, some suppliers are also stakeholders in the industry or service in question and therefore have a stake in the success of the industry as a whole, even though they do business with only parts of it at one time.

For example, a UK-based supplier of oil drilling pumping equipment has a contract with two large oil companies. This supplier has a direct stake not only in these companies performance but also in the performance of the whole industry.

When suppliers fail to perform well there are often problems in the relationship that are the fault of the buying organisation. Suppliers may therefore feel entitled to a view as to how business is conducted, an opportunity to add value to the process, and perhaps even an opportunity to measure the effectiveness of the purchasing department. The organisation may also support this view!

The attitude and contribution of suppliers can have a major impact both on a business and on how the purchasing team with whom they deal is perceived, so it should be in the interests of the purchasing team to involve willing suppliers in this way.

Suppliers' contributions to measuring purchasing performance can be broadly divided into two elements.

How is purchasing's operational performance?

This is where the supplier passes judgement on the day-to-day performance of purchasing. We can see several potential issues here:

- Is the purchasing organisation dealing well with the transactional and basic operational process involved in servicing the buying arrangement?
- Does the supplier find purchasing easy to deal with and accessible?
- Is day-to-day communication good?
- Are queries dealt with promptly?
- Are payments processed quickly?
- Are tenders and bids (where used) handled in a supplier-friendly manner?

What value does purchasing add?

This is where the supplier passes judgement on the added value that purchasing contributes to the relationships the supplier has with the buying organisation:

- Is purchasing trying to work with the supplier in a positive way to bring additional benefits?
- Does purchasing respond to savings opportunities when offered?
- Will they let suppliers contribute to value analysis and value engineering studies?
- Is there a role for suppliers in the development of specifications?
- Will they allow suppliers to train and develop users and purchasing staff?
- Do they respond to ideas on manufacturing or process improvements, or on new technologies and materials?
- Will they accept ideas on ways to improve communications?

Suppliers who wish to work in this way should receive active support from the purchasing department, and together they can provide a better service to the customer. This type of supplier relationship will enhance the image of procurement within an organisation, so there should be mutual benefit. Including the supplier in the performance measurement process may help to create the right environment.

Purchasing (with the customer's help) remains responsible for measuring and monitoring that the service proved is satisfactory, but the customer (the stakeholder) will also express their view through an input to the measurement and appraisal process.

The process is shown diagrammatically in figure 20..

20

Figure 20.2: Input to the performance measurement process

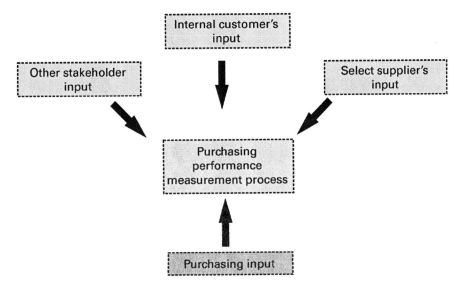

Attempting to introduce a measurement system with this kind of involvement can create a number of potential problems. These might include the following:

- Selling the idea in the business. Will other stakeholders and management accept the idea?
- Selling the idea to the staff involved. How will it be received by the staff dealing with this supplier?
- Choosing appropriate suppliers. Clearly not all suppliers will wish to work in this way, and only a few with a major stake in the business or the industry are likely to be suitable.
- Control and audit. How can we ensure the information is accurate?

Care should also be taken to ensure this is a bona fide wish on the part of the supplier, and not just an attempt to weaken or bypass procurement!

Self-assessment question 20.3

Following on from learning activity 20c, write a short report on the potential benefits of introducing an approach involving suppliers in measuring purchasing performance. What difficulties would you envisage?

Feedback on page 330

20.4 Performance links with other stakeholders

We have seen that typically there can be three major stakeholders for a purchasing team, and we have considered in some detail the contribution that suppliers can make. The other stakeholders may also be able to provide a useful perspective on how purchasing is performing (apart from any views

20

as customers), which should also be included in the measurement and appraisal process.

These other stakeholders could include:

- Finance: Are all budget targets being met, and is there sufficient emphasis on real savings and margin improvements?
- Operational management: Is purchasing adding real value to the organisation, and are the contributions ensuring minimum adverse reactions or bad publicity?
- Human resources: Are staffing issues and problems being dealt with effectively, and are appraisal and development programmes operated well?
- Risk management: Are the products and services supplied contributing to, and in line with, risk management strategies?
- Specialist departments, eg health and safety: Do all products and services supplied comply fully with heath and safety policies and guidance?
- Staff associations: Does purchasing have good employee relations, and manage and develop staff well?
- The wider public: Is the organisation perceived to procure in a public-minded way, including environmental and ethical issues, eg exploiting child labour?

Learning activity 20.4

Consider to what extent – if any – other stakeholders already influence procurement performance measurement in your organisation. List some of those involved, and the contribution they make.

Feedback on page 330

Now go on to tackle the following self-assessment question.

Self-assessment question 20.4

Write a second report, following on from your views on involving suppliers, that looks at the potential benefits of introducing other stakeholders into the assessment process.

Feedback on page 331

Summary

In study sessions 15 to 19 we have considered the benefits of performance management for the organisation and the employees, and have looked at how this links to training and development, including continuous professional development. We have also considered the issues that can arise if the information flow necessary for good performance management does not work effectively.

In all these study sessions we have been looking at what might be considered as the conventional model of performance management and appraisal, based on cascaded objectives and a departmental or organisational appraisal system.

In this session we have tried to move away from the conventional model by involving those who have a stake in an effective purchasing and supply department in the performance measurement process. If this is done well, the final outcome should be a much fairer measure of the true contribution that purchasing is making.

Suggested further reading

Students will find Neely et al (2002) especially relevant for an overview of approaches that may be of use in considering the subject of this session.

Feedback on learning activities and self-assessment questions

Feedback on learning activity 20.1

You should identify those that are the biggest issues in your organisation. These could include the following:

- The programme is too inward-looking.
- There is too much information'
- Unachievable targets are set.
- The process is not suitable for this department.
- Nobody wants to drop it!
- There is a blame culture.

Did you identify the need to involve external stakeholders?

Feedback on self-assessment question 20.1

mechanistic – wider picture – relationships – effectively – unachievable – stakeholders – inward looking – suppliers – customers

Feedback on learning activity 20.2

Your analysis should nominate some stakeholders who could participate in the measurement process, and indicate the contribution they could make.

Table 20.1

Stakeholder	Potential Contribution

20

Feedback on self-assessment question 20.2

1 FALSE. Conflicting stakeholder ambitions are not a function of poor management but of the different roles each stakeholder has.
2 FALSE. Decisions made by purchasing teams (especially in the public sector) can sometimes impact directly on the public, eg disposal of waste in a service contract.
3 TRUE. Shareholders have increasing expectations of company performance.
4 TRUE. Bad procurement can lead to visible rows, overspends or bad news stories.
5 TRUE. In some organisations the real measure of a successful supplier is one who keeps the customer happy.

Feedback on learning activity 20.3

You should comment on whether or not any suppliers are involved in measuring purchasing performance and, if so, what impact and issues it has created.

Feedback on self-assessment question 20.3

There is no specific right answer; you should look for issues of real benefit to your organisation. Try to bring out some of the points highlighted in this section, if they are relevant.

Show who the suppliers could be, the degree of contribution they could make, and what the contribution could be.

Feedback on learning activity 20.4

Your list of stakeholders might include:

- operational/production management
- finance
- HR
- risk management
- specialist, eg health and safety
- staff associations or trade unions
- the public.

Table 20.2

Stakeholder	Involved in your organisation Y/N	Comment on contribution
Stakeholder Operational/production management		
Finance		
HR		
Risk management		
Specialist, eg health and safety		
Staff associations or trade unions		
The public		

Feedback on self-assessment question 20.4

There is no specific right answer; you should look for issues of real benefit to your organisation. Try to bring out some of the points or stakeholders highlighted in this section if they are relevant, but consider others that are applicable in your business.

Show who the stakeholder could be, the degree of contribution, and what the contribution could be.

Revision questions

Revision question for study session 1

You have been recently appointed as the supply chain manager to a medium-sized manufacturing company producing engineering components and employing a workforce of some 1,500.

Your remit is to source all goods and services for the business, and manage the supply chain for your business.

You have line responsibility for three managers: the purchasing and contracts manager, the stores and stock control manager, and the transport and distribution manager.

You are preparing a report to be submitted to the Board to recommend new targets for, and reporting of, key performance indicators (KPIs) for your department.

Draft the outline of this report. The report should have a clear introduction of the issues, and should detail the performance indicators for each manager in your team. The report should state the methodology you would use to identify the KPIs, and should conclude with some management recommendations linked to your business.

Feedback on page 341

Revision question for study session 2

Your company has a programme of cross-functional training sessions planned to ensure a good understanding of departmental principles and processes.

As the purchasing manager, you have been asked to deliver a one-hour presentation to a group of internal operational managers and user departments on the subject of 'total cost of acquisition', and how this relates to costs and performance.

The presentation timescale is:

Introduction – 10 minutes

Subject presentation – 35 minutes

Questions – 15 minutes.

You have decided to prepare six PowerPoint slides for the subject presentation, and you now have to draft the bullet points for each slide, together with brief trainer's notes, which will be given out with the slides as handouts.

Describe the content and points that you will include in your presentation.

Feedback on page 341

Revision question for study session 3

The management of a business operates at various levels: strategic management, tactical/operational management, and transactional management.

Write an essay discussing how a purchasing manager would select key performance indicators (KPIs) for each level of management under his or her control, and how these KPIs interface with corporate plans.

Feedback on page 342

Revision question for study session 4

As purchasing manager for your organisation you have identified your top 20% of products by spend value.

You have decided that in future your requests for quotation (RFQs) will request detailed cost information from your suppliers rather than just unit selling prices.

You need to give the suppliers a brief guidance note on what you want and how you need the information.

Taking an example of a manufactured engineering component, what information will you ask a supplier to detail in future offers?

Set out how you will present this guidance note to suppliers bidding for future supply contracts.

Feedback on page 342

Revision question for study session 5

You are the stores and stock control manager for your organisation. Your managing director is concerned about the level of stock held and the cost of holding stock.

The stores is being set up as a cost centre, and you are to identify all costs of holding stock in order to set a stores on-cost percentage.

Describe how you will calculate the real cost of stockholding and, having set this, how you will manage the stores and stock control performance indicators for the future.

Feedback on page 343

Revision question for study session 6

Your organisation is reviewing its IT systems, and discussions are under way with two suppliers who offer corporate integrated IT management systems.

As purchasing manager you have been asked what are the most important elements for you to operate the purchasing system within the proposed corporate IT process.

Prepare a set of headers and brief notes on each point as part of your response to the IT manager.

Feedback on page 343

Revision question for study session 7

You are the purchasing and supply manager for a medium-sized manufacturing company that has a few problems with supplier deliveries and pricing, but some major concerns over quality are your biggest worry. Currently your supplier measurement systems are poor to non-existent.

Write a report for your board to:

- demonstrate how introducing systems for measuring supplier performance might impact on different aspects of the five basic 'rights' of purchasing
- analyse the particular impact it might have on solving your quality problems
- make some brief recommendations for consideration by the board.

Feedback on page 344

Revision question for study session 8

You are the deputy supplies manager for a large trust hospital. About 60% of procurement comes through your department, and you have some good supplier measurement systems in place. Your manager has asked you to make a presentation to the estates, pharmacy and TSSU departments who manage the rest of the spend, clarifying in particular:

- where supplier performance measurement fits into a typical procurement process
- the differences between pre-award assessments and post-award evaluation
- the basic steps to be taken to implement each.

Your final presentation will be in PowerPoint form, but your manager wants to see your rough draft of the text and diagrams first. You should prepare this in writing in the following format:

- Slide 1: Title; points or paragraph to be presented, with diagram if required
- Slide 2: Title; points or paragraph to be presented

and so on to the end of your presentation.

Feedback on page 345

Revision question for study session 9

You are probably familiar with the concept of the buyer's 'toolkit', and also with the idea that not all performance management activity can be desk based.

Write an essay discussing the merits of the different kinds of tool that are available for supplier performance management, and clarify the base through which they could be applied.

Feedback on page 345

Revision question for study session 10

You work in the purchasing department of a large university, which is just outsourcing its office cleaning services.

Your manager has asked you to prepare a management report for him outlining the generic post-award performance measurement systems that could be used to monitor the supplier, with some simple examples. He also wants you to make a recommendation in the report as to which system might be most appropriate, and give your reasons why.

Feedback on page 346

Revision question for study session 11

You are the senior buyer in a medium-sized food processing company that is currently experiencing disputes and conflicts with its supplier base. To provide some background for a meeting of departmental managers your managing director has asked you to prepare a short paper that:

- classifies the communications links and relationships that *can* be established across the different levels in the business
- appraises the nature of disputes and conflicts
- selects some appropriate ways for helping to resolve these disputes and conflicts.

Feedback on page 347

Revision question for study session 12

Kieran is head of the purchasing department of a large local authority. The authority has recently undergone a large reorganisation, and has moved much of the transactional activity (order placing, expediting etc) to the users, leaving the central team free to concentrate on higher-value, longer-term contracts.

As part of this restructuring the head of finance (Kieran's boss) wishes to outplace one of his staff to provide full-time support to Kieran, as he believes there is a valuable role to fill. Kieran is less sure, believing this is the start of financial interference in procurement.

Discuss this scenario in an essay, and demonstrate the benefits you think will come from such a placement.

Feedback on page 347

Revision question for study session 13

Your organisation has recently announced plans to implement joint performance measurement initiatives with a number of key suppliers, starting with the setting up of some cross-functional teams. After this was announced, several questions were raised at your team meeting, and you have agreed to write an explanatory paragraph on each question for the next purchasing newsletter. The questions raised were:

1 Why do we need joint initiatives? Isn't our existing measurement system enough?
2 Isn't this going to be very expensive to implement?
3 If we have a team and they have a team, aren't we just going to end up arguing?
4 Why would the suppliers want to participate in this process?

Your response should have a short introduction clarifying (for other readers) what joint performance measurement is, plus four specific answers to the questions (do not restate the question).

Feedback on page 348

Revision question for study session 14

You are buying in a difficult market, and have identified a supplier who is not performing well. You are surprised by this, as the supplier seems keen, and showed promise during the initial pre-award assessments.

Write an essay discussing the options you have for dealing with this supplier, and demonstrate why developing the supplier might be beneficial for your business.

Feedback on page 348

Revision question for study session 15

You are working in defence procurement, and your HR department has decided to extend the departmental performance review scheme to procurement staff, linking it to performance-related pay and advancement opportunities.

Using a report style, prepare an information bulletin for issue to staff that highlights the positive benefits that both they and the department will gain from having such a performance review scheme in place.

Feedback on page 349

Revision question for study session 16

It is essential to write good, clear objectives if performance measurement for buyers is to work effectively.

(a) Describe four common elements found in typical simple objectives.

(b) Classify the five key principles used when writing objectives.
(c) Demonstrate the application of the elements and principles you have identified in (a) and (b) by writing one objective for each of the following activities:
   (i) achieving purchasing savings
   (ii) improving the quality of a product
   (iii) writing objectives for members of your team
   (iv) producing a departmental newsletter.

Feedback on page 350

Revision question for study session 17

Consider the process of staff appraisal/evaluation, which is often at the heart of performance management for purchasing and supply staff. Organisations can have very different views on how this is done, and on who should be involved in the process.

Write an essay that:

- discusses the advantages and disadvantages of the different levels of formality and administration
- demonstrates the practicality of involving other parties than the line manager.

Feedback on page 351

Revision question for study session 18

Your organisation is planning to identify a targeted training programme for purchasing and supply staff, and intends to undertake a training needs analysis (TNA) to help establish exactly what training is required.

Planning is still in the early stages, but to help keep staff informed you have been asked to write an internal memo/email that:

- introduces the TNA concept
- demonstrates to staff the reasoning behind the decision to use a TNA, and tells more about the steps involved
- classifies a selection of potential training solutions that might be used once the outputs of the TNA are available.

Feedback on page 351

Revision question for study session 19

In procurement there is often an ongoing requirement for information and data to allow effective buyer performance measurement, and this information and data will be both qualitative and quantitative in nature.

(a) There are four main categories of performance. State what these categories are, and demonstrate the different characteristics of each. (33% of marks)

(b) Using the categories you have identified, select at least four example measures for each category, providing a brief description of the measure and whether it is qualitative or quantitative in nature. (66% of marks)

There is no set requirement for a style of response, but you may find a table-type format useful.

Feedback on page 352

Revision question for study session 20

'A supplier is a major stakeholder in the performance of the buying team it deals with.'

Discuss this concept in an essay, demonstrating how the buying team performance may be viewed by the supplier, and evaluating the issues that might occur if suppliers are brought into the measurement process for buyers.

Feedback on page 353

Feedback on revision questions

Feedback on revision question for study session 1

Your report could have the following structure. The writing times are for guidance only.

(a) *Introduction*
     Explain the principles and importance of setting KPIs for the supply chain. This should be only a summary for the benefit of Board members who may not be familiar with the value of KPIs (say 15% of writing time).

(b) *Identify the role of each element in the supply chain*
     There are three elements in the flow of goods through the supply chain:
     •   inbound contracts and purchasing
     •   intra-site stores and stock control
     •   outbound transport and distribution.
     (This will need about 25% of writing time.)

(c) *Methodology*
     Explain how the three department managers work together and with other operational managers on the flow of goods into, through and out from the business.
     State a model or methodology of how you will review, coordinate, identify, set and report on KPI targets.
     This is the largest section of your report (say 35% of writing time).

(d) *Recommendations*
     State how you will report the results, and how you will interface with other operational managers and systems. For example, in this business you may well be working on an MRP system with production management. Ensure that the issue of continuous improvement is covered in the recommendations
     Around three recommendations will do (say 25% of writing time).

Note: This question is focused on the following sections in study session 1:

•   1.1 The importance of performance management in business
•   1.6 The importance of measuring purchasing and supply chain performance in public and private sector organisations

Feedback on revision question for study session 2

The main headers would need to cover the following six points:

(a) Setting the scene; definition of total cost of acquisition (TCA).
(b) Why all managers need to understand this concept.

(c) How user departments and purchasing can work together to add value to TCA solutions.

(d) How you would measure TCA performance over time.

(e) How you would learn from decisions and operations to ensure continuous improvement for the organisation.

(f) How this best practice process benefits the organisation as a whole.

Note: This question is focused on the following sections in study session 2:

- 2.1 Added value performance management in corporate business operations: general principles
- 2.5 Added value opportunities of negotiating improved procurement and contract terms with suppliers

Feedback on revision question for study session 3

Your essay could contain:

(a) *Introduction*
A brief explanation of the key issues for a purchasing manager at each level and the relationship to the wider corporate plans (say 20% of writing time).

(b) *The main issues*
The purchasing issues as developed from a model similar to table 3.3. An explanation that the KPIs need to pass the SMART criteria set out in the course book, with purchasing examples.
How each management level interfaces with the departmental plan.
How the departmental plan is a part of the wider company plan.
(This part of the essay would take some 60% of writing time.)

(c) *Conclusion*
Confirming what you have said, emphasising the business benefits and closing the essay (say 20% of writing time).

Note: This question is focused on the following sections in study session 3:

- 3.1 How do purchasing and supply managers contribute to the KPI targets set by corporate management?
- 3.2 How do purchasing and supply managers select and set KPIs for their core business operation?

Feedback on revision question for study session 4

(a) *Introduction*
It would be useful to explain why more detailed cost analysis data is of use to a purchasing manager (say 20% of writing time).

(b) *The main body*
Your main areas are likely to be as follows:
- Give suppliers a brief definition of the cost categories: fixed, variable, other costs
- The main elements of cost for which you require a breakdown: see section 4.2.
- How the base costs are set for labour and materials.

- Create a pricing table for the suppliers to complete. This will set the standard for comparison against your definitions outlined in the introduction.
- Identify the main basis of indexing on price elements: labour/material indexes.
- Set out how you will manage price reviews over time on longer contracts.

Some 80% of your writing will be in this main body section.

Note: this question is focused on the following sections in study session 4:

- 4.2 How are costs allocated and accounted for in a commercial organisation?
- 4.3 Introduction to cost price analysis: how are variable costs managed?
- 4.4 Using cost analysis and measuring your purchasing performance

Feedback on revision question for study session 5

Your report could have the following structure. The writing times are for guidance only.

(a) *Introduction*
An explanation of the main costs involved in holding stock, based on the model illustrated in section 5.2 (say 25% of writing time).

(b) *The cost elements*
- financial opportunity costs
- physical opportunity costs
- calculation of a stores on-cost based on annual turnover.
(This will need about 35% of writing time.)

(c) *KPIs*
Identify a set of KPIs for stores, stock control and management (say 20% of writing time).

(d) *Recommendations*
State how you will report the results, and how you will interface with other operational managers and systems.
Around three recommendations will do (say 20% of writing time).

Note: this question is focused on the following sections in study session 5:

- 5.2 The cost of holding stock
- 5.3 Building up the stockholding cost base and identifying links to performance management
- 5.4 Stores and inventory key performance indicators

Feedback on revision question for study session 6

Your report could have the f\lowing structure. The writing times are for guidance only.

(a) *Introduction*
An outline of the links with the organisation, both upstream and downstream A summary of the data needed for purchasing decisions (see figure 6.2) (say 15% of writing time).

(b) *Identify some details in purchasing management reports you wish to generate*
- inbound contracts and purchasing management
- intra site stores and stock control operations
- outbound transport and distribution operations.

(This will need about 25% of writing time.)

(c) *State how purchasing information links to the corporate system*
Identify the interdepartmental links (see learning activity 6.2) (say 35% of writing time).

(d) *Recommendations*
State how you would need the system to be set up for transactions, contract records and strategic data analysis.
Around three recommendations will do (say 25% of writing time).

Note: this question is focused on the following sections in study session 6:

- 6.1 Information systems in business, and the links with supply chain systems used to measure performance
- 6.2 The key elements of a purchasing IT system
- 6.6 Best practice: which KPIs will help supply chain managers reduce cost and improve service?

Feedback on revision question for study session 7

Your report could have the following structure. The writing times are for guidance only.

(a) *Introduction*
Explain the background and problems you face. This is a report, so it needs an introduction, but this has mostly been given to you, so keep it relatively short (say 10% of writing time).

(b) *Impact on the five 'rights'*
The five 'rights' are price, quality, quantity, place and time. You should not spend time here commenting on quality, as you will pick this up later; a brief reference will show you are aware of it. You should then give a brief explanation of the impact that performance measurement could have on each of the remaining four 'rights' (say 30% of writing time).

(c) *Contribution to improving quality*
Here you could use two or three themes to emphasise the importance of this element. For example:
- an introductory theme on basic quality measurement issues
- a comment on how this can move quality further up the supply chain, and the benefits this brings
- some of the wider issues to be measured, such as workforce training or investment in technology.

This is the largest 'section' of your report (say 40% of writing time)

(d) *Some recommendations*
These will be very much down to you, but should provide the board with some good ideas. There are no clues in the question, so use your knowledge of supplier performance management. Around three recommendations will do (say 20% of writing time)

Note: this question is focused on the following sections in study session 7:

- 7.1 Supplier performance and business success
- 7.3 Performance measurement and 'quality management'

Feedback on revision question for study session 8

Your PowerPoints might read as follows:

- Slide 1: Introduction and purpose of presentation.
- Slide 2: Brief description of supplier performance management.
- Slides 3–4: Explain a typical public sector procurement process, showing all the stages from project planning to closure. Emphasise the points at which performance management has particular relevance. You might use diagrams here as well.
- Slides 5–7: Explain in a little more depth the difference between pre-award and post-award measurements. For example, post-award measurements are often sustained over time with the chosen supplier, whereas pre-award measurement is concerned with helping to select suitable suppliers.
- Slides 7–9: Pick up the stages in the process, emphasising particularly that post-award assessment is a 'live' process and one that can change and develop through review and feedback.

Note: this question is focused on the following sections in study session 8:

- 8.1 The key stages in the buying process
- 8.2 Steps in a pre-award assessment
- 8.3 Steps in a post-award evaluation

Feedback on revision question for study session 9

Your essay could contain:

(a) *Introduction*
    Showing you know what the question is about, and outlining how you intend to cover it (say 15% of writing time).
(b) *Section on performance management tools*
    A description of the available toolkit, which should pick up the three main categories of tool, with a description and at least one example (say 40% of writing time):
- systems and information tools: a wide range of data and information tools that may be available to support performance measurement and which may be particularly useful at the pre-award assessment stage, eg corporate IT systems
- performance measurement and accreditation tools
- management, theoretical and support tools:
(c) *A section on 'base'*
    This should highlight the three main types of activity:
    1 desk based: activity best undertaken in the office, eg Internet research
    2 meeting based: activities best undertaken by meetings, eg planning and communication session

3   visit based: activities best undertaken through visits, eg supplier's process and material flows.

Be sure to have cross-linkage to the tools. The use of different examples would be a bonus. (Say 30% of writing time.)

(d) *Conclusion*

Confirm what you have said, and close the essay (say 15% of writing time). Try to make a telling point at the end. For example:

'We can see that in determining which tools and techniques to use we are also to some extent deciding the degree to which our activities will be focused outside the office.'

Note: this question is focused on the following sections in study session 9:

- 9.1 Using the right performance measurement 'tools'
- 9.5 A desk-based or visit-based approach?

Feedback on revision question for study session 10

Your report will need to cover those methodologies detailed in the course material but selecting only those suitable for use post-award. In the section on recommendations there is no right answer: you may choose whichever method you feel is appropriate, as long as you can justify this sensibly and in line with the course content, or a university scenario.

Your report might contain:

(a) *Introduction*

Explain the background, and the problems you face. This is a report, so it needs an introduction, but this has mostly been given to you, so keep it relatively short (say 10% of writing time).

(b) *The main body*

Your main areas are likely to be
- statistics based, eg simple rating, complex rating, weighted rating
- perception based, eg categorical rating, the 7Cs
- self-assessment.

You will need some detail of each example, and should show a simple calculation or form design if you think it necessary, as the manager has asked for examples. Keep any maths simple. (Say 60% of writing time.)

(c) *Recommendations*

As indicated, you cannot be wrong, but your answer should reflect the given situation. A weighted complex rating system, heavily dependent on external support to deliver, would probably be too expensive for this type of project.

Therefore you might recommend a simple six-point category-based approach using a small team, undertaken on a monthly basis. This would be practical, not too expensive, easy to establish, and not too time-consuming.

Note: this question is focused on the following sections in study session 10:

- 10.1 Generic methodologies for post-award performance measurement
- 10.2 Simple vendor rating

- 10.3 Perception based rating
- 10.4 The benefits of using weighted measurements

Feedback on revision question for study session 11

Your paper will have three main sections, but may benefit from a short introduction.

(a) *Introduction*
The question is suggesting a link between conflict and disputes and communications, and you should pick this up, as well as the loss of time and effort that conflict can cause (say 10% of writing time).

(b) *Classifying communications*
Relationships can develop at all levels in a business, but a four-part breakdown into director, management, supervisory and operative levels will be sufficient. Show the nature of the relationship at each level, perhaps linking it to disputes and conflicts (say 35% of writing time).

(c) *Nature of disputes and conflicts*
Explain the difference between disputes and conflict, and show how disputes can lead to conflict (say 20% of writing time).

(d) *Resolution of disputes and conflicts*
Solutions can range from normal course of business up to litigation, and you should provide an indication of a preferred route, with explanations (say 35% of writing time).

Note: this question is focused on the following sections in study session 11:

- 11.1 Communication and business relationships at strategic, tactical and operational levels.
- 11.4 Good communications and the resolution of disputes and management of conflict

Feedback on revision question for study session 12

Your essay should support the placement, because there several benefits from close collaboration, especially on longer-term, higher-value purchasing. Your essay could include:

(a) *Introduction*
Showing you know what the question is about, and outlining how you intend to cover it (say 10% of writing time).

(b) *Some of the roles and inputs*
A description of the available tools, such as balance sheet analysis, annual report analysis, and cost control analysis (say 25% of writing time).

(c) *The benefits of corporate financial appraisal*
(Say 25% of writing time.)

(d) *Some specific financial appraisal tools*
For example, return on capital employed (ROCE), profit margin on sales (margin) (say 25% of writing time).

(e) *Conclusion*
Confirm what you have said, and close the essay (say 15% of writing time). Try to make a firm conclusion. For example:

We can see that Kieran will gain substantially from this new appointment, which will....

Note: this question is focused on the following sections in study session 12:

- 12.1 The role and input for the finance department
- 12.2 The benefits of undertaking corporate financial appraisal
- 12.4 Financial appraisal measurement tools

Feedback on revision question for study session 13

(a) *Introduction*
Will emphasise the positive benefits of working with the suppliers rather having than one-sided measurement (say 12% of writing time).

(b) *Question 1*
Could include comment on improving relationships, creating a partnership style, getting early supplier involvement, going a step beyond the existing system (say 22% of writing time).

(c) *Question 2*
Could include comment on cost versus expected benefits, application only where business justifies it, the need to take a longer-term view, the cost being shared between the parties (say 22% of writing time).

(d) *Question 3*
Could say this is possible at first, but there is a likelihood that the teams will start to work together as time goes on. Emphasise the need for good management of the process and real empowerment of the teams (say 22% of writing time).

(e) *Question 4*

Could include:

- market advantage and reduced selling effort
- improved technological capability and product development
- enhanced innovativity in what the organisation offers
- improved and secured payment arrangements
- improved financial stability and security
- opportunities to improve and refocus management capability
- ability to plan resources over the longer period.

(Say 22% of writing time.)

Note: this question is focused on the following section in study session 13:

- 13.3 Joint performance measurement initiatives

Feedback on revision question for study session 14

Your essay could contain:

(a) *Introduction*
Showing you understand the question, and that you have identified the two themes that you need to consider in detail (say 15% of writing time).

(b) *A section discussing the options you have*
There is no correct answer, but you may develop the following options (say 35% of writing time):
- terminate – but this is a difficult market
- 'discipline' and penalise the supplier in some way – but this may not help if the supplier is trying hard
- take no action at all, and hope for improvement – not very proactive in a difficult market
- take some simple steps to see what the supplier's problems are – worth considering, and has no major resource implications
- look at introducing a 'supplier development' approach.

This leads you into:

(c) *A section on supplier development*
The question is leading you into arguing in favour, but you should not ignore some of the potential negatives. You could cover:
- what supplier development means.
- what it might include: eg advice, technology and even finance
- some key requirements: eg good communications, establishing benchmarks, multi-functional approach, could be part of a programme
- some disadvantages: eg needs good management, costly in time and resources, must be reviewed regularly, can be applied only to a limited number of suppliers.

(Say 35% of writing time.)

(d) *Conclusion*

Confirm what you have said, and close the essay (say 15% of writing time). Try to make a telling point at the end. For example:

'Supplier development should not be undertaken lightly, but in the right situation it can bring positive benefits both to the buyer and to the supplier.'

Note: this question is focused on the following section in study session 14:

- 14.3 About supplier development

Feedback on revision question for study session 15

Your bulletin could contain the following:

(a) *Introduction*
Explain the purpose of the bulletin, and how it is intended that both parties will benefit – it should be 'win–win' (say 10% of writing time).

(b) *The employees*
Could include comment on:
- improved skills and knowledge
- training opportunities
- career prospects
- making a better contribution
- having a better view of overall aims and business strategy
- improved motivation and morale.

(Say 25% of writing time.)
(c) *The department*
Could include comment on:
- improved departmental performance
- improved prices, deals or contracts, improved quality and service, and a 'bottom-line' improvement
- improved perception and profile of the procurement function
- better communication and feedback with staff
- meeting procedural or legal requirements.

(Say 25% of writing time.)
(d) *Links to rewards and advancement*
Could comment on:
- developing talent
- improved motivation and innovation
- financial reward
- organised bonus schemes
- need for careful management.

(Say 25% of writing time.)
(e) *Conclusion and summary*
This will wrap up the bulletin, and needs a positive 'spin' to inspire the target audience and give them confidence (say 15% of writing time).

Note: this question is focused on the following sections in study session 15:

- 15.1 Performance management and the buyer
- 15.2 Performance management and the organisation
- 15.4 The links with reward and advancement

Feedback on revision question for study session 16

There is no set style for this question, and each part should be treated as roughly equal in terms of writing time.

(a) Common elements (with description):
- the overall task or area of activity
- the objective
- the performance measures
- the timescale, by when, milestones and review timetable:

(b) Key principles (with description):
S = Specific
M = Measurable
A = Achievable
R = Realistic
T = Timed.

(c) Examples
As an example you might have:
(iii) Writing objectives for members of your team
Performance management – to write at least five good quality objectives for each member of the team, in line with the departmental strategies and objectives: to be agreed and in place by 1 April with a schedule of three review meetings in the following 12 months.

Note: this question is focused on the following section in study session 16:

- 16.3 Designing positive and SMART objectives

Feedback on revision question for study session 17

Your essay could contain:

(a) *Introduction*
Showing you understand the question, and that you have identified the two themes that you need to consider in detail (say 15% of writing time).

(b) *A section discussing levels of formality*
You should develop the following options (say 35% of writing time). Some topics are suggested below, but you will need to decide whether they are advantages or disadvantages.
- *Formal*. Include comments on: organisational, rules and requirements, written objectives, set interview requirements, standards for measurement of achievement, timetables, scoring mechanisms, preparation. Suitable for which type of organisation?
- *Informal*. Include comments on: less structured and disciplined, based on regular day-to-day discussion, shorter, more relaxed meetings, less paperwork, can still be demanding. Suited to which type of organisation?
- *Structured*: a mix of the two.

(c) *A section demonstrating the potential for involving others*
The question is leading you into arguing in support of involving others, but you should not ignore some of the potential negatives (say 35% of writing time). You could cover:
- why involve others?
- who might be involved (team and/or peers, internal customers, suppliers, etc)?

(d) *Conclusion*
Confirm what you have said, and close the essay (say 15% of writing time). Try to make a telling point at the end. For example:
'I believe that in general the very formal style of appraisal should be avoided, and that, wherever possible, appraisal should include input from outside the procurement team'

Note: this question is focused on the following sections in study session 17:

- 17.1 Formal and informal appraisal and evaluation techniques
- 17.5 Involving others in the appraisal process

Feedback on revision question for study session 18

Your memo/email should contain:

(a) *The introduction section*
The key word here from the question is 'targeted', and you can outline why a TNA can provide a more accurate appreciation of staff training needs than some other ways of selecting training (say 30% of writing time).

(b) *A section on the TNA and a typical process*

Remember nothing is yet agreed, so you are concerned only with a typical TNA. The steps can include:

(i) Agree the method to be used (and recruit external interviewers if needed).

(ii) Agree the group(s) of staff involved.

(iii) Agree and prioritise the areas of performance, skills and competences required.

(iv) Undertake the interviews or assessment.

(v) Compare the results with the benchmark requirements and identify any major problem areas (the skills gaps).

(vi) Devise and implement suitable training to remedy those skill gaps.

(vii) Review and feed back as appropriate.

(Say 35% of writing time.)

(c) *A section on potential training solutions*

You are asked for a selection. Choose which ones you like, but your reasoning must be sound and logical. Some options are:

• job based: orientation or induction, learning by doing, buddying, mentoring, rotational

• specific skills based: training aimed at learning how to do something specific, such as operate a new machine or computer program

• generic: training aimed at broadening generic skills used in the job and which form a 'toolbox' for the employee that grows over time

• professional or academic.

(Say 35% of writing time.)

Note: this question is focused on the following sections in study session 18:

• 18.1 Developing a training needs analysis

• 18.4 The different types of training available

Feedback on revision question for study session 19

The marking schedule has indicated how you should allocate your writing time, and there is no need for an introduction or conclusion if you use a list- or table-type format.

(a) The four categories are:

• Transactional activity: data relating to basic, day-to-day activity such as orders placed, invoices cleared.

• Budgetary conformance: data relating to adherence to departmental or project budget activities, often at management level and including pay and staffing levels etc

• Operational performance: data relating to more advanced 'tasks' of procurement, including the real added value issues such as savings targets, supplier appraisal.

• Strategic contributions: data relating to strategic and organisational contributions that help drive the business, such as margin improvements, supplier rationalisation programmes.

Examples are not asked for here but will add value to your answer if they do not overlap with part (b).

(b) Examples would be:

Table 21.1

Basic or transactional activity	
Number of requisitions handled, orders placed etc	Quantitative
Speed of turn-round (purchasing lead time)	Quantitative
Overall lead time (request to receipt)	Quantitative
Number of complaints	Mix
Number of invoice queries	Quantitative
Expediting activity	Quantitative
Quality and effectiveness of the service	Mix
Internal and external customer satisfaction	Mix

Table 21.2

Departmental or internal performance	
Staffing costs and levels to budget or targeted reductions	Quantitative
Non-pay cost to budget or targeted reductions	Quantitative
Staff appraisal and development/training targets	Mix
Activity ratios per employee	Quantitative
Personnel and welfare issues	Qualitative
Staff recruitment/retention targets	Mix

Table 21.3

Operational performance	
Savings or margin contribution	Quantitative
Amount of delegated procurement activity	Quantitative
Use of procurement cards	Mix
Inventory reduction	Quantitative
Quality or service improvements	Qualitative
Environmental targets	Quantitative
Impact on current business objectives	Mix
Performance against corporate milestones	Mix
Legislative and process compliance targets	Mix
Project milestones	

Table 21.4

Strategic performance	
New sourcing strategies	Mix
Product and materials development	Mix
Supplier relationships and development	Mix
Contribution to company performance	Mix
Make or buy strategies	Mix
Value analysis and value engineering	Mix
Globalisation targets	Mix

Note: this question is focused the following section in study session 19:

- 19.3 Types of data used

Feedback on revision question for study session 20

Your essay could contain:

(a) *Introduction*

showing you understand the question, and that you have identified the three themes you need to cover (say 10% of writing time):

- Discuss the concept.
- Demonstrate the supplier's view.
- Evaluate the issues.

(b) *The concept*

Argue whether the supplier is a stakeholder showing ('discuss') you can see two sides (say 25% of writing time).

- *For* the argument you could cite the service received, the need for good specifications, involvement in the whole industry etc
- *Against* you might suggest the supplier simply wants a sale, is not a real stakeholder, might like procurement out of the way etc

(c) *The supplier's view*

A section showing how the supplier sees procurement. You could cover:

- operational performance – its impact on making business work smoothly and payments happen on schedule.
- value added performance – is the relationship being developed? is there early supplier involvement? etc

(Say 25% of writing time.)

(d) *The issues*

Relationship with the customer, vested interests, staff reactions, choosing the suppliers etc (say 25% of writing time).

(e) *Conclusion*

Confirm what you have said, and close the essay (say 15% of writing time). Try to make a telling point at the end. For example: 'Involving suppliers in a buyer's performance measurement system is likely to be controversial, but there may be some real benefits to be gained for both the buyers and the buying organisation.'

Note: this question is focused the following section in study session 20:

- 20.3 Performance measurement links to suppliers

References and bibliography

This section contains a complete A-Z listing of all publications, materials or websites referred to in this course book. Books, articles and research are listed under the first author's (or in some cases the editor's) surname. Where no author name has been given, the publication is listed under the name of the organisation that published it. Websites are listed under the name of the organisation providing the website.

Association of British Certification Bodies (ABCB) http://www.abcb.demon.co.uk/.

Bailey, D (Associates) (2001) *The Training Handbook,* London: Gee Publishing.

British Electro-technical and Allied Manufacturers Association (BEAMA) http://www.beama.org.uk/.

Christopher, M (1985) *The Strategy of Distribution Management.* Aldershot: Gower.

Deming, WE (1982) *Quality, Productivity and Competitive Position.* MIT Press.

Det Norske Veritas (DNV) http://www.dnv.com/.

Drucker, P (2003) *The Essential Drucker,* 2004 edition, Harper Collins.

Dun and Bradstreet http://www.dnb.com/.

Goodworth, C (1989) *The Secrets of Successful Staff Appraisal and Counselling,* 1st edition, UK: Butterworth /Heinemann.

Institute of Civil Engineers (ICE) http://www.ice.org.uk/.

International Standards Organisation (ISO) http://www.iso.org/.

Investors in People http://www.investorsinpeople.co.uk/.

Ishikawa, K (1985) *What is total quality control? The Japanese Way.* Prentice Hall.

Kirkpatrick, D (1975) *Techniques for Evaluating Training Programmes,* Alexandria, VA: American Society of Training Directors (originally published in the *Journal of the American Society of Training Directors,* 1958/59).

Kirkpatrick, DL and JD Kirkpatrick (2005) *Evaluating Training Programmes – the four levels,* 3rd edition. USA: Berrett-Koehler.

Little, N (2004) *Price, Cost, Value, Benefit, Gain, Worth … which way do I turn.* Eli Broad Graduate School, Michigan State University, USA.

Lysons, K (2000) *Purchasing and Supply Chain Management,* 5th edition, London: Pearson/Prentice Hall.

Lysons, K and B Farrington (2006) *Purchasing and Supply Chain Management,* 7th edition, London: Pearson/Prentice Hall.

Neely, A, C Adams and M Kennerley (2002) *The Performance Prism,* 1st edition Pearson/Prentice Hall.

Poister, T (2003) *Measuring performance in public and non-profit organisations* 1st edition. San Francisco: Wiley.

Porter, ME (1985) Competitive Advantage. Free Press.

Taguchi, G (1986) *Introduction to Quality Engineering.* Asian Productivity Association.

Index

80/20 analysis, 80, 144
ABC *see* activity-based costing
academic training, 297
accounting measures, 194
accreditation, 144, 159
accuracy in data, 307
achievable objectives, 264
acid test, 204
acquisition costs, 163
actioning assessments, 130, 132
activity-based costing (ABC), 66,
    81, 144
added value, 19
    administration, 25
    buyer performance, 98
    consignment stocks, 25
    contract terms, 26
    definition, 20
    inventory costs, 25
    inventory management, 73
    measuring, 23
    negotiation, 26
    operational efficiency, 28
    opportunities, 22, 26
    procurement negotiation, 26
    purchasing function, 95
    purchasing performance , 326
    supplier performance, 96
annual reports, 195
annual reviews, 247
appraisals, 275
    formal appraisals, 276
    informal appraisals, 276, 277
    interview-based, 279
    involving others, 282
    performance management, 245
    problems with, 284
    structured appraisals, 277
    training evaluation , 300
    training needs analysis, 290
arbitration , 185
asset turnover, 203
audits, 168, 195, 268
award schemes, 188

balance sheet analysis, 194
BEAMA *see* British Electrotechnical
    and Allied Manufacturers
    Association
benchmarking, 211, 220, 291
bespoke requirements , 310
best practice, 64, 80, 99
bonus schemes, 249
bottom line, 108
British Electrotechnical and Allied
    Manufacturers' Association
    (BEAMA), 64
buddying, 296
business development, 119
business infrastructures, 47
business objectives, 49
business plans, 263
business strategy participation, 244
business success, 108
buyer performance, 98, 319
buying process
    key steps, 126
capability measures, 111
capacity, 163
Carter's model, 157, 162
cascading targets, 259
cash resources, 163
categories of key performance
    indicators, 37
category rating, 159, 162
closedown, 132
commercial cost model, 6
commercial pricing strategy, 59
commercial relationships, 212
commitment, 163
commodity prices, 60

communication, 175
  business relationships, 176
  channels, 186
  conflicts, 183
  contracts, 181
  dispute resolution, 183
  performance management, 145,
    178, 247
  types, 186
competency, 49, 163
conferences, 187
confidence, 284
conflicts, 177, 183, 184, 185, 200
consignment stocks, 25
consistency, 163
consultations, 152
continuity of supply, 10
continuous improvement, 8
continuous measurements, 265
continuous professional
  development (CPD), 99, 298
continuous reviews, 136
contracts, 26, 181
contribution development, 244,
  245
controls
  communication, 187
  performance measurements,
    163
  suppliers, 228
core business activities, 1, 41, 119
corporate business, 20
corporate financial appraisals, 197
corporate management, 38, 323
corporate planning, 263, 308
corporate software tools, 143
corrective action, 134
correspondence, 187
cost accountancy, 60
cost allocation, 60
cost analysis, 7, 60
cost control history analysis, 195
cost management, 6, 43, 99
cost measures, 57
cost of acquisition, 163
cost price analysis (CPA), 61, 62,
  64, 67
cost ratio ratings, 159

costs
  financial appraisals, 199
  fixed costs management, 66
  market forces, 59
  stockholding , 73
cost savings, 44
CPA see cost price analysis
CPD see continuous professional
  development
credit rating checks, 195
cross-functional teams, 218
cross-organisational teams, 218
cultures, 322
current ratio, 203
current relationships, 236
customers, 324
data
  availability, 148
  importance, 306
  management, 89
  overload, 321
  quality, 305
  sources, 313
  types, 311
delivery performance, 111
Demming's continuous
  improvement, 8
departmental costs, 45
departmental planning, 263, 308
desk-based approaches, 151
directors, 177
discussion techniques, 152
dispute resolution, 177, 183, 184,
  185
distribution planning (DRP), 102
Dun & Bradstreet report analysis,
  195
early purchasing involvement, 108
ECC see Engineering and
  Construction Contract
economy
  inventory, 73, 80
effectiveness
  added value, 24
  inventory management, 73, 80
  key performance indicators, 46
  performance management, 3
efficiency
  added value, 24, 28
  inventory management, 73, 80
  key performance indicators, 46
  performance management, 3

electronic data exchange, 188
email, 187
employee objectives, 261
employee performance, 246
employee plans, 263
employees, 216
empowerment, 284
Engineering and Construction
    Contract (ECC), 64
enterprise resource planning (ERP),
    29, 102
ERP *see* enterprise resource
    planning
escalating disputes, 185
evaluation techniques, 117, 130,
    131, 275, 299
exhibitions, 187
exploitable relationships, 119
external commercial relationships,
    212
external supplier feedback, 134
fair data, 308
fast tracking employees, 249
feedback
    definition, 134
    objective-setting, 268
    performance management, 247
    post-award evaluations, 132
    pre-award assessments, 130
    supplier performance, 134
finance
    appraisals, 193, 198, 201
    department input/roles, 194
    IT/IS systems, 102
    key performance indicators , 80
    rewards, 249
    stability, 163
    stakeholder performance, 328
    status ratios, 201, 203
    strength, 111
fixed costs, 66
focused training, 295
formal appraisals, 276
forms
    data sources, 314
    self-assessments, 281
fraud prevention, 195
frequency of reviews, 247
future relationship objectives, 236
general financial support, 195
generic methodologies, 158
generic training, 297

geography factors, 200
health and safety, 328
high-level plans, 187
holding stock costs, 73
human resources (HR), 102, 328
ICE *see* Institution of Civil
    Engineers
identifying key suppliers, 230
impartiality, 200, 308
inbound supply issues, 5
income statement analysis, 194
individual performance
    management, 305
individual pre-award assessments ,
    130
induction, 296
informal appraisals, 277
information overload, 321
information sourcing, 247
information systems (IS), 90
information technology (IT), 89
    best practices, 99
    capability, 148
    purchasing systems, 93
    supply chains, 90
information tools, 143
innovation, 111, 200
Institution of Civil Engineers
    (ICE), 64
intelligent enterprises, 90
internal commercial relationships,
    212
internal customers, 314, 324
internal financial appraisals, 198
internal supplier feedback, 134
Internet research, 187
interviews, 279, 291
intra-site management, 5
inventory
    costs, 25, 77
    key performance indicators, 79
    management measures, 73
    performance management, 78
    stores, 79
    supplier performance, 109
Investors in People, 252
involving others, 149, 297
IS *see* information systems
Ishikawa's continuous
    improvement, 8
ISO 14000 , 144
ISO 9000, 144

IT *see* information technology
Japanese philosophy, 9
JIT *see* just-in-time
job-based training, 296
job descriptions, 292, 293
job specification, 293
joint performance measurement,
    211, 217
just-in-time (JIT) culture, 9, 25
kaizen, 9
key performance indicators (KPI)
    business infrastructures, 47
    categories, 37
    core business operations, 41
    corporate management, 38
    departmental purchasing costs,
      45
    inventory management, 79
    performance management, 3
    supplier performance, 116
    supply chains, 45, 99
key supplier identification, 230
Kirkpatrick, Donald, 300
knowledge development, 244, 245
KPI, 116
Kraljic's 'four box' matrix, 144, 231
labour rates, 60
law of supply and demand, 57
lean supply culture, 9
learning by doing, 296
legal requirements, 185, 247
library research, 187
litigation, 185
location factors, 109, 200
management
    communication, 177
    executive summary, 237
    performance, 243
    supplier performance, 215
management by objectives (MBO),
    259, 260
market forces, 59
materials requirements planning
    (MRP), 25, 102
MBO *see* management by objectives
measurable objectives, 264
measurement reasons, 243
measurement weaknesses, 320
mediation, 185
meetings, 152, 188
mentoring , 296
minutes , 188

mission statements, 262
monitoring post-award evaluations ,
    132
morale, 244, 245
motivation
    appraisal problems, 284
    performance management, 244,
      245, 249
MRP *see* materials requirements
    planning
mutual advantages, 118
NEC *see* New Engineering Contract
negotiation, 26, 185
New Engineering Contract (NEC),
    64
newsletters, 188
notes, 188
nuisance customers, 119
objective-setting, 146, 259
    audits, 268
    feedback, 268
    performance measurement, 321
    problems with, 267
    reviews, 268
    timescales, 266
objectives-setting, 264
ongoing information requirements,
    309
ongoing reviews , 247
open days, 187
operational efficiency, 28
operational key performance
    indicators, 80
operational management, 328
operational performance, 326
operational plans, 187
operational relationships, 176
opportunity costs, 25
organisationally driven CPD, 299
organisations and performance
    management, 246
original equipment manufacturer
    (OEM), 129
overall aims participation, 244, 245
overhead costs, 66
Pareto analysis, 80, 144, 228
participation in appraisals, 284
partner development, 115
partnership sourcing, 114
partner suppliers, 128
percentage profitability, 6
perception-based ratings, 159, 162

performance *see also* key
    performance indicators
    appraisals, 275
    evaluation, 275
    history, 144
    indicators, 95
    ratios, 201, 202
    statistics, 187
performance management, 1, 2
    buyers, 319
    continuity of supply, 10
    continuous improvement, 8
    cost management, 6
    data quality, 305
    data types, 311
    measurement, 37, 141, 243
    organisations, 246
    private sector organisations, 12
    problems and difficulties, 250
    public sector organisations, 12
    supply, 1
    tools, 141
personally driven CPD, 299
personally managed systems, 314
PESTLE, 144
PFI *see* Private Finance Initiative
place factors , 109
planning assessments, 130, 132,
    148
politics, 200
Porter, Michael, 21
positive objective design, 263
post-award evaluations, 123, 128,
    131, 132, 158
pre-award assessments, 123, 127,
    129
preparing assessments , 130
price factors, 57, 108, 111
    analysis, 60
    market forces, 59
primary suppliers, 110
prime bidders, 197
Private Finance Initiative (PFI),
    199, 200
private sector organisations, 12
procedural factors, 200, 247
process audits, 169
procurement functions, 110
product portfolios, 231
professionally driven CPD, 299
professional publications, 188
professional training, 297, 298

profit, 43, 202
pro formas, 314
public sector organisations, 12
published documents, 187, 188
purchasing, 126
    bottom-line profit, 43
    competence, 49
    function, 22, 95
    IT systems, 93
    joint performance, 217
    key performance indicators, 38,
      47
    managers, 38, 43
qualitative data, 131
qualitative information, 311
qualitative measures, 145, 277
qualitative objectives, 267, 268
quality factors, 108, 111, 112, 144
quantitative data, 131
quantitative information, 311
quantitative measures, 145, 277
quantity factors , 109
questionnaires, 281, 300
quick ratio, 204
ratio analysis, 194, 201
recommendations in assessments,
    130
re-engineering evaluations , 132
relationships
    building, 114
    communication, 176
    planning assessments, 310
relevance of data, 307
reporting pre-award assessments ,
    130
research, 159, 187, 315
resolving disputes, 177, 183, 184,
    185
return on capital employed
    (ROCE), 6, 202
reviews
    frequency, 247
    objective-setting, 268
    training evaluation, 300
rewards, 249
risk management, 181, 182, 328
ROCE *see* return on capital
    employed
rotational training, 297
safety, 328
self-assessments, 144, 159, 281, 291
service improvements, 99

service levels, 43, 73, 80
service performance history, 111
six-point guide, 40
six sigma, 122
size factors, 200
skills
    based training, 297
    development, 244, 245
    financial appraisals, 199
SMART criteria, 41, 263, 267, 268
software tools, 143
specialist departments, 328
specific objectives, 264
staff associations, 328
staff development, 289
stakeholders, 149, 282, 319
    involvement, 322
standards, 159
statistics-based measurement, 159
stock
    place in business operations, 75
    turnover, 81
    value, 75
stockholding costs, 73
stores, 79
strategic performance, 42
strategic relationships, 176
structured appraisals, 277
subjective measures *see* qualitative
    measures
supervisors, 178
supplier performance, 1, 319, 324
    added value issues, 96
    audits, 168
    benchmarking, 211, 220
    business success, 108
    commercial relationships, 212
    continuous reviews, 136
    corrective action, 134
    evaluation, 117
    feedback, 130, 132, 134
    financial appraisals, 193
    key steps, 125
    mutual advantages, 118
    post-award evaluations, 128,
      131
    pre-award assessments, 127,
      129
    procurement functions, 110
    quality management, 112
    relationship building, 114
    surveys, 222

sustained improvement, 157
    tools, 108
    vendor rating, 128, 131
suppliers
    account management, 235
    assessments, 123
    award schemes, 188
    categorisation, 127
    contract terms, 26
    controlling, 228
    data sources, 314
    development, 128, 227, 232
    evaluation, 117
    identifing key suppliers, 230
    joint performance, 217
    relationships, 230
    selection, 117, 127, 128
supply chains
    costs, 45
    information systems, 90
    key performance indicators, 45,
      82, 99
    management, 5
supply managers, 38
support tools, 144
surveys, 222
SWOT analysis, 144
tactical performance, 42
tactical relationships, 176
Taguchi's continuous
    improvement, 8
talent development, 249
targets *see* cascading targets
    achievability, 321
    appraisals, 284
    data measurement data, 307
    objective-setting, 259
TCA *see* total cost of acquisition
TCO *see* total cost of ownership
technical assessments, 144
telephones, 187
testing procedures, 166
third parties, 166, 198
time factors, 109, 200, 264, 266,
    308
TNA *see* training needs analysis
total cost of acquisition (TCA), 26,
    44, 46, 95
total cost of ownership (TCO), 26,
    44, 46, 95
total opportunity costs, 77, 78

total quality management (TQM), 122

trade publications, 188

traditional audits, 168

traditional sourcing, 114

training, 289
    evaluation, 299
    financial appraisals, 199
    types, 296

training needs analysis (TNA)
    development, 290
    job descriptions, 292, 293
    job profiles, 292

transactional costs, 54

transactional performance, 42

unfocused training, 295

usable data, 308, 313

value *see also* added value
    chains, 21
    purchasing performance , 326
    stock, 75

value for money (VFM), 73, 169

variable costs, 61, 62

vendor rating
    communications, 186
    performance measurements, 160, 164
    supplier performance, 123, 128, 131

verbal feedback, 300

VFM *see* value for money

visits, 151, 152, 188

weaknesses in measurement, 320

weighting, 164

wider view, 252

zero based measurements, 265